Symbolism,
the Sacred,
and the Arts

Mircea Eliade

Symbolism, the Sacred, and the Arts

Edited by
Diane Apostolos-Cappadona

CROSSROAD • NEW YORK

1985
The Crossroad Publishing Company
370 Lexington Avenue, New York, N.Y. 10017

The Introduction and the following English translations—
"The Symbolism of Shadows in Archaic Religions," "Reflections on Indian Art,"
"Sacred Architecture and Symbolism," "Barabudur, the Symbolic Temple,"
"From the Portuguese Journal, 1941–1943," "Folkloric Themes and Artistic Creation,"
"Marthe Bibesco and the Meeting of Eastern and Western Literature"—
are copyright 1985 by The Crossroad Publishing Company.

Printed in the United States of America

Library of Congress Cataloging in Publication Data

Eliade, Mircea, 1907–
  Symbolism, the sacred, and the arts.

  Bibliography: p.
  Includes index.
  1. Symbolism—Addresses, essays, lectures. 2. Arts
and religion—Addresses, essays, lectures.
I. Apostolos-Cappadona, Diane. II. Title.
BL603.E45 1985   291.1'75   85-14037
ISBN 0-8245-0723-1

For Isamu Noguchi
whose art transcends time. . . .

Contents

Acknowledgments

To PREPARE A COLLECTION OF ESSAYS by Mircea Eliade is a Prome-
thean task on two accounts: the richness and vastness of the materials
to be considered, and the stature of the scholar himself. I am deeply
grateful to Professor Eliade for his interest, time, and encouragement in
the preparation of this volume. I also wish to thank Mac Linscott Ricketts
for his translations and critical additions to the bibliography. And I am
happy to acknowledge the collaboration of my former student, Frederica
Adelman, in the translation of several of the essays selected for this
collection.

Through the sponsorship of the 700–Series Committee of The
George Washington University, I was able to co-chair a special seminar,
"Mircea Eliade: The Scholar as Artist, Critic, and Poet," during the 1985
Spring Semester. I am indebted to my colleagues in that seminar:
Thelma Z. Lavine, of the Department of Philosophy; Suzanne L.
Simons, of the Department of Anthropology; Arthur Hall Smith, of the
Department of Fine Arts; and, most especially, Alf Hiltebeitel, of the
Department of Religion, who served as co-chair and shared with me the
preparation and presentations. I would also like to acknowledge the
students who participated in that seminar. In the best sense of what
scholarship is about, it was a mutual endeavor in intellectual exchange.
We were extremely fortunate to conclude the semester with Professor
Eliade serving as scholar in residence.

My own scholarship has benefited from the opportunities to present
my "Eliade research" at several professional meetings. I am grateful to
Thaddeus J. Gurdak, of West Virginia Wesleyan College, chair of the
Spirituality East-West Session, College Theology Society 1981 Annual
Meeting; Dennis E. Owen, of the University of Florida, chair of the Ritual
Aspects of the Arts and Literature Session, American Academy of
Religion 1982 Annual Meeting; and Albert C. Moore, of the University
of Otago, chair of the Religion and Art Section of the XVth Congress of
the International Association of the History of Religions.

Of course, no publication is possible without the continued interest of those engaged in the business of publishing. I am pleased to acknowledge the continued support and critical admonitions of Werner Mark Linz and Frank Oveis of The Crossroad Publishing Company. I am especially grateful for their interest in bringing this collection of Professor Eliade's work to a larger audience.

Finally, there are always those individuals whose intellectual and personal encouragement becomes paramount during the difficult moments when one is engaged in a project of this nature. Without the continued sustenance of the friendship and counsel of Dorothy Norman and Stephen Happel, I would have found it difficult, if not impossible, to complete this volume.

In acknowledging intellectual and personal debts, perhaps the greatest of all is acknowledged in the dedication of this volume to Isamu Noguchi. Professor Eliade and I join in this dedication to one of the world's singular and universal artists whom we are both privileged to call friend. This volume then serves as some tangible acknowledgment of the vision that undergirds and unites our mutual tasks.

Diane Apostolos-Cappadona
The George Washington University
Washington, D.C.

Introduction: Mircea Eliade:
The Scholar as Artist, Critic, and Poet

MAJOR WORK IS DISTINGUISHED by an intensity of inspiration and an overwhelming sense of personal vision. This merging of inspiration and vision permits the creation of a classic oeuvre whose creator is deemed to be a "master of his craft," or perhaps better, "a seminal mind." Such is the work of the historian of religions, Mircea Eliade.

In his lifelong quest to understand the presence of the Sacred throughout human history, Eliade has been fascinated by two central themes: Creation and Time. He has examined the temporal structures and meanings of cosmogonic myths and rituals of initiation. His writings begin and end with an attempt to understand Creation and Time. At the moment of Creation, Time is first encountered; and from that encounter, light and matter come to be known.

Eliade is both a historian and a writer. He advocates the primacy of cosmogonic myths for the understanding of Creation and Time. As a writer, he is an artist: one who creates an aesthetic interpretation of reality which allows for the temporary suspension of the traditional sense of time and space. Eliade's world includes the scholarly and the creative, or as he refers to it, the diurnal and the nocturnal imagination:

> I said to myself that my spiritual equilibrium—the condition which is indispensable for any creativity—was assured by this oscillation between the research of a scientific nature and the literary imagination. Like many others, I live alternatively in a diurnal mode of the spirit and in a nocturnal one. I know, of course, that these two categories of spiritual activity are interdependent and express a profound unity, because they have to do with the same "subject"— *man* or, more precisely, with the mode of existence in the world specific to man, and his decision to assume this mode of existence.[2]

For Eliade, artists succeed in circumventing fate.[3] They suspend the traditional perception of time and space by the act of "making," an act in which we share through participating in the environment of that artwork. During the moments of artistic creation, artists fulfill the fundamental human instinct for transcendence. The craving to be freed from the limitations of one's humanness is satisfied by the experience of passing over into the Other. Momentarily tasting transcendence, artists break the iron band of individuality and experience universality. They are freed not only from the limitations of human individuality and fallibility but also from human frailty and, precisely the most powerful form of that frailty, death. Artistic creation suspends Time.

Eliade's mode of artistic creation is verbal: he is a writer of essays, fiction, and literary criticism.[4] But his words are not simply words. They are, as David Tracy has so astutely pointed out, words of manifestation. Eliade's words express the existential dimension of the cosmic and ritual character of Christianity. His are words that manifest logos; words that are grounded in and that create an experience. As Tracy suggests, Eliade's choice of words of manifestation distinguishes him from other contemporary religious thinkers.[5]

Mircea Eliade is a poet in the fullest Heideggerian sense of the word. He deconceals and reveals the presence of Being, thus making it possible for one to find a place of dwelling in this world in the time between the gods.[6] And this Eliade is able to do not simply because he lives both diurnally and nocturnally with the ever-present manifestation of the Sacred. For him, then, the sacramental possibility of the natural order is always present. As an artist and as a historian of religions, he seeks to make that presence more accessible to others.

Whether he is functioning as a historian of religions or as a *littérateur*, Eliade is first and foremost a story-teller. Here he stands in the tradition of the mythologists of the archaic and folk traditions that he has studied with such passion. The stories he tells heal and reveal, suspend time and space, presence a dimension of cosmic sacredness. One of his favorite stories, which is in the genre of a homecoming story, is that of Rabbi Eisik of Cracow.[7]

There are several layers of interpretation and meaning to this tale of Rabbi Eisik of Cracow. One possible interpretation falls within the tradition of Paul Ricoeur's dictum that ". . . the interpreter's interpretation is an interpretation of the interpreter." As one who spent his childhood and youth in Romania, Eliade was raised in a cultural tradition ". . . that does not accept the idea of incompatibility between scientific investigation and artistic, especially literary, activity."[8] But more than that, Eliade was nurtured in a world which was Eastern Orthodox in its religious orientation. This worldview senses the aesthetic dimensions of religion, a sacramental understanding of matter, and places an aesthetic and spiritual importance on light. In order to understand that perspective and its implications for his own perceptions of reality, Eliade [like Rabbi Eisik of

Cracow] had to travel outside of himself to encounter and know himself.

In *Ordeal by Labyrinth*, Eliade recounts his recognition of the role of the icon in Eastern Orthodox spirituality.

> The second discovery, the second part of the lesson I learned, is the meaning of symbols. In Romania, I hadn't been particularly attracted to religion; to my eyes, all those icons in the churches seemed merely to clutter them up. I didn't exactly regard the icons as idols, of course, but still. . . . Well, in India I happened to live for a time in a Bengali village, and I saw the women and girls touching and decorating a *liṅgam*, a phallic symbol, or, more precisely, an anatomically very accurate stone phallus; and, naturally, the married women at least could not be unaware of what it was, of its physiological function. So I came to understand the possibility of "seeing" the symbol in the *liṅgam*. The *liṅgam* was the mystery of life, of creativity, of the fertility that is manifested at every cosmic level. And that manifestation of life was Shiva, not the anatomical member that we know. So this possibility of being religiously moved by the image and the symbol—*that* opened up a whole world of spiritual values to me. I said to myself: it is clear that in looking at an icon the believer does not perceive simply the figure of a woman holding a child; he is seeing the Virgin Mary and therefore the Mother of God and Sophia, Divine Wisdom. This discovery of the importance of religious symbolism in traditional cultures —well, you can imagine its importance in my training as a historian of religions.[9]

Predominant among the religious symbolisms of world religions is the icon of the Eastern Orthodox tradition. Through these icons the conjunction of light and matter is profoundly experienced in a sacramental encounter.[10] Icon is distinguished from idol. Worshiping an icon is not an idolatrous activity, for the devout pray *through* the icon to the sacred presence manifested therein. In that sense, the icon is a threshold, a window to a sacramental encounter.[11] It is a centering point for meditation and contemplation that leads towards the possibility of a spiritual encounter that is fundamentally grounded in an aesthetic experience. The gold leaf backgrounds of Eastern Orthodox icons visually enhance the sacramental interpretation of light and matter.

One of the most significant contributions of Eastern Orthodox theology is its teaching of *theosis* (deification). Eliade notes its relevance in terms of this discussion of light and matter:

> [T]he central doctrine of Eastern theology, notably the idea of the deification (*theosis*) of man, is of great originality, even though it depends on Saint Paul, the Gospel of John, and other biblical texts. The equivalence between salvation and deification derived from the mystery of the Incarnation. . . . The Incarnation of the Logos had made *theosis* possible, but it is always the grace of God which effectuates it. It is this which explains the importance of the interior prayer (later "uninterrupted prayer"), the contemplation, and the monastic life

in the Eastern Church. Deification is preceded or accompanied by an experience of mystical light.[12]

The writings of Gregory Palamas on the radiant and transformative light of the Transfiguration also enhance the Eastern Orthodox sensibility of the interpenetration of light and matter, of the spiritual and the aesthetic that is a natural part of the sensibility of Mircea Eliade.[13] As David Tracy has commented, it is Eliade's retrieval of an Eastern Orthodox orientation that has enabled him to challenge traditional Western Christian thinking. Tracy credits Eliade's spiritual sensitivity to Eastern Christian theology as a constant source for his awareness of the possibility of participating in the manifestation of the Sacred through our "divinized" humanity.[14]

Moreover, the transformative and disclosive conjunction of light and matter is best expressed by Eliade himself in his *Autobiography:*

> But I remember especially a summer afternoon when the whole household was sleeping. I left the room my brother and I shared, creeping so as not to make any noise, and headed towards the drawing room. I hardly knew how it looked, for we were not allowed to go in except on special occasions or when we had guests. Besides, I believe that the rest of the time the door was locked. But this time I found it open and entered, still crawling. The next moment I was transfixed with emotion. It was as if I had entered a fairy-tale palace. The roller blinds and the heavy curtains of green velvet were drawn. The room was pervaded by an eerie iridescent light. It was as though I were suddenly enclosed within a huge grape. I don't know how long I stayed there on the carpet, breathing heavily. When I came to my senses, I crept carefully across the floor, detouring around the furniture, looking greedily at the little tables and shelves on which all kinds of statuettes had been carefully placed along with cowry shells, little crystal vials, and small silver boxes. I gazed into the large venetian mirrors in whose deep and clear waters I found myself looking different—more grown up, more handsome, as if ennobled by that light from another light.[15]

Here clearly for Eliade the experience of the interpenetration of light and matter was felt in a singular and transformative manner. Substitute the terms transcendence and immanence for light and matter respectively, and a religious interpretation of this experience reveals the structure of a ritual of initiation. Similar experiences of the conjunction of light and matter are recounted by Eliade in *Autobiography, No Souvenirs, Ordeal by Labyrinth,* and in several of his scholarly texts.[16] Eliade's scientific interest in investigating matter as a source of sacrality would then appear to have an experiential base.[17] Consider the possible connections between Eliade's theme of "cosmic Christianity" and the Eastern Orthodox theology of the Incarnation, Transfiguration and *theosis;* or his interest in the transmutation of matter to his classic study of yoga.[18]

Once the experiential base of Eliade's scholarly and creative texts has been acknowledged, the formative but subliminal influence of an Eastern Orthodox sensibility upon his thought is recognizable. Thus, the central role of images and symbols in his scientific study of religions is apparent. His continued examination of the "Center of the World" relates to his interest in the interpenetration of light and matter in terms of a geographic site. A study of his writings on the rituals of initiation suggests a continued interest in the architectural structures created for these rites as well as the special costumes of the ritual participants. His study of myths and mythical structures has to do with the primal human need to hear and to tell stories. And his interest in searching for and analyzing the hidden but continual presence of the Sacred in modern art and literature characterizes one who accepts the divinization of matter.

And at the heart of all this is an interest in light—as a spiritual source, as divine illumination, and as a means of revelation. As if to highlight this interest, Eliade selects visual artists like Constantin Brancusi and Marc Chagall whose artworks are permeated with what has been described as a "radiant form of light."[19] Such a luminosity infuses its object with a glow which radiates throughout the artwork and outside of its boundaries. It is a light which invites attention and participation, and which suggests that the perceiver is able to pass through this object to an encounter with the Other. This is the type of light present in an Eastern Orthodox icon, a Śiva liṅgam, a Brancusi sculpture, and a Chagall painting. This is the same quality of light that transfixed the young Eliade in his parents' drawing room. This is the light that conjoins light and matter in the writings of Mircea Eliade. This is the light that suffused Mount Tabor at the Transfiguration. It is a transformative light which is the interpenetration of Creation and Time, and which is made known to us through the arts.

Consider the following entry Eliade made in his journal in September 1957 during a stay in Florence:

> Of the frescoes that decorate the monks' cells I remember—for reasons other than artistic—the *Transfiguration* and the *Two Marys at the Tomb* (nos. 6 and 8). In these two compositions the Christ is shown to us in his glory, as though in an immense egg of dazzling whiteness. I feel a limitless admiration for the metaphysical and theological genius of Angelico. In this image of the Divine Glory, similar to the Cosmogonic Egg, he says more than could be said in a whole book. The intuition of Angelico is truly stupefying: the light of the transfiguration, which blinded the apostles on Mount Tabor, is the same glorious light of the cosmos on the eve of the creation, when the world was still in its embryo state, not yet detached from God.[20]

And so the worlds of Mircea Eliade merge—the personal, the

aesthetic, the imaginative, the scholarly, and the spiritual. It is almost impossible to see where the one ends and the other begins. Yet it is the integral unity and universality of the oeuvre which makes it accessible. For as reflected in the following passage of dialogue by Constantin Brancusi in Eliade's play, "The Endless Column," each of us is the initiate being brought into a new mode-of-being-in-the-world when we encounter the imaginative vision of the arts.

> But I can tell you that in the Labyrinth, as in the Monument at Indore, you can enter only by first *descending under the earth,* and that in the Labyrinth and also in my Monument, you must enter it alone in order to reach the light in the center. . . .[21]

Symbolism, the Sacred, and the Arts is a collection of Mircea Eliade's essays examining the interrelationships between religion and the arts. They reflect Eliade's recognition of ". . . [the] possibility of being religiously moved by the image and the symbol."[22] He appears to have carefully considered Martha Graham's testimony:

> There is a fragment of poetry which has always had deep meaning for me. It referred to a long lost civilization: They had no poet and so they died. For the record of history lives in the arts.[23]

So, too, for Mircea Eliade a record of religious history lives in the symbols and images of the arts.

This collection begins by exploring Eliade's understanding of symbol: its origins, its functions, its role in human experience, and its aesthetic expression. "The Symbolism of Shadows in Archaic Religions," published here for the first time in English, is a significant essay for understanding not only Eliade's interpretation of symbol but also his hermeneutics of symbolism.

"Cultural Fashions and the History of Religions" examines the importance of the historian of religions in deciphering the hidden meanings in a cultural milieu. For Eliade, the spiritual sense of a people can be understood by a study of their culture, and especially of those persons or ideas that are "popular." His thesis that popular cultural expressions are revelatory of spirituality is no less possible or meaningful in a secular century. In "Survivals and Camouflages of Myths," Eliade comments upon the structural analogies between classical mythology and the modern narrative with the latter fulfilling a mythic function in contemporary culture.

Part II of this collection surveys Eliade's interest in the visual arts. "Divinities: Art and the Divine" focuses on the heart of the matter: the relationship between religion and art. Archaic and folk cultures translate their religious experiences into concrete images. The Sacred allows itself to be manifested in but not limited to these images. In "Masks: Mythical and Ritual Origins," Eliade considers the relationship between the ritual-maker (in this case, either the maker or wearer of the mask) and Time; in particular, the power of the mask to allow its wearer to experience the loss of the traditional sense of Time, space and individuality. The mystery of the transformation of art into ritual and ritual into art is analyzed in terms of myth and magic.

In "Reflections on Indian Art," Eliade reveals his early interest in religious iconography and aesthetic expressions of the Sacred. These reflections on aesthetic expressions of spirituality suggest the fundamental pattern of Eliade's mature reflections on religion and the arts.

Like modern literature, modern art interests Eliade for its expression of the camouflaged survival of the Sacred in a secular century. In "The Sacred and the Modern Artist," he applies his analysis of modern literature to the visual arts. Eliade finds that although artists would decry traditional religious art, their art is no less an expression of the presence of the Sacred. Eliade sees affinities between the non-representational art of many modern artists and the cosmic religiosity of archaic societies.

The exchange between Marc Chagall and Mircea Eliade highlights the interrelationship between religion and art in a personal way. In his verbal reflections on the power and spirituality of art, Chagall reveals the prophetic side of the artist. His statement, like his paintings, resonates with a powerful authenticity from his deepest human experiences. Eliade's response is a reflection on the spirituality inherent in Chagall's paintings.

"Brancusi and Mythology" is an insightful analysis of the Romanian sculptor's aesthetic inspiration and the spiritual possibilities of his oeuvre. In his interpretation of Brancusi, Eliade reveals himself as a historian of religions in identifying and discussing the visualization of primordial myths, the *coincidentia oppositorum*, the conjunction of light and matter, and the elements of alchemy in Brancusi's sculptures. The continual presence of the Sacred in human experience accounts for Brancusi's retrieval of the cosmic sacrality of matter, in this case, the primal stone.

Part III surveys Eliade's continued interest in the "Center of the World" through his essays on architecture. "Sacred Architecture and Symbolism" is an in-depth analysis of the "Center of the World"—its mythical and ritual origins, its transformations in various societies, and its camouflaged contemporary expressions. Eliade is also concerned here with important methodological issues, and he suggests his own hermeneutic development *vis à vis* the work of other scholars. The cosmological and soteriological functions of architecture are examined in a cross-cultural, trans-historical context.

In "Barabudur, the Symbolic Temple," Eliade applies the afore-mentioned iconological analysis to this study of one specific religious edifice. This in-depth analysis of the Temple of Barabudur delineates the relationship between art and ritual, the transformation of space from Profane to Sacred, and Buddhist iconology. Eliade carefully examines the meaning and value of this singular religious edifice through his own categories of *axis mundi*, "Center of the World," Sacred and Profane, *coincidentia oppositorum*, and Creation and Time.

Eliade accents his experience of particular places in Portugal in "From the Portuguese Journals, 1941–1944." Although he delves deeply into an examination of several Portuguese master paintings, it is the spatial environment and ambiance of these paintings that has the most marked effect upon him. This essay is an appropriate conclusion to Parts II and III for we are reminded that as the placement of the religious edifice requires the appearance of a hierophany or the presence of a "Center of the World," so too the experience of an artwork is effected by its location and the sense of environment the artwork creates.

With Part IV, our attention turns to that art form that Mircea Eliade knows best—literature. We begin with an early (1937) essay, "Folkloric Themes and Artistic Creations." Eliade examines the lack of "folk inspiration" in the work of Romanian artists and writers. Decrying this situation, Eliade calls for a retrieval of the authentic creativity that first inspired the folklore of Romania. Implicit in this essay are several of the themes which are more fully developed in Eliade's mature studies of the structure and source of the literary imagination.

The next two essays in Part IV deal specifically with the work of two Romanian expatriate writers. In "Marthe Bibesco and the Meeting of Eastern and Western Literature," Eliade analyzes the relationship between Princess Bibesco's life and her oeuvre. Mutual interest is at the heart of Eliade's study of Princess Bibesco: her interest in the Romanian folk traditions, her study of mythology, her passion for history, her nostalgia for paradise, and her search for the spiritual unity that grounds a universal "cosmic Christianity." Even Eliade's analysis of Princess Bibesco's sense of being an "exile" has an autobiographical ring to it.

In "Eugene Ionesco and 'The Nostaglia for Paradise,'" Eliade examines the playwright's work from the perspective of a religious sensibility. For Ionesco, literature (especially the theatre) has a soterio-logical function. The theme of light—the mystic light of Mount Tabor to be exact—is juxtaposed to the theme of sinking in the mud. Eliade's analysis of the theme of light in Ionesco's oeuvre again has an autobio-graphical quality. Here as elsewhere in this collection and throughout Eliade's entire oeuvre—creative and scholarly—appears the consistent theme of the nostalgia for paradise.

The concluding essay of this collection, "Literary Imagination and Religious Structure" is autobiographical. The interdependency of the literary imagination and the scientific intellect *is* the dialectical world of Mircea Eliade. For him the writing of fiction is "an experience in method" and "an instrument of knowledge." Simultaneously, his primal experi-ence of the *mundus imaginalis* grounds and enriches his scientific intellect.

This collection formally ends with a selected bibliography of critical essays analyzing Mircea Eliade's fiction, art and literary criticism, and their relationship (or lack thereof) to his scholarly world. This may prove a helpful starting point for more critical or fully developed examinations of the worlds and oeuvre of Mircea Eliade—artist, critic, poet and scholar.

NOTES

1. I am happy to acknowledge my indebtedness to those who were my colleagues and students in the seminar "Mircea Eliade: The Scholar as Artist, Critic, and Poet," at The George Washington University, Spring 1985. Much of those varied interpretations and conversations of Eliade's oeuvre are woven into this introductory esay. I am especially grateful to Alf Hiltebeitel, Professor of Religion, for closing our seminar with his own interpretation of the significance of light and matter in Eliade's work. Happily, his perceptions of Eliade balanced my own as his interests lie in the "scientific" and mine in the "aesthetic." I am also grateful to Arthur Hall Smith, Associate Professor of Painting, for our conversation about the aesthetic dimensions of Eliadean thought and for the distinctions between radiant and retinal light. In the end, of course, this inter-pretation of Eliade [and its inherent flaws] are totally my own.

2. Mircea Eliade, "Literary Imagination and Religious Structure," see p. 171 of this collection.

3. Mircea Eliade, "Foreword—Literature and Fantasy," *Tales of the Sacred and the Supernatural* (Philadelphia: Westminster Press, 1981), 7–13.

4. For more detailed analyses of the literary writings of Mircea Eliade, see the critical bibliography that concludes this collection.

5. David Tracy, *The Analogical Imagination* (New York: The Crossroad Pub-lishing Company, 1981), 207.

6. For example, see any of the following essays by Martin Heidegger, "The Origin of the Work of Art," "What Are Poets For?," and ". . . Poetically Man Dwells. . ." in his *Poetry, Language, Thought* (New York: Harper Colophon Books, 1975 [1971]).

7. The story of Rabbi Eisik of Cracow is recounted by Mircea Eliade in

"Brancusi and Mythology," see pp. 93–94 of this collection.

8. Eliade, "Literary Imagination and Religious Structure," p. 171. See also his interpretation of the life and oeuvre of Princess Marthe Bibesco, also an expatriate Romanian writer living in Paris, in "Marthe Bibesco and the Meeting of Eastern and Western Literature," pp. 154–163 of this collection.

9. Mircea Eliade, *Ordeal by Labyrinth* (Chicago: University of Chicago Press, 1982), 55.

10. For a detailed theological discussion of the role of the icon in Eastern Orthodox theology, see either *Saint John of Damascus, On the Divine Images* (Crestwood, NY: St. Vladimir's Seminary Press, 1980); or, *Saint Theodore the Studite, On the Holy Icons* (Crestwood, NY: St. Vladimir's Seminary Press, 1981). See also, Mircea Eliade, *A History of Religious Ideas*, Volume 3: *From Muhammad to the Age of Reforms*, translated by Alf Hiltebeitel and Diane Apostolos-Cappadona (Chicago: University of Chicago Press, 1985), 55–61, esp. 59–61.

11. My interpretation of icon as a threshold experience has an affinity to Victor Turner's notion of liminality. See Victor Turner, *The Forest of Symbols* (Ithaca, NY: Cornell University Press, 1977 [1967]), 93–111.

12. Eliade, *A History of Religious Ideas*, Volume 3, 57.

13. See Gregory Palamas, *Triads for the Defense of the Hesychasts Saints*, esp. 1:2, 2; 3:1, 12–17 from the translations and summaries by John Meyendorff, *Saint Gregory Palamas and Orthodox Spirituality* (Crestwood, NY: St. Vladimir's Seminary Press, 1974). See also any of Meyendorff's studies in French on Palamas, e.g., *Introduction á l'étude de Grégoire Palamas* (which includes a complete exposition of the published and unpublished works of Palamas). See also Vladimir Lossky, "La Théologie de la Lumière chez Grégoire Palamas de Thessalonique," *Dieu Vivant* 1 (1945), 93–118; and Jaroslav Pelikan, *The Spirit of Eastern Christendom* (Chicago: The University of Chicago Press, 1974), 261ff. As to Eliade's own interpretation of Palamas, see his *A History of Religious Ideas*, Volume 3, 57, 219–220; and his essay, "Experiences of Mystic Light" in Eliade, *The Two and the One* (New York: Harper Torchbook, 1969), 19–77, esp. 61–65. Also consider note #6 of Eliade's essay, "Eugene Ionesco and 'The Nostalgia for Paradise,'" p. 169 of this collection.

14. Tracy, *The Analogical Imagination*, 208.

15. Mircea Eliade, *Autobiography I: Journey East, Journey West 1907–1937* (San Francisco: Harper and Row, 1982), 6. See also Eliade, *Ordeal by Labyrinth*, 6–11, for further discussion of this incident.

16. See any of the following by Eliade: *Autobiography*, 28–30, 72–73; *No Souvenirs* (New York: Harper and Row, 1977), 116–117, 300; and, *Ordeal by Labyrinth*, 6–11. See also Eliade's scholarly works on the conjunction of light and matter; for example, "Spirit, Light and Seed" in *Occultism, Witchcraft and Cultural Fashions* (Chicago: University of Chicago Press, 1976), 93–119; "Experiences of Mystic Light" in *The Two and the One*, 19–77; and the passages in *A History of Religious Ideas*, Volumes 1–3, dealing with various traditions of religious

mysticism. Consider also the role of light and matter in Eliade's play, "The Endless Column," *Dialectics and Humanism* 1 (1983), 43–88.

17. See Eliade's description of the story of the lead soldier in his *Autobiography*, 64–65.

18. Mircea Eliade, *Yoga, Immortality and Freedom* (Princeton: Princeton University Press, Bollingen Series No. 56, 1973 [1958]).

19. See my doctoral dissertation, "The Emergence of Christian Romanticism in Nineteenth-Century American Art and Theology: A Comparative Study of Thomas Cole's 'Voyage of Life' and Horace Bushnell's *Christian Nurture*," for a detailed discussion of the aesthetic and theological dimensions of radiant light.

20. Eliade, *No Souvenirs*, 23.

21. Mircea Eliade, "The Endless Column," 79.

22. Eliade, *Ordeal by Labyrinth*, 55.

23. From Martha Graham's testimony before the Senate Appropriations Subcommittee on the N.E.A. Appropriations, March 1979.

Diane Apostolos-Cappadona

Part I:

Theories of Symbolism

I / 1

The Symbolism of Shadows in Archaic Religions

Preliminary Remarks

THERE IS NO QUESTION of beginning a detailed analysis of symbolism in these few pages.[1] We will content ourselves to present briefly certain aspects which directly pertain to the subject of this article, namely, the symbolism of Shadows in primitive traditions.

First of all, let us say that at the level of archaic societies, all symbolism is, or at least was, a religious symbolism. Symbols reveal a modality of the real or a deep structure of the World, and in the spiritual horizon of primitive man, the real mingles with the Sacred and the World is considered the creation of the Gods. Consequently, every revelation bearing on the structure of the Universe, or on different modes of existence in the world, and especially on human existence, is at the same time a revelation of religious nature. From the beginnings of archaic cultures, a *hierophany* is simultaneously an *ontophany*, the manifestation of the Sacred is equivalent to an unveiling of Being and vice versa.

It follows that archaic religious symbolism is dependent upon an ontology. From a particular point of view, the symbol itself may be considered as a language which, although conceptual, is nevertheless capable of expressing a coherent thought on existence and on the World. The symbol reveals a pre-systematic ontology to us, which is to say an expression of thought from a period when conceptual vocabularies had not yet been constituted. To give only one example, the terms designating "becoming" appear fairly late in history, and only in some languages of high culture: Sanskrit, Greek, Chinese. But the symbolism of "becoming," the images and the myths which place it in motion are already

"The Symbolism of Shadows in Archaic Religions" was first published as "Le symbolisme des ténèbres dans les religions archaiques" in *Polarités du symbole, Études Carmélitaines* 39 (1960), 15–28. It is translated from the French by Diane Apostolos-Cappadona and Frederica Adelman.

evidenced in the archaic strata of culture. All the images of the spiral, of weaving, of the emergence of light from shadow, of the phases of the moon, of the wave, etc., express the ideas of movement, of cycle, of duration, of passage from one mode of being into another (passage of the "unformed," the shadow, into the "formed," to the light). These symbols and myths of "becoming" have a lunar structure. It is the Moon which discloses *par excellence* the flow, passage, waxing and waning, birth, death and rebirth, in short the cosmic rhythms, the eternal becoming of things, Time.[2] This is to say that due to lunar symbolism, predialectic man was able to become conscious of the temporal modality of the Cosmos well before systematic thought had succeeded in extricating the concept of "becoming" and expressing it in adequate terms.

Other examples can be given illustrating the fact that the symbol is capable of expressing the "truths" of the theological order; once again from the period of predialectic thought, the essential function of the symbol is precisely in disclosing the structures of the real inaccessible to empirical experience. The words expressing the concepts of *transcendence* and *freedom* were witnessed to relatively late in the history of philosophy. And still, in primitive cultures, many symbols and myths relating to "magical flight" and celestial ascent are used to signify these spiritual experiences. "Magical flight" expresses the fact that weight is abolished, that ontological mutation has occurred in the human being itself. On the other hand, an entire set of symbols and meanings having reference to the spiritual life, and especially to the powers of intelligence, are simultaneously images of "flight" and "wings."

"Flight" translates as intelligence, comprehension of secret things or metaphysical truths. "Intelligence [*manas*] is the most rapid of birds," says the *Rig Veda*, VI, 9, 5. And the *Pañcaviṃça Brāhmaṇa*, VI, 1, 13 specifies: "He who understands has wings." If one considers "flight" and all its parallel symbolism in its totality, their significance is immediately disclosed: all translate as a rupture effected in the Universe of daily experience. The double intentionality of this rupture is evident: we gain at once both *transcendence* and *freedom* through "flight."

This fact has its importance. It proves that the roots of freedom must be sought in the depths of the psyche and not in the conditions created by certain historical moments; in other words, that the desire for absolute freedom ranks among the essential nostalgias of man, whatever his cultural period and his form of social organization. The rupture caused by the "flight" also signifies an act of transcendence. It is not difficult to encounter already among the "primitives" the desire to surpass the human condition "from on high," to transmute it by an excess of "spiritualization." Because we can translate all the myths and symbolisms of "magical flight" by the nostalgia to see the human body behave like a "spirit," to transmute the corporeal modality of the human into a modality of the spirit.[3]

When we say that symbols succeed in disclosing structures of the real, which much later and in certain cultures had been signified by concepts, we do not intend to homologize symbols with concepts. Their essence and their function are different. Symbols still maintain contact with the deep sources of life; they express, we may say, the "lived" spiritual. This is the reason why symbols have a numinous aura: they disclose that the modalities of the Spirit are at the same time manifestations of Life, and, by consequence, directly engage human existence. Symbols not only disclose a structure of the real or even a dimension of existence, at the same time they carry a significance for human existence. This is why even symbols bearing on ultimate reality conjointly constitute some existential revelations for the man who deciphers their message. Here we can measure the entire distance which separates conceptual language from symbolic language. Not only because wherever it strives to grasp the contradictory aspects of ultimate reality, conceptual language sometimes runs afoul of considerable difficulties; but also because it does not succeed in communicating the existential significance which accompanies the disclosures of the deep structures of reality.

We know the desperate efforts of the diverse Oriental as well as Occidental theologies and metaphysics to conceptually express the *coincidentia oppositorum*, that is to say the mode of being of Ultimate Reality, of the Absolute or of the Divinity. But this mode of being is fairly easily expressed by religious images and symbols. For example, the conjunction of the Serpent (symbol of the chthonic Shadows and the non-manifested), and the Eagle (symbol of the solar light and the manifested), or the Chinese diagram of the *Yin-Yang*, or the paradoxical coexistence, in the same divinity of polar and antagonistic principles. In Vedic India, the Sun, prototype of the Gods, is also the "Serpent";[4] Agni, the god of fire, is at the same time an "Asura priest" (*Rig Veda*, VII, 30, 3), i.e., essentially a "demon."[5]

It is also necessary not to lose sight of one characteristic which is specific to a symbol: its *multivalence*, which is to say the multiplicity of meanings which it expresses simultaneously. This is why it is sometimes so difficult to explain a symbol, to exhaust its significations; it refers to a plurality of contexts and it is valuable on a number of levels. If we retain only one of its significations, in declaring it the only "fundamental" or "first" or "original" signification, we risk not grasping the true message of the symbol. Whatever a symbol tries to show us, it is precisely the unity between the different levels of the real, and to us, this unity is rationally accessible with difficulty. The interpretations of symbols by the reductive method, that is to say the reduction of all possible significations to only one proclaimed "fundamental," appears erroneous to us. The cognitive function of the symbol is precisely to disclose to us a perspective from whence things appear different and very distinct activities are revealed as equivalent and united. The Sanskrit term, *liṇga* (literally, phallus), so important in Hinduism, connected with the term *lāṇgula* (plough), derives from an Austro-Asiatic root, *lak,* designating both a spade and the male generative organ.[6] Woman is compared to the soil, the phallus to the spade, and the generative act to agrarian labor. But as the spade is called phallus and sowing is homologous to the sexual act, it does not follow that the "primitive" farmer is ignorant of the specific function of his labor and the immediate concrete value of his tool. Symbolism *adds* a new value to an object or to an action without however disturbing their own proper and immediate values. In applying itself to an object or an action, symbolism renders it "open." Symbolic thought makes the immediate reality "shine," but without diminishing or devaluating it: in its perspective the Universe is not closed, no object is isolated in its own existentialness; everything holds together in a closed system of correspondences and assimilations.

Structures of a Symbol

Now we understand why we must approach the symbolism of Shadows simultaneously in all the levels where it occurs: we have the opportunity to perceive its significance in the measure where we bear in mind all its contexts at once. The first level is cosmological: Shadows symbolize the Cosmic Night, the undifferentiated totality, the unformed, the secret. From one perspective, Shadows are homologizable with Chaos, since no form is discernible, no structure is disengaged; this is the modality of the pre-formed. Shadows symbolize at the same time that which is *before* the manifestation of forms and *after* their disappearance, when the forms are reintegrated into the primordial mass. This is why the cosmological symbolism of Shadows approximates that of the Waters. The Waters also express the undifferentiated, the pre-formed, the unmanifested.[7] The act of manifestation is signified by the emergence from the Waters, the exemplary image of Creation is the island or the lotus which rises about the waves. In Asiatic, Oceanic and American Indian iconography, the passage from Shadows into Light, of the non-manifested into the cosmogony is signified by the masks of the *t'ao-t'ieh,* the symbol of obscurity, the monster allows a solar sign to escape from its mouth, this is the symbol of light or of a child (=mythic Ancestor, symbolizing the foundation of one "humanity" or the beginning of a new Age[8]).

In this last example, we see that the cosmological valence of the symbolism of Shadows surpasses its plane of reference and extends into a neighboring level: a "form" rising from Shadows can signify not only the manifestation of a World, but also the appearance of a "humanity" (a race, a people). The emergence of Light out of Shadows symbolizes the creation of the Universe as well as the beginnings of History. In one case as in the other, it is a matter of the "form" emerging from the un-manifested. But the strict relation between the symbols of Shadows (chthonic monster, tiger, etc.) and the Light (sun, pheasant, etc.), teaches us that Shadows are not valued solely in a negative sense (non-being) but also in a positive sense: the sum of the "unformed," "seeds." The pre-cosmogonic Chaos is not the non-being, but the totality, the fusion of all forms.

This becomes even more apparent when we examine the second context of the symbolism of Shadows: the initiatory context. It is known that in the majority of traditional societies, initiation rites at puberty essentially involve a ceremony of symbolic death and rebirth for the initiate. The "death" is signified by tortures and initiatory mutilations, or by a ritual interment, or by the forgetting (obviously feigned) of the "unillumined" existence which preceeded the initiation, and the forget-ting of the mother tongue, etc.; but also by isolation in the bush or in a solitary hut, which is to say segregation in Shadows.[9] The forest, the jungle, Shadows symbolize the beyond, Hell. In this context, Shadows signify simultaneously death (=Hell) and the Cosmic Night, the regres-sion to the unformed, pre-cosmogonic mode. On the other hand, to be enclosed in the initiatory hut symbolizes the maternal womb.[10] The "death" of the initiate signifies at once a *regressus ad uterum* and a return to the pre-cosmogonic state.

Many a time, the hut where the initiates are enclosed represents the body or the open mouth of a sea monster; for example, a crocodile or a serpent.[11] In certain regions of Ciram, the opening through which the novices penetrate is properly called the "serpent's mouth." To be en-closed in the cabin is equivalent to finding oneself imprisoned in the monster's belly. In New Guinea for the circumcision of boys, a special hut is built which has the form of the monster Barlun (who is thought to swallow the novices), that is to say presents a "belly" and a "tail."[12] The novices' entry into the hut is equivalent to the penetration into the monster's belly. The initiatory hut of the Kai and of the Jabim have two entries; the first, shaped like the monster's mouth, is very large; the other symbolizing the tail is much smaller.[13]

An equivalent rite is the entry into a mannequin which resembles an aquatic monster (crocodile, whale, large fish). And so, for example, among the Papua of New Guinea, a monstrous hamper called *kaiemunu* is built of raffia; at his initiation, the boy is brought into the monster's belly. But the initiatory feeling has been lost in our day: the novice enters into the *kaiemunu* while his father is completing its construction.[14]

The initiation constitutes a "new birth"; it thus reiterates symbolically the *regressus ad uterum*. But the exemplary model of embryology, as moreover of all "creation," of all "making,"[15] is cosmogony. Consequently in many ways, initiation imitates cosmogony. To enter into the belly of the monster is also equivalent to a regression into the primordial void, into the Cosmic Night, and to exit from the monster is equivalent to a cosmogony: it is the passage from "chaos" into "creation." The initiatory death reiterates this exemplary return to Chaos in order to make possible the repetition of the cosmogony, that is to say to prepare for a new birth. The regression to Chaos oftentimes confirms itself by being taken literally; this is the case, for example, in the initiatory illness of future shamans which has been a number of times considered as true madness. In effect, we are witness to a total crisis often leading to the disintegration of personality.[16] In the horizon of archaic spirituality, "psychic chaos" is valued as a reply to "pre-cosmogonic chaos," the amorphic and indescribable state which precedes all cosmogony. But we know that, for archaic and traditional cultures, the symbolic return to Chaos is indispensable to all new creation, whatever the level of manifestation, every new sowing, or every new harvest is preceeded by a collective orgy which symbolizes the reintegration of "pre-cosmogonic Night," of total "confusion"; every New Year is comprised of a series of ceremonies which signify the reiteration of the primordial Chaos and of the cosmogony.[17] But the same symbolism can be deciphered in the "madness" of future shamans, in their "psychic chaos," in Shadows where they have strayed: this is the sign that profane man is in the process of "dissolution" and that a new personality is on the point of being born.

Maui, Väinämöinen, Ilmarinen

From a certain perspective, we can homologize the initiatory "madness" of future shamans to the dissolution of the old personality which follows the entry into the monster's belly or the descent into Hell. In all these contexts, we are concerned with a total immersion into Shadows. Each initiatory event of this type always ends by *creating* something, by founding a "world" or a new mode of being. A Polynesian myth admirably illustrates what we have just said. At the end of a life rich in adventures, Maui, the great Maori hero, returns to his country to his grandmother, Hine-nui-te-po, the Great Lady of the Night. He finds her asleep, and quickly shedding his clothes penetrates her giant body. He traverses her without incident, but when he is ready to leave, that is to say still having over half of his body in the giant's mouth, the birds who had accompanied him, broke out in laughter. Awakening abruptly, the Great Lady of the Night clenches her teeth and cuts in half the hero who died. The Maoris say that it is for this reason that man is mortal; if Maui had succeeded in leaving his grandmother's body uninjured, men would have become immortal.[18]

Maui's grandmother is *Mater Terra*. Entering into her belly is equivalent to descending alive into the subterranean depths, that is to say into Hell. This is a matter then of a *descensus ad infernos*, like that which is evidenced for example in the myths and sagas of the ancient Orient and the Mediterranean worlds. But we ascertain in this myth a new significance to initiatory entry into the body of a giant or a monster: this is no longer death followed by rebirth, a theme common to all initiations, but the quest for immortality. In other words, this time it is a matter of confronting death without dying, of descending into the Kingdom of the Night and of the Dead, and of returning from there *alive*—like the shamans still do in our own day during their trances. But as the shaman enters the Kingdom of the Dead *in spirit* only, Maui gives himself up to a descent in the material sense of the word. This is the well-known difference between shamanic ecstasy and the adventures of flesh-and-blood heroes.

We recognize the same difference in northern Arctic-Eurasia, where religious experience is dominated by shamanism. For example, following certain versions of the *Kalevala*, the hero Väinämöinen undertakes a journey to the Land of the Dead, Teconala. The daughter of Teroni, the Lord of the Underworld, swallows him but once arrived in the giant's stomach, Väinämöinen builds himself a boat and as the text says, rowed vigorously "from one end of her intestine to the other." The giantess was finally forced to vomit him into the sea.[19]

During their trances, Lapp shamans are reputed to enter into the intestine of a large fish or a whale. A legend tells us that, the son of a shaman woke his father, who had been asleep for three years, with these words, "Father, wake-up and return from the fish's intestine, return from the third mouth of his intestine!"[20] In this case, it is a matter of an ecstatic voyage, that is to say, in spirit, into the stomach of a marine monster. We will try to understand in good time why the shaman remains for three years in "the third mouth of the intestine." For the moment, recall several other initiatory adventures of this same type.

Still following the Finnish tradition, the blacksmith Ilmarinen courted a young girl who imposed as a condition of marriage that Ilmarinen should "wander among the teeth of the old witch Hiisi." Ilmarinen left to search for her, as he approached the sorceress she swallowd him. She then asked him to leave by her mouth, but Ilmarinen refused. "I will make my own door!" he responded, and with blacksmith tools which he magically forged for himself, he cracked the old woman's stomach and left. In another version, the condition imposed by the young girl was to catch a large fish. But the fish swallows him. Once in its stomach, Ilmarinen struggled about until the fish burst.[21]

This myth has several versions. Lucien of Samosate recounts in his "True History" that a sea monster swallowed an entire ship and its crew. The men lit a great fire which killed the monster, and in order to get out they opened its mouth with poles. A similar story is told in Polynesia. The hero Nganaoa's boat had been swallowed by a type of whale, but the hero took the mast and forced it into its mouth in order to keep it open. Then he descended into the monster's stomach where he found both his parents still alive. Nganaoa lit a fire, killed the whale and left through its mouth. This folkloric motif is widespread in Oceania.[22]

Let us note the ambivalent role of the sea monster. There is no doubt that the fish that swallowed Jonah and the other mythical heroes symbolizes death: his stomach represents Hell. In medieval visionary literature, Hell is frequently imaged in the form of an enormous sea monster, perhaps having the Biblical Leviathan as a prototype. To be swallowed then is equivalent to dying, to entering Hell; which is what all primitive initiation rites make very clearly understood. On the other hand, the entry into the monster's belly also signifies the reintegration of a pre-formed, embryonic state. As we have already said: the shadows which prevail in the monster's interior correspond to the Cosmic Night, to Chaos before Creation. In other words, we are dealing with a dual symbolism: that of Death which is to say the end of a temporal existence, and consequently, the end of Time—and the symbolism of the return to the germinal modality, which precedes all form and all temporal existence. On the cosmological plane, this dual symbolism refers to *Urzeit* and *Endzeit*.

"Shadows," "Madness," "Wisdom"

We recall that in penetrating into his grandmother's body, Maui sought immortality. This is to say that he believed that he was able by this initiatory exploit to found a new human condition, simliar to that of the gods. We also recall the legend of the Lapp shaman who in spirit remained for three years in the intestine of an enormous fish. Why had he undertaken this adventure? An old Finnish myth, in relation to Väinämöinen, may give us the answer. Väinämöinen created by magic, that is to say by singing, a boat; but he was unable to finish it because he lacked three words. To learn them, he went to find a renowned sorcerer, Antero, a giant who remained immobile for many years, like a shaman during his trance, so still that a tree grew from his shoulder and birds had made their nests in his beard, Väinämöinen fell into the giant's mouth and was soon swallowed. But once in Antero's stomach, he forged an iron suit for himself and threatened to stay for as long a time as it would take for him to obtain the three magic words to complete the boat.[23]

In this case, we are dealing with an initiatory adventure undertaken to gain secret knowledge. One descends into the belly of a giant or a monster to learn *science, wisdom*. It is for this reason that the Lapp shaman remains in the fish's belly for three years: to learn the secrets of Nature, to decipher the enigma of life, and to learn the future. But if entry into the monster's belly is equivalent to the descent into Hell, among Shadows and the Dead; if it symbolizes regression into the Cosmic Night as well as into Shadows of "madness" where all personality is dissolved, if we bear in mind all of these homologizations and correspondences among Death, Cosmic Night, Chaos, "madness," regression to the embryonic condition, then we understand why Shadows symbolize also Wisdom, why the future shamans ought to first know "madness," why creativity is always in relation to a certain "madness" or "orgy," unifying the symbolism of death and Shadows. It is during the period of segregation, that is to say when they are reputed to be swallowed up into the monster's stomach or found in the Shadows of Hell, that the initiates are instructed in the religious traditions of the tribe. The sacred science is only accessible in the course of or following the process of spiritual regeneration achieved by the initiatory death and rebirth.

"To Decipher" a Symbol

The multiple values of the symbolism of Shadows can be classified as follows:
(1) on the cosmological level: Cosmic Night; the pre-formed; the totality; the fusion of forms, Chaos;
(2) on the anthropocosmic level: the hereafter, Hell, but also the maternal Womb, the *regressus ad uterum*; the Land of the Dead, but also the "unformed," seed;

(3) on the anthropological level: death, but also initiation, i.e., ritual
    death followed by mystical rebirth; "chaos" in which the apprentice
    shaman is "broken up," i.e., initiatory "madness"; Hell where the
    Hero descends to obtain a new condition (eternal youth, immor-
    tality).

As we see it, these valences are considered interdependent, each
one implies all the others in some way, and considered together, form
a structure. The meaning of the symbolism of Shadows becomes comprehensible to us only in the measure that we succeed in grasping the
structure in its entirety. If we stop at one significance, as it is revealed
on only one level, we cannot say that we have "deciphered" the symbolism. If we interpret the symbolism of Shadows by insisting only on
its embryological or cosmological values, the meaning that we draw is
incomplete, indeed, incorrect. Because the symbol's function is precisely
to "open" simultaneously multiple and complementary perspectives on
the world and on existence. The symbolism of Shadows reveals at first
the unity between modes of being not easily homologizable in a conceptual perspective: Night, Chaos (cosmogonic or psychological), Death
(actual or ritual), the embryonic state (real or initiatory).

Considered together, the cosmological and initiatory valences of the
symbolism of Shadows (e.g., the Sun leaving the Night, the *regressus ad
uterum* in the monster's stomach, the entry of Maui into his grandmother's body, etc.) reveal a significance which was not obvious in any
one level taken separately: the positive value, "redemptory," of Shadows. In other words, we now understand not only that Shadows
precede Forms and periodically swallow them, when "being" rises and
returns to "non-being," when Death precedes Life and defeats it, but as
when the return to Shadows is beneficial; what's more, when in certain
cases (initiation, foundation of a new mode of being), it is even indispensable. Shadows symbolize in the end the universal *Urgrund*, the
primordial Totality, the paradoxical fusion of Being and Non-Being; thus
the sum total of all possibilities. A provisional regression into Shadows
is equivalent to an immersion in the inexhaustible source, where all
modes of being are already found *in potentia*. In studying the Indian
initiation of the *regressus ad uterum* type, we understand that their goals
were the *recommencement* of existence on a superior level and, especially,
with the sum of all possibilities intact, that is to say, as if the Time passed
between birth and the moment of initiation no longer existed, as if it
were abolished.[24] In effect, we retrieve in the symbolism of Shadows the
note of atemporality, of "eternity," of the suspension of becoming. Time
begins with the apparition of Forms, thus with the Light. Time is mea-
sured following the lunar rhythm and the path of the sun. The return to

Shadows implies then the immersion into the pre-formed, contact with that which was not worn away by Time.

The Function of Symbols

This brief analysis allows us to understand better the function of the symbol in the activity of the spirit. The symbol translates a human situation into cosmological terms; and reciprocally, more precisely, it discloses the interdependence between the structures of human existence and cosmic structures. This means that primitive man does not feel "isolated" in the Cosmos, that he is "open" to the World which symbolically is "familiar" to him. On the other hand, the cosmological valence of symbolism permits him to step out of a subjective situation, to recognize the objectivity of his personal experiences. Of course, it is not a question of reflections, but of intuitions, of immediate seizures of reality. The initiate shut in the initiatory hut finds himself simultaneously in the monster's belly and in the maternal womb, he is at once "dead" and "in the process of birth" (embryo), but he "feels" at the same time that his particular condition is also the condition of the world in the Cosmic Night, of the embryo-World which is not yet born. This is to say that he assumes the objectivity of his own experiences because he recognizes them outside of himself, identifies them in his cosmic life.

An important consequence proceeds from this cosmological valence of symbolism: we who understand symbols not only "open" ourselves to the objective world, but at the same time succeed in leaving our unique condition and acceding to a comprehension of the universal. The initiate isolated in the initiatory hut or the one who contemplates a t'ao-t'ieh mask and understands its significance, or the one who hears the myth of Maui or a story of the Jonah type intuitively perceives the unity of structure between his particular "nocturnal condition," and all the others. As we have already said, the symbol makes a concrete object "explode" by disclosing dimensions which are not given in immediate experience. Likewise, the symbol "explodes" a particular condition by revealing it as exemplary, i.e., indefinitely repeated in multiple and varied contexts. Consequently, "to live" a symbol and to decipher the messages correctly is equivalent to gaining access to the universal. To transform an individual experience by symbolism is equivalent to opening it to the Spirit. (We understand the importance of this function of the symbol for psychotherapeutic techniques; an image lived on multiple levels, especially the cosmological level, is likely to "awaken" the patient to the life of the Spirit.)

But there is still more: as the World is the divine creation *par excellence* it reveals the cosmological valences of a symbol (i.e., to discover the cosmological values in the lived experience of a symbol), is equivalent to participating, although in a mediated manner, in the Sacred. In revealing the cosmic context of the symbol, man is placed in the presence of the mystery of Creation. The World being a divine work, all understanding bearing these deep structures is accompanied by a religious experience. It is the encounter with this irreducible and mysterious fact: that the World came to be by the intervention of a superhuman Figure.

The general remarks suggested by the symbolism of Shadows will end here. A proper discussion requires an entire volume. But there is still a point which must be stressed. The interdependence of the valences of a symbol and the homology of its different contexts ought not to be understood as a monotonous repetition of the same message on different levels. The fact that the symbol of Shadows governs birth, puberty rites, death, mystical initiation (shamanistic or heroic) does not mean that there is no difference between these levels of experience. What we obtain through initiation is not accessible through physical birth. Of course, the initiation permits new birth, but it is a matter of a *mystical rebirth* of the spiritual order, i.e., access to another mode of existence (sexual maturity, participation in the Sacred and in the culture; in brief, "opening" to the Spirit). Each context of a symbol reveals *something more* which was only unformed and allusive in the neighboring contexts. Shadows of the initiatory hut do *not exactly repeat* Shadows of the fetal state as distinguished from the embryo; the initiate symbolically transformed into an embryo, assumes this ritual condition, in order to acquire a new mode of being, superior to simple biological existence. Concisely, to throw into relief the structure of the symbol with the help of a considerable number of contexts, does not intend to confuse its valences nor to reduce them to a single significance.

NOTES

1. The bibliography is considerable. See several references in Mircea Eliade, *Patterns in Comparative Religions* (New York: World Publishing, 1970 [1958]), 47ff.; and idem, *Images and Symbols* (New York: Search Books, 1969 [1961]).

2. Cf. Eliade, *Patterns*, 154ff.

3. On this problem, see Mircea Eliade, "Symbolisme du Vol magique," *Numen* III.12 (1956), 1–13, esp. 8–9.

4. Cf. e.g., *Rig Veda*, I, 24, 8; cf. Eliade, *Patterns*, 154.

5. Cf. ibid., 417, and especially the studies of Ananda K. Coomaraswamy, "Angel and Titan. An Essay on Vedic Ontology," *Journal of the American Oriental*

Society 55 (1935), 373–419; idem, "The Darker Side of the Dawn," *Smithsonian Miscellaneous Collections* 94 (1935). See also Mircea Eliade, *Mitul Reintegrarii* (Bucharest, 1942).

6. Cf. Mircea Eliade, *Yoga, Immortality and Freedom* (Princeton: Princeton University Press, Bollingen Series 56, 1973 [1954]), 352ff., 422.

7. On the symbolism of the Waters, see Eliade, *Patterns*, 18ff.; see also idem, *Images and Symbols*, 164ff., 199ff.

8. Carl Hentze has dedicated several important works to the exegesis of the complex of the mythico-iconography of the *t'ao-t'ieh*. See especially Carl Hentze, *Mythes et Symboles lunaires* (Anvers: Editions "De Sikkel," 1952); idem, *Objets rituels, Croyances et Dieux de la Chine antique et de l'Amérique* (Anvers: Editions "De Sikkel," 1936); idem, "Le culte de l'ours ou du tigre et le *t'ao-t'ien*," *Zalmoxis* I (1938), 50–68; and idem, *Die Sakralbronzen und ihre Bedeutung in den frühchinesischen Kulturen* (Anvers: Editions "De Sikkel," 1941).

9. For all that follows, see Mircea Eliade, "Mystère et Régénération spirituelle dans les Religions extra-européenes," *Eranos-Jahrbuch* XXIII (1955), 57–98; and idem, *Patterns of Initiation* (Chicago: University of Chicago Press, 1956).

10. Cf. R. Thurnwald, "Primitive Initiations und Wiedergeburtsriten," *Eranos-Jahrbuch* VII (1940), 321–398, esp. 393; see also Sir James Frazer, *Spirits of the Corn and the Wild* (New York: St. Martin's Press, 1955).

11. Ad. E. Jensen, *Beschneidung und Reifezeremonien bei Naturvölken* (Stuttgart: Strecker und Schroder, 1933), 94; Otto Zerries, *Das Schwirrholz. Untersuchung über die Verbreitung und Bedeutung des Schwirren im Kult* (Stuttgart: Strecker und Schroder, 1942), 44.

12. H. Schurtz, *Alterklassen und Männerbünde* (Berlin: G. Reimer, 1902), 224; Hans Nevermann, *Masken und Geheimbünde Melanesian* (Leipzig: Reimer-Hobbing, 1933), 24, 40, 56.

13. Jensen, op. cit., 87 (the Kai), 89 (the Jabim). Among the Karesau, the candidates are isolated in two huts, and it is said that they are in the Belly of the Spirit; cf. Wilhelm Schmidt, "Die geheime Junglingswiche du Karesau-Insulanern," *Anthropos* II (1907), 1029–1056, esp. 1032ff.

14. F. E. Williams, "The Pairama Ceremony in the Purari Delta, Papua," *Journal of the Anthropological Institute* LIII (1923), 361–382, esp. 363ff.

15. In the last place, see Mircea Eliade, "La vertu créatice du mythe," *Eranos-Jahrbuch* XXV (1956).

16. See Mircea Eliade, *Shamanism* (Princeton: Princeton University Press, Bollingen Series 76, 1974 [1951]), 33ff.; idem, "Expérience sensorielle et expérience mystique chez les primitifs," *Études Carmélitaines: Nos Sens et Dieu*, (1954), 70–99, esp. 77ff.

17. On this symbolism, see Eliade, *Patterns*, 345ff., 400; and idem, *The Myth of the Eternal Return, or Cosmos and History* (Princeton: Princeton University Press, Bollingen Series 46, 1977 [1949]), 36, 51ff.

18. W. D. Westervelt, *Legends of Maui the Demi-god* (Honolulu: The Hawaiian Gazette Co., Ltd., 1910), 128ff.; J. F. Stimson, *The Legends of Maui and Tabaki* (Honolulu: The Museum, 1934), 46ff.

19. Martti Naavio, *Väinämöinen, Eternal Sage* (Helsinki: FF Communications, Number 144, 1952), 117ff.

20. Ibid., 124.

21. Ibid., 114ff.

22. Cf. L. Rademacher, "Walfischmythen," *Archiv für Religionswissenschaft* IX (1906), 246ff.; F. Graebner, *Das Weltbild der Primitiven* (Munich: E. Reinhardt, 1924), 62ff.

23. Haavio, op. cit., 106ff.

24. Cf. Eliade, *Patterns*.

I / 2

Cultural Fashions and the History of Religions

The Artist's Unsuspected Mythologies

THE QUESTION THAT I should like to discuss is the following: what does a historian of religions have to say about his contemporary milieu? In what sense can he contribute to the understanding of its literary or philosophical movements, its recent and significant artistic orientations? Or even more, what has he to say, as a historian of religions, in regard to such manifestations of the *Zeitgeist* as its philosophical and literary vogues, its so-called cultural fashions? It seems to me that, at least in some instances, his special training should enable him to decipher meanings and intentions less manifest to others. I am not referring to those cases in which the religious context or implications of a work are more or less evident, as, for example, Chagall's paintings with their enormous "eye of God," their angels, severed heads, and bodies flying upside down—and his omnipresent ass, that messianic animal par excellence. Or Ionesco's recent play, *Le Roi se meurt,* which cannot be fully understood if one does not know the *Tibetan Book of the Dead* and the *Upanishads.* (And I can testify to the fact that Ionesco *did* read these texts; but the important thing for us to determine is what he accepted and what he ignored or rejected. Thus it is not a question of searching for *sources,* but a more exciting endeavor: to examine the renewal of Ionesco's imaginary creative universe through his encounter with exotic and traditional religious universes.)

But there are instances when only a historian of religions can discover some secret significance of a cultural creation, whether ancient or contemporary. For example, only a historian of religions is likely to

"Cultural Fashions and the History of Religions" was originally published in *The History of Religions. Essays in the Problem of Understanding,* edited by Joseph M. Kitagawa (Chicago: The University of Chicago Press, 1967), 21–38; and reprinted in *Occultism, Witchcraft and Cultural Fashions* by Mircea Eliade (Chicago: The University of Chicago Press, 1976), 1–17. It is reprinted here by permission.

perceive that there is a surprising structural analogy between James Joyce's *Ulysses* and certain Australian myths of the totemic-hero type. And just as the endless wanderings and fortuitous meetings of the Australian cultural heroes seem monotonous to those who are familiar with Polynesian, Indo-European, or North American mythologies, so the wanderings of Leopold Bloom in *Ulysses* appear monotonous to an admirer of Balzac or Tolstoi. But the historian of religions knows that the tedious wanderings and performances of the mythical ancestors reveal to the Australian a magnificent history in which he is existentially involved, and the same things can be said of the apparently tedious and banal journey of Leopold Bloom in his native city. Again, only the historian of religions is likely to catch the very striking similarities between the Australian and Platonic theories of reincarnation and anamnesis. For Plato, learning is recollecting. Physical objects help the soul withdraw into itself and, through a sort of "going back," to rediscover and repossess the original knowledge that it possessed in its extraterrestrial condition. Now, the Australian novice discovers, through his initiation, that he has already been here, in the mythical time; he was here in the form of the mythical ancestor. Through initiation he again learns to do those things which he did at the beginning, when he appeared for the first time in the form of a mythical being.

It would be useless to accumulate more examples. I will only add that the historian of religions is able to contribute to the understanding of writers as different as Jules Verne and Gérard de Nerval, Novalis and García Lorca.[1] It is surprising that so few historians of religions have ever tried to interpret a literary work from their own perspective. (For the moment I can recall only Maryla Falk's book on Novalis and Stig Wikander's studies of French writers from Jules Michelet to Mallarmé. Duchesne-Guillemin's important monographs on Mallarmé and Valéry could have been written by any excellent literary critic, without any contact with the history of religions.) On the contrary, as is well known, many literary critics, especially in the United States, have not hesitated to use the findings of the history of religions in their hermeneutical work. One need only call to mind the frequent application of the "myth and ritual" theory of the "initiation pattern" in the interpretation of modern fiction and poetry.[2]

My purpose here is more modest. I will try to see whether a historian of religions can decipher some hidden meanings in our so-called cultural fashions, taking as examples three recent vogues, all of which originated in Paris but are already spreading throughout western Europe and even the United States. Now, as we all know well, for a particular theory or philosophy to become popular, to be à la mode, *en vogue*, implies neither that it is a remarkable creation nor that it is devoid of all value. One of the fascinating aspects of the "cultural fashion" is that it does not matter whether the facts in question and their interpretation are true or not. No amount of criticism can destroy a vogue. There is something "religious" about this imperiousness to criticism, even if only in a narrow-minded, sectarian way. But even beyond this general aspect, some cultural fashions are extremely significant for the historian of religions. Their popularity, especially among the intelligentsia, reveals something of Western man's dissatisfactions, drives, and nostalgias.

"Totemic Banquets" and Fabulous Camels

To give only one example: Fifty years ago, Freud thought that he had found the origin of social organization, moral restrictions, and religion in a primordial murder, namely, the first patricide. He told the story in his book *Totem and Taboo*. In the beginning, the father kept all the women for himself and would drive his sons off as they became old enough to evoke his jealousy. One day, the expelled sons killed their father, ate him, and appropriated his females. "The totemic banquet," writes Freud, "perhaps the first feast mankind ever celebrated, was the repetition, the festival of remembrance, of this noteworthy criminal deed."[3] Since Freud holds that God is nothing other than the sublimated physical father, it is God himself who is killed and sacrificed in the totemic sacrifice. "This slaying of the father-god is mankind's original sin. This blood-guilt is atoned for by the bloody death of Christ."[4]

In vain the ethnologists of his time, from W. H. Rivers and F. Boas to A. L. Kroeber, B. Malinowski, and W. Schmidt, demonstrated the absurdity of such a primordial "totemic banquet."[5] In vain they pointed out that totemism is not found at the beginnings of religion and is not universal: not all peoples have passed through a "totemic stage"; that Frazer had already proved that, of the many hundred totemic tribes, only *four* knew a rite approximating the ceremonial killing and eating of the "totem-god" (a rite assumed by Freud to be an invariable feature of totemism); and, finally, that this rite has nothing to do with the origin of sacrifice, since totemism does not occur at all in the oldest cultures. In vain did Wilhelm Schmidt point out that the pretotemic peoples knew nothing of cannibalism, that patricide among them would be a

sheer impossibility, psychologically, sociologically, and ethically [and that] . . . the form of the pre-totemic family, and therefore of the earliest human family we can hope to know anything about through ethnology, is neither general promiscuity nor group-marriage, neither of which, according to the verdict of the leading anthropologists, ever existed at all.[6]

Freud was not in the least troubled by such objections, and this wild "gothic novel," *Totem and Taboo,* has since become one of the minor gospels of three generations of the Western intelligentsia.

Of course, the genius of Freud and the merits of psychoanalysis ought not to be judged by the horror stories presented as objective historical fact in *Totem and Taboo.* But it is highly significant that such frantic hypotheses could be acclaimed as sound scientific theory in spite of all the criticism marshaled by the major anthropologists of the century. What lay behind this victory was first the victory of psychoanalysis itself over the older psychologies and then its emergence (for many other reasons) as a cultural fashion. After 1920, then, the Freudian ideology was taken for granted in its entirety. A fascinating book could be written about the significance of the incredible success of this "roman noir frénétique," *Totem and Taboo.* Using the very tools and method of modern psychoanalysis, we can lay open some tragic secrets of the modern Western intellectual: for example, his profound dissatisfaction with the worn-out forms of historical Christianity and his desire to violently rid himself of his forefathers' faith, accompanied by a strange sense of guilt, as if he himself had killed a God in whom he could not believe but whose absence he could not bear. For this reason I have said that a cultural fashion is immensely significant, no matter what its objective value may be; the success of certain ideas or ideologies reveals to us the spiritual and existential situation of all those for whom these ideas or ideologies constitute a kind of soteriology.

Of course, there are fashions in other sciences, even in the discipline of history of religions, though evidently they are less glamorous than the vogue enjoyed by *Totem and Taboo.* That our fathers and grandfathers were fascinated by *The Golden Bough* is a comprehensible, and rather honorable, fact. What is less comprehensible, and can be explained only as a fashion, is the fact that between 1900 and 1920 almost all the historians of religions were searching for mother-goddesses, corn-mothers, and vegetation demons—and of course they found them everywhere, in all the religions and folklores of the world. This search for the Mother—mother earth, tree-mother, corn-mother, and so on— and also for other demonic beings related to vegetation and agriculture is also significant for our understanding of the unconscious nostalgias of the Western intellectual at the beginning of the century.

But let me remind you of another example of the power and prestige of fashions in history of religions. This time there is neither god nor goddess involved, neither corn-mother nor vegetation spirit, but an animal—specifically, a camel. I am referring to the famous sacrifice of a camel described by a certain Nilus who lived in the second part of the fourth century. While he was living as a monk in the monastery of Mount Sinai, the Bedouin Arabs raided the monastery. Nilus was thus able to observe at first hand the life and beliefs of the Bedouins, and he recorded many such observations in his treatise *The Slaying of the Monks on Mount Sinai*. Particularly dramatic is his description of the sacrifice of a camel, "offered," he says, "to the Morning Star." Bound upon a rude altar of piled-up stones, the camel is cut to pieces and devoured raw by the worshipers—devoured with such haste, Nilus adds, "that in the short interval between the rise of the Day Star, which marked the hour for the service to begin, and the disappearance of its rays before the rising sun, the entire camel, body and bones, skin, blood and entrails, is wholly devoured."[7] J. Wellhausen was the first to relate this sacrifice in his *Reste arabischen Heidenthumes* (1887). But it was William Robertson Smith who established, so to speak, the unique scientific prestige of Nilus' camel. He refers to this sacrifice innumerable times in his *Lectures on the Religions of the Semites* (1889), considering it "the oldest known form of Arabian sacrifice,"[8] and he speaks of the "direct evidence of Nilus as to the habits of the Arabs of the Sinaitic desert."[9] From then on, all the followers of Robertson Smith's theory of sacrifice—S. Reinach, A. Wendel, A. S. Cook, S. H. Hooke—abundantly and untiringly referred to Nilus' account. It is still more curious that even those scholars who did not accept Robertson Smith's theory could not—or dared not—discuss the general problem of sacrifice without duly relating Nilus' story.[10] In fact, no one seemed to doubt the authenticity of Nilus' testimony, even though a great number of scholars rejected Robertson Smith's interpretation of it. Thus, by the beginning of this century Nilus' camel had become so exasperatingly omnipresent in the writings of historians of religions, Old Testament scholars, sociologists, and ethnologists that G. Foucard declared, in his book *Histoire des religions et méthode comparative*,

> It seems that no author has any longer the right to treat of history of religions if he does not speak respectfully of this anecdote. For it is indeed an anecdote . . . , a detail related as an "aside"; and on a unique fact, so slender, one cannot really build up a religious theory valid for all humanity.[11]

With great intellectual courage, Foucard summed up his methodological position:

> Concerning Nilus' camel, I persist in the belief that it does not deserve to carry on its back the weight of the origins of a part of the history of religions.[12]

Foucard was right. Meticulous textual and historical analysis has proved that Nilus was not the author of the treatise *The Slaying of the Monks on*

Mount Sinai, that this is a pseudonymous work, probably written in the fourth or fifth century, and, what is more important, that the text is full of literary clichés borrowed from Hellenistic novels; for example, the description of the killing and devouring of the camel—"hacking off pieces of the quivering flesh and devouring the entire animal, body and bones"—has no ethnological value but reveals only a knowledge of the rhetorical-pathetic genre of these novels. Nonetheless, although these facts were already known soon after the First World War, thanks especially to Karl Heussi's painstaking analysis,[13] Nilus' camel still haunts many recent scientific works.[14] And no wonder. This short and colorful description of what is presumed to be the original form of sacrifice and the beginnings of religious communion was tailor-made to gratify all tastes and inclinations. Nothing could be more flattering to Western intellectuals, convinced, as so many of them were, that prehistoric and primitive man was very nearly a beast of prey and consequently that the origin of religion should reflect a troglodytic psychology and behavior. Furthermore, the communal devouring of a camel could not but substantiate the claim of many sociologists that religion is merely a social fact, if not just the hypostatic projection of the society itself. Even those scholars who called themselves Christians were somehow happy with Nilus' account. They would readily point out the immense distance that separates the total consumption of a camel—bones and skin included— from the highly spiritualized, if not merely symbolic, Christian sacraments. The splendid superiority of monotheism and especially of Christianity as over against all preceding pagan creeds and faiths could not be more convincingly evident. And, of course, all these scholars, Christians as well as agnostics or atheists, were supremely proud and happy to be what they were: civilized Westerners and champions of infinite progress.

I do not doubt that the analysis of the three recent cultural fashions which I referred to at the beginning of this paper will prove no less revealing for us, although they are not directly related to history of religions. Of course, they are not to be considered equally significant. One of them, at least, may very soon become obsolete. For our purposes, it does not matter. What matters is the fact that during the past four or five years—the early 1960s—Paris has been dominated—one might almost say conquered—by a magazine called *Planète* and by two authors, Teilhard de Chardin and Claude Lévi-Strauss. I hasten to add that I do not intend to discuss here the theories of Teilhard and Lévi-Strauss. What interests me is their amazing popularity, and I will refer to their ideas only insofar as they may explain the reasons for that popularity.

A Magazine Called Planète

For obvious reasons, I shall begin with the magazine *Planète*. As a matter of fact, I am not the first to have pondered the cultural meaning of its unheard-of popularity. Some time ago the well-known and extremely serious Parisian paper *Le Monde* devoted two long articles to this very problem, the unexpected and incredible success of *Planète*. Indeed, some 80,000 subscribers and 100,000 buyers of a rather expensive magazine constitute a unique phenomenon in France—and a problem for the sociology of culture. Its editors are Louis Pauwels, a writer and a former disciple of Gurdjiev, and Jacques Bergier, a very popular scientific journalist. In 1961 they published a voluminous book, *Le Matin des sorciers*, which rapidly became a best-seller. In fact *Planète* was launched with the royalties earned by *Le Matin des sorciers*. The book has also been translated into English, but it has not made a comparable impact on the Anglo-American public. It is a curious mélange of popular science, occultism, astrology, science fiction, and spiritual techniques. But it is more than that. It tacitly pretends to reveal innumerable vital secrets—of our universe, of the Second World War, of lost civilizations, of Hitler's obsession with astrology, and so on. Both authors are well read, and, as I have already said, Jacques Bergier has a scientific background. Consequently, the reader is convinced that he is being given *facts*, or at least responsible hypotheses—that, in any case, he is not being misled. *Planète* is constructed on the same premises and follows the same pattern: there are articles on the probability of inhabited planets, new forms of psychological warfare, the perspectives of *l'amour moderne*, H. P. Lovecraft and American science fiction, the "real" keys to the understanding of Teilhard de Chardin, the mysteries of the animal world, and so on.

Now, in order to understand the unexpected success of both the book and the magazine, one should recall the French cultural milieu of the late 1950s. As is well known, existentialism became extremely popular immediately after the liberation. J.-P. Sartre, Camus, Simone de Beauvoir, were the guides and models inspiring the new generation. Sartre in particular enjoyed a popularity equaled by no other French writer since the days of Voltaire and Diderot, Victor Hugo, or Zola during the Dreyfus affair. Marxism itself had not become a real attraction for the young intellectuals before Sartre proclaimed his own Communist sympathies. Very little was left of the French Catholic renaissance of the early 1920s. Jacques Maritain and the neo-Thomists had already gone out of fashion at the beginning of the Second World War. The only living movements within Catholicism, aside from the Christian existentialism of Gabriel Marcel, were those which produced at that time the rather modest group of *Études Carmélitaines* (stressing the importance of mystical experience and encouraging the study of the psychology of religion and of symbolism) and the *Sources Chrétiennes*, with their reevaluation of Greek patristics and their insistence on liturgical renewal. But, of course, these Catholic movements had neither the glamor of Sartre's existentialism nor the charisma of communism. The cultural milieu, from philosophy and political ideology to literature, art, cinema, and journalism, was dominated by a few ideas and a number of clichés: the absurdity of human existence, estrangement, commitment, situation, historical moment, and so on. It is true that Sartre spoke constantly of freedom; but in the end *that* freedom was meaningless. In the late 1950s the Algerian war prompted a profound malaise among the intellectuals. Whether existentialists, Marxists, or liberal Catholics, they had to make personal decisions. For many years the French intellectual was forced to live almost exclusively in his "historical moment," as Sartre had taught that any responsible individual should do.

In this gloomy, tedious, and somehow provincial atmosphere—for it seemed that only Paris, or rather Saint-Germain-des-Prés, and now Algeria, really counted in the world—the appearance of *Planète* had the effect of a bombshell. The general orientation, the problems discussed, the language—all were different. There was no longer the excessive preoccupation with one's own existential "situation" and historical "commitment" but a grandiose overture toward a wonderful world: the future organization of the planet, the unlimited possibilities of man, the mysterious universe into which we are ready to penetrate, and so on. It was not the scientific approach as such that stirred this collective enthusiasm but the charismatic impact of "the latest scientific developments" and the proclamation of their imminent triumphs. Of course, as I have said already, science was supplemented with hermeticism, science fiction, and political and cultural news. But what was new and exhilarating for the French reader was the optimistic and holistic outlook which coupled science with esoterism and presented a living, fascinating, and mysterious cosmos, in which human life again became meaningful and promised an endless perfectibility. Man was no longer condemned to a rather dreary *condition humaine*; instead he was called both to conquer his physical universe and to unravel the other, enigmatic universes revealed by the occultists and gnostics. But in contrast to all previous gnostic and esoteric schools and movements, *Planète* did not disregard the social and political problems of the contemporary world. In sum, it propagated a *saving* science: scientific information which was at the same time soteriological. Man was no longer estranged and useless in an absurd world, into which he had come by accident and to no purpose.

The Cultural Significance of Teilhard's Popularity

I must stop here with my rapid analysis of the reasons for *Planète's* success, for I realize that many of the things which I have said in connection with this magazine can be applied almost identically to the vogue of Teilhard de Chardin. It should be unnecessary to add that I am not speaking of the scientific and philosophic merits of Teilhard, which are unquestionable, but of the tremendous success of his books, all of which, as is well known, were published posthumously. And it is a strange paradox that the only Roman Catholic thinker who has gained a responsible and massive audience was prevented by his ecclesiastical authorities from publishing those very books which today are best-sellers in both the Old World and the New. What is even more important, at least one hundred volumes and many thousands of articles have been published all over the world, in less than ten years, discussing, in most cases sympathetically, Teilhard de Chardin's ideas. If we take into consideration the fact that not even the most popular philosopher of this generation, J.-P. Sartre, attained so massive a response after twenty-five years of activity, we must acknowledge the *cultural* significance of Teilhard's success. We have no books at all, and only a very few articles, about the ideas of Louis Pauwels and Jacques Bergier (both articles in *Le Monde* are concerned with the popularity of their magazine, *Planète*), but the majority of books and articles written about Teilhard discuss his philosophy and his religious conceptions.

Probably the readers of *Planète* and of Teilhard de Chardin are not the same, but they have many things in common. To begin with, all of them are tired of existentialism and Marxism, tired of continual talk about history, the historical condition, the historical moment, commitment, and so on. The readers of both Teilhard and *Planète* are not so much interested in history as in *nature* and in *life*. Teilhard himself considers history to be only a modest segment in a glorious cosmic process which started with the appearance of life and which will continue for billions and billions of years, until the last of the galaxies hears the proclamation of Christ as Logos. Both the ideology of *Planète* and the philosophy of Teilhard de Chardin are fundamentally optimistic. As a matter of fact, Teilhard is the first philosopher since Bergson who has dared to express faith and confidence both in life and in man. And when critics attempt to prove that Teilhard's basic conceptions are not a legitimate part of the Christian tradition, they usually point to his optimism, his belief in a meaningful and infinite evolution, and his ignoring of original sin and evil in general.

But, on the other hand, the agnostic scientists who read Teilhard admit that for the first time they have understood what it can mean to be a religious man, to believe in God and even in Jesus Christ and in the sacraments. It is a fact that Teilhard has been the first Christian author to present his faith in terms accessible and meaningful to the agnostic scientist and to the religiously illiterate in general. For the first time in this century the agnostic and atheistic masses of scientifically educated Europeans know what a Christian is speaking about. This is not due to the fact that Teilhard is a scientist. Before him there were many great scientists who did not conceal their Christian faith. What is new in Teilhard, and explains his popularity at least in part, is the fact that he has grounded his Christian faith in a scientific study and understanding of nature and of life. He speaks of the "spiritual power of matter" and confesses an "overwhelming sympathy for all that stirs within the dark mass of matter." This *love* of Teilhard's for the cosmic substance and the cosmic life seems to impress scientists greatly. He candidly admits that he had always been a "pantheist" by temperament and "less a child of heaven than a son of earth." Even the most refined and abstruse scientific tools—the electronic computer, for example—are exalted by Teilhard because he considers them to be auxiliaries and promoters of life.

But one cannot speak simply of the "vitalism" of Teilhard, for he is a religious man, and life for him is *sacred;* moreover, the cosmic matter as such is susceptible of being sanctified in its totality. At least this seems to be the meaning of that beautiful text entitled "The Mass on the Top of the World." When Teilhard speaks of the penetration of the galaxies by the cosmic Logos, even the most fantastic exaltation of the bodhi-sattvas seems modest and unimaginative by comparison. Because for Teilhard the galaxies in which Christ will be preached millions of years hence are *real,* are living matter. They are not illusory and not even ephemeral. In an article in the magazine *Psyché,* Teilhard once confessed that he simply could not believe in a catastrophic end of the world—not now, and not after billions of years; he could not even believe in the second law of thermodynamics. For him the universe was real, alive, meaningful, creative, sacred—and, if not eternal in the philosophical sense, at least of infinite duration.

We can now understand the reason for Teilhard's immense popularity: he is not only setting up a bridge between science and Christianity; he is not only presenting an optimistic view of cosmic and human evolution and insisting particularly on the exceptional value of the human mode of being in the universe; *he is also revealing the ultimate sacrality of nature and of life.* Modern man is not only estranged from himself; he is also estranged from nature. And of course one cannot go back to a "cosmic religion" already out of fashion in the time of the prophets and later persecuted and suppressed by the Christians. One cannot even go back to a romantic or bucolic approach to nature. But the nostalgia for a lost mystical solidarity with nature still haunts Western man. And Teilhard has laid open for him an unhoped-for perspective, where nature is charged with religious values even while retaining its completely "objective" reality.

The Vogue of Structuralism

I will not say too much about the third recent vogue, that of Claude Lévi-Strauss, because it is interrelated with a broader interest in structural linguistics and structuralism in general. Whatever one may think of Lévi-Strauss's conclusions, one cannot but recognize the merits of his work. I personally consider him to be important primarily for the following reasons: (1) Although an anthropologist by training and profession, he is fundamentally a philosopher, and he is not afraid of ideas, theories, and theoretical language; therefore, he forces anthropologists to *think*, and even to think hard. For the empirically minded anthropologist, this is a real calamity, but the historian of religions cannot help but rejoice in the highly theoretical level on which Lévi-Strauss chooses to discuss his so-called primitive material. (2) Even if one does not accept the structuralist approach *in toto*, Lévi-Strauss's criticism of anthropological historicism is very timely. Too much time and energy have been expended by anthropologists in trying to reconstruct the *history* of primitive cultures, and very little on *understanding their meaning*. (3) Finally, Lévi-Strauss is an excellent writer; his *Tristes tropiques* is a great book, in my opinion his most important work. Furthermore, Lévi-Strauss is what I might call a "modern encyclopedist," in the sense that he is familiar with a great number of *modern* discoveries, creations, and techniques; for example, cybernetics and communication theory, Marxism, linguistics, abstract art and Béla Bartók, dodecaphonic music and the "new wave" of the French novel, and so forth.

Now, it is quite probable that some of these achievements have contributed to the popularity of Lévi-Strauss. His interest in so many modern ways of thinking, his Marxian sympathies, his sensitive understanding of Ionesco or Robbe-Grillet—these are not negligible qualities in the eyes of the younger generation of intellectuals. But in my opinion the reasons for Lévi-Strauss's popularity are primarily to be found in his antiexistentialism and his neopositivism, in his indifference to history and his exaltation of material "things"—of matter. For him, "la science est déjà faite dans les choses": science is already effected in things, in material objects. Logic is already prefigured in nature. That is to say, man can be understood without taking *consciousness* into consideration. *La Pensée sauvage* presents to us a thinking without thinkers and a logic without logicians.[15] This is both a neopositivism and a neonominalism, but at the same time it is something more. It is a reabsorption of man into nature—not, evidently, dionysiac or romantic nature or even the blind, passionate, erotic drive of Freud, but the nature which is grasped by nuclear physics and cybernetics, a nature reduced to its fundamental structures; and these structures are the same in both the cosmic substance and the human mind. Now as I have already said, I cannot discuss Levi-Strauss's theories here. But I would like to remind the reader of one of the most distinctive characteristics of the French "new-wave" novelists, particularly Robbe-Grillet: the importance of "things," of material objects—ultimately, the primacy of space and of nature—and the indifference to history and to historical time. Both in Lévi-Strauss, for whom "la science est déjà faite dans les choses," and in Robbe-Grillet we witness a new epiphany of "les choses," the elevation of physical nature to the rank of the one all-embracing reality.

Thus all three recent vogues seem to have something in common: their drastic reaction against existentialism, their indifference to history, their exaltation of physical nature. Of course, there is a great distance between the rather naïve scientific enthusiasm of *Planéte* and Teilhard's mystical love for matter and life and his confidence in the scientific and technological miracles of the future, and there is an even greater distance between Teilhard's and Lévi-Strauss's conceptions of man. But what we might call their "worlds of image" are somehow similar: in all three instances we are confronted with a kind of *mythology of matter*, whether of an imaginative, exuberant type (*Planéte*, Teilhard de Chardin) or a structuralist, algebraic type (Claude Lévi-Strauss).

If my analysis is correct, then the antiexistentialism and the anti-historicism patent in these fashions and their exaltation of physical nature are not without interest for the historian of religions. The fact that hundred of thousands of European intellectuals are enthusiastically reading *Planéte* and the works of Teilhard de Chardin has another meaning for the historian of religions than it might have for a sociologist of culture. It would be too simple for us to say that the terror of history is again becoming unbearable and that those European intellectuals who can neither take refuge in nihilism nor find solace in Marxism are looking hopefully toward a new—because scientifically approached—and charismatic cosmos. We certainly cannot reduce the meaning of these vogues to the old and well-known tension between "cosmos and history." The cosmos presented in *Planéte* and the works of Teilhard de Chardin is itself a product of history, for it is the cosmos as understood by science and in the process of being conquered and changed by technology. But what is specific and new is the almost religious interest in the structures and values of this natural world, of this cosmic substance so brilliantly explored by science and transformed by technology. The antihistoricism which we have identified in all three fashions is not a rejection of history as such; it is rather a protest against the pessimism and nihilism of some recent historicists. We even suspect a nostalgia for what might be called a macrohistory—a planetary and, later, a cosmic history. But whatever may be said about this nostalgia for a more comprehensive understanding of history, one thing remains certain: the enthusiasts for *Planéte*, for Teilhard de Chardin, and for Lévi-Strauss do not feel the Sartrean *nausée* when they are confronted with natural objects; they do not feel themselves to be *de trop* in this world; in brief, they do not experience their own situation in the cosmos as an existentialist does.

Like all fashions, these new vogues will also fade out and finally disappear. But their real significance will not be invalidated: the popularity of *Planéte*, of Teilhard de Chardin, and of Claude Lévi-Strauss reveals to us something of the unconscious or semiconscious desires and nostalgias of contemporary Western man. If we take into consideration the fact that somehow similar intentions can be deciphered in modern art, the significance of these recent vogues for the historian of religions becomes even more startling. Indeed, one cannot fail to recognize in the works of a great number of contemporary artists a consuming interest in matter as such. I will not speak of Brancuşi, because his love for matter is well known. Brancuşi's attitude toward stone is comparable to the solicitude, fear, and veneration of a Neolithic man when faced with certain stones that constitute hierophanies for him; that is to say, they also reveal a sacred and ultimate reality. But in the history of modern art, from cubism to *tachisme*, we have been witnessing a continuing effort on the part of the artist to free himself from the "surface" of things and to penetrate matter in order to lay bare its ultimate structures. I have already discussed elsewhere the religious significance of the contemporary artist's effort to abolish form and volume, to descend, as it were, into the interior of substance while disclosing its secret or larval modalities.[16] This fascination for the elementary modes of matter betrays a desire to deliver oneself from the weight of dead forms, a nostalgia to immerse oneself in an auroral world.

If our analysis is correct, there is a decided convergence between the artist's attitude toward matter and the nostalgias of Western man, such as they can be deciphered in the three recent vogues we have discussed. It is a well-known fact that through their creations artists often anticipate what is to come—sometimes one or two generations later—in other sectors of social and cultural life.

NOTES

1. See, e.g., Léon Cellier, "Le Roman initiatique en France au temps du romantisme," *Cahiers Internationaux de Symbolisme*, No. 4 (1964), 22–44; Jean Richer, *Nerval: Expérience et création* (Paris: Hachette, 1963); Maryla Falk, *I "Misteri" di Novalis* (Naples: Casa Editrice Rondinella Alfredo, 1938); Erika Lorenz, *Der metaphorische Kosmos der modernen spanischen Lyrik, 1936–1956* (Hamburg: Cram, De Gruyter, 1961).

2. I discussed some of these interpretations in my article, "Initiation and the Modern World," reprinted in Mircea Eliade, *The Quest: History and Meaning in Religion* (Chicago: The University of Chicago Press, 1969), 112–126.

3. Sigmund Freud, *Totem und Tabu* (1913), 110, quoted by A. L. Kroeber, "Totem and Taboo: An Ethnological Psychoanalysis," *American Anthropologist* 22 (1920): 48–55.

4. Wilhelm Schmidt, *The Origin and Growth of Religion,* translated by H. J. Rose (New York: MacVeagh, 1931), 112.

5. See Mircea Eliade, "The History of Religions in Retrospect: 1912–1962," reprinted in Eliade, *The Quest*, 12–36.

6. Schmidt, *Origin and Growth of Religion*, 112–115.

7. Summarized by William Robertson Smith, *Lectures on the Religions of the Semites* (London: A. & C. Black, 1894), 338.

8. Ibid.

9. Ibid., 281.

10. See the bibliography in Joseph Henninger, "Ist der sogennante Nilus-Bericht eine brauchbare religionsgeschichtliche Quelle?" *Anthropos* 50 (1955): 81–148, esp. 86ff.

11. George Foucardt, *Histoire des religions et méthode comparative*, (Paris: A. Picard, 1912, 2nd ed.), 132ff.

12. Ibid., lxv: "Et pour le chameau de saint Nil, je persisterai à croire qu'il ne mérite pas de porter sur son dos le poids des origines d'une partie de l'histoire des religions."

13. Karl Heussi, *Das Nilusproblem* (Leipzig: J. C. Hinrichs, 1921). The bibliography of Heussi's work on Nilus is presented and discussed by Henninger, "Ist der sogenannte Nilus-Bericht . . . ," 89ff.

14. See the bibliography in Henninger, "Ist der sogenannte Nilus-Bericht," 86ff.

15. For a critical appraisal of the neopositivism of Lévi-Strauss, see Georges Gusdorf, "Situation de Maurice Leenhardt ou l'ethnologie française de Lévy-Bruhl à Lévi-Strauss," *Le Monde Non Chrétien*, 71/72 (July/December, 1964): 139–192. See also Paul Ricoeur, "Symbolique et temporalité," in *Ermeneutica e Tradizione*, edited by Enrico Castelli (Rome: Bocca, 1963), 5–31; Gaston Fessard, S.J., "Symbole, Surnaturel, Dialogue" in *Demitizzazione e Morale*, edited by Enrico Castelli (Padua: CERAM, 1965), 105–154.

16. Mircea Eliade, "The Sacred and the Modern Artist," *Criterion* (1965), 22–24; reprinted in *Art, Creativity and the Sacred: An Anthology in Religion and Art*, edited by Diane Apostolos-Cappadona (New York: The Crossroad Publishing Company, 1984), 179–183, and also reprinted in Part II of this collection. This article was originally published as "Sur la permanence du sacré dans l'art contemporain," *XXᵉ Siècle* 24 (1964), 3–10.

I / 3

Survivals and Camouflages of Myths

Christianity and Mythology

THE RELATIONS BETWEEN CHRISTIANITY and mythical thought can hardly be presented in a few pages. For the fact is that their relations raise several quite separate problems. First of all, there is the equivocal use of the term "myth." The earliest Christian theologians took the word in the sense that had become current some centuries earlier in the Greco-Roman world, i.e., "fable, fiction, lie." They therefore refused to see a "mythical" figure in Jesus and a "myth" in the Messianic drama. From the second century on, Christian theologians had to defend the historicity of Jesus against the Docetists and the Gnostics as well as against the pagan philosophers. We shall presently see the arguments they employed to support their thesis and the difficulties they had to meet.

The second problem is in some measure bound up with the first. It does not impugn the historicity of Jesus but questions the validity of the literary documents that illustrate it. Origen was already aware how difficult it is to prove a historical event with incontrovertible documents. In our day a Rudolf Bultmann, though he does not doubt the historical existence of Jesus, insists that we can know nothing about his life and character. This methodological position assumes that the Gospels and other primitive documents are full of "mythological elements" (taking myth, of course, to mean "what cannot exist"). It is beyond doubt that "mythological elements" abound in the Gospels. In addition, symbols, figures, and rituals of Jewish or Mediterranean origin were early assimilated by Christianity. We shall later see the significance of this twofold process of "Judaization" and "paganization" of primitive Christianity.

We may add for the moment that the vast number of symbols and elements that Christianity shares with solar cults and Mystery religions has prompted some scholars to deny the historicity of Jesus. They have,

"Survivals and Camouflages of Myths" was published in *Myth and Reality* by Mircea Eliade (New York: Harper and Row, Vol. 31 of World Perspectives planned and edited by Ruth Nanda Ashen, 1963), 161–193, and is here reprinted by permission.

for example, taken the position opposite to Bultmann's. Instead of postulating, at the beginning of Christianity, a historical person of whom we can know nothing because of the "mythology" with which he was soon overlaid, these scholars have postulated a "myth" that was imperfectly "historicized" by the earliest generations of Christians. To mention only the moderns, from Arthur Drews (1909) and Peter Jensen (1906, 1909) to P. L. Couchoud (1924) scholars of sundry orientations and sundry degrees of competence have laboriously attempted to reconstruct the "original myth" which they hold to have given birth to the figure of Christ and finally to Christianity. This "original myth," be it said, varies from author to author. A fascinating study could be made of these at once scholarly and daring reconstructions. They betray a certain nostalgia in modern man for the "primordially mythical." (In the case of P. L. Couchoud the exaltation of the nonhistoricity of myth at the expense of the poverty of the historically concrete is glaringly obvious.) But none of these nonhistorical hypotheses has been accepted by the specialists.

Finally there is a third problem that arises when one studies the relations between mythical thought and Christianity. It can be stated as follows: If Christians have refused to see in their religion the desacralized *mythos* of the Hellenistic period, what is the situation of Christianity in respect to the *living myth*, as known in the archaic and traditional societies? We shall see that Christianity as understood and practiced during the nearly two thousand years of its history cannot be completely separated from mythical thinking.

History and "Enigmas" in the Gospels

Let us now see how the Fathers attempted to defend the historicity of Jesus both against pagan unbelievers and against "heretics." Faced with the problem of presenting the authentic life of Jesus, that is, his life as it was known and orally transmitted by the Apostles, the theologians of the primitive Church found themselves confronting a certain number of texts and oral traditions circulating in different milieux. The Fathers displayed both critical faculty and "historicistic" leanings by refusing to accept the apocryphal Gospels and the "unwritten sayings" as authentic documents. However, they opened the way to long controversies within the Church, and facilitated attacks on the part of non-Christians, by accepting not one Gospel but four. Since differences existed between the synoptic Gospels and the Gospel of John, they had to be explained, and justified, by exegesis.

The exegetical crisis was precipitated by Marcion, in 137. Marcion proclaimed that there was only one authentic Gospel, orally transmitted in the beginning, then written down and sedulously interpolated by enthusiastic partisans of Judaism. Actually this "only valid" Gospel was Luke's, reduced by Marcion to what he considered the authentic kernel.[1] Marcion had used the method of the Greco-Roman grammarians, who claimed to be able to separate the mythological excrescences from antique theological texts. In defending themselves against Marcion and the other Gnostics, the orthodox were forced to employ the same method.

At the beginning of the second century Aelius Theon, in his *Progymnasmata*, showed the difference between myth and narrative: the myth is "a false account portraying truth," whereas the narrative is "an account descriptive of events which took place or might have taken place."[2] The Christian theologians, of course, denied that the Gospels were "myths" or "wonder stories." Justin, for example, could not believe that there was any danger of confusing the Gospels with "wonder stories": on the one hand, the life of Jesus was the accomplishment of the Old Testament prophecies and, on the other, the literary form of the Gospels was not that of myth. More than this: Justin held that the non-Christian reader could be given material proofs of the historical truth of the Gospels. The Nativity, for example, could be proved by the "tax declarations submitted under the procurator Quirinius and (*ex hypothesi?*) available at Rome a century later."[3] So too, a Tatian or a Clement of Alexandria considered the Gospels historical documents.

But for our purpose the greatest importance attaches to Origen. For, on the one hand, Origen was too convinced of the spiritual value of the stories preserved by the Gospels to admit that they could be taken in a crudely literal sense, as simple believers and heretics took them—and for this reason he was a partisan of allegorical exegesis. But, on the other hand, when he was forced to defend Christianity against Celsus, he insisted on the historicity of the life of Jesus and attempted to substantiate all the historical testimonies. Origen criticizes and rejects the historicity of the cleansing of the Temple. "In Origen's systematic treatment of inspiration and exegesis he tells us that where spiritual truths did not correspond to historical events, 'the scripture wove into the historical narrative what did not take place—at some points what cannot take place and at others what can take place but did not.'"[4] Instead of "myth" and "fiction," he uses "enigma" and "parable"; but there is no doubt that for Origen the terms are equivalent.[5]

Origen, then, admits that the Gospels contain episodes that are not "authentic" historically though they are "true" on the spiritual plane. But in answering Celsus' criticisms, he also admits the difficulty of proving the historicity of a historical event. "An attempt to substantiate the truth of almost any story as historical fact, even if the story is true, and to produce complete certainty about it, is one of the most difficult tasks and in some cases impossible."[6]

Origen believes, however, that certain events in the life of Jesus are adequately substantiated by historical testimonies. For example, Jesus was crucified in the presence of a crowd of people. The earthquake and the darkness can be confirmed by the historical narrative of Phlegon of Tralles.[7] The Last Supper is a historical event that can be dated with absolute precision.[8] So is the ordeal in Gethsemane, though the Gospel of John does not mention it (but Origen explains the reason for this silence: John is more concerned with the divinity of Jesus and he knows that God the Logos cannot be tempted). The resurrection is "true" in the historical sense of the word, because it is an event, even though the resurrected body no longer belonged to the physical world. (The resurrected body was made of air and was spiritual.)[9]

Though he does not doubt the historicity of the life, passion, and resurrection of Jesus Christ, Origen is more concerned with the spiritual, nonhistorical meaning of the Gospel text. The true meaning is "beyond history."[10] The exegetist must be able to "free himself from the historical materials," for these are only a "steppingstone." To overstress the historicity of Jesus and neglect the deeper meaning of his life and message is, in fact, to mutilate Christianity. "People marvel at Jesus," he writes in his *Commentary on the Gospel of John*, "when they look into the history about him, but they no longer believe when the deeper meaning is disclosed to them; instead, they suppose it to be false."[11]

Historical Time and Liturgical Time

Origen rightly understood that the originality of Christianity lies above all in the fact that the Incarnation took place in a historical Time and not in cosmic Time. But neither does he forget that the Mystery of the Incarnation cannot be reduced to its historicity. Besides, by proclaiming the divinity of Jesus Christ "to the nations," the earliest Christian generations implicitly proclaimed his trans-historicity. This did not mean that Jesus was not a historical figure, but the emphasis was put primarily on the fact that he was the Son of God, the universal Saviour who had redeemed not only Man but Nature too. Nay, more—the historicity of Jesus had already been transcended by his Ascension to Heaven and by the fact that he had returned into the divine Glory.

In proclaiming the Incarnation, Resurrection, and Ascension of the Word, the Christians were sure that they were not putting forth a new myth. Actually, they were employing the categories of mythical thought.

Obviously they could not recognize this mythical thought in the desacralized mythologies of the pagan scholars who were their contemporaries. But it is clear that for Christians of all creeds the center of religious life is constituted by the drama of Jesus Christ. Although played out in History, this drama first established the possibility of salvation; hence there is only one way to gain salvation—to reiterate this exemplary drama ritually and to imitate the supreme model revealed by the life and teaching of Jesus. Now, this type of religious behavior is integral with genuine mythical thought.

It must at once be added that, *by the very fact that it is a religion*, Christianity had to keep at least one mythical aspect—liturgical Time, that is, the periodical recovery of the *illud tempus* of the "beginnings." "The religious experience of the Christian is based upon an *imitation* of the Christ as *exemplary pattern*, upon the liturgical repetition of the life, death, and resurrection of the Lord, and upon the *contemporaneity* of the Christian with *illud tempus* which begins with the Nativity at Bethlehem and ends, provisionally, with the Ascension." Now, as we have seen, "the imitation of a transhuman model, the repetition of an exemplary scenario and the breakaway from profane time through a moment which opens out into the Great Time, are the essential marks of 'mythical behavior'—that is, the behavior of the man of the archaic societies, who finds the very source of his existence in the myth."[12]

However, though liturgical Time is a circular Time, Christianity, as faithful heir of Judaism, accepts the linear Time of History: the World was created only once and will have only one end; the Incarnation took place only once, in historical Time, and there will be only one Judgment. From the very first, Christianity was subjected to various and conflicting influences, especially those from Gnosticism, Judaism, and "paganism." The Church's reaction was not always the same. The Fathers fought relentlessly against the acosmism and esotericism of the Gnosis; yet they kept the Gnostic elements found in the Gospel of John, in the Pauline Epistles, and in certain primitive texts. But, despite persecutions, Gnosticism was never wholly extirpated, and certain Gnostic myths, in more or less camouflaged form, reappeared in the oral and written literatures of the Middle Ages.

As for Judaism, it gave the Church not only an allegorical method of interpreting the Scriptures, but, most importantly, the outstanding model for "historicizing" the festivals and symbols of the cosmic religion. The "Judaization" of primitive Christianity is equivalent to its "historicization," that is, to the decision of the first theologians to connect the history of Jesus' preaching and of the earliest Church to the Sacred History of the people of Israel. But Judaism had "historicized" a certain number of seasonal festivals and cosmic symbols by connecting them with important events in the history of Israel (cf. the Feast of Tabernacles, Passover, the Hanukkah Feast of Lights, etc.). The Church Fathers took the same course: they "Christianized" Asianic and Mediterranean rites and myths by connecting them with a "Sacred History." Obviously, this "Sacred History" exceeded the bounds of the Old Testament and now included the New Testament, the preaching of the Apostles, and, later, the history of the Saints. A certain number of cosmic symbols—Water, the Tree and the Vine, the plow and the ax, the ship, the chariot, etc.—had already been assimilated by Judaism,[13] and they could easily be incorporated into the doctrine and practice of the Church by being given a sacramental or ecclesiological meaning.

"Cosmic Christianity"

The real difficulties arose later, when the Christian missionaries were faced, especially in Central and Western Europe, by *living* popular religions. Willy-nilly, they ended by "Christianizing" the "pagan" divine Figures and myths that resisted extirpation. A large number of dragon-slaying Gods or Heroes became St. Georges; storm Gods were transformed into St. Eliases; the countless fertility Goddesses were assimilated to the Virgin or to female Saints. It could even be said that a part of the popular religion of pre-Christian Europe survived, either camouflaged or transformed, in the feasts of the Church calendar and in the cult of the Saints. For more than ten centuries the Church was obliged to fight the continual influx of "pagan" elements—that is, elements belonging to the cosmic religion—into Christian practices and legends. The success of this intensive struggle was not very great, especially in the South and Southeast of Europe. In the folklore and religious practices of the rural populations at the end of the nineteenth century there still survived figures, myths, and rituals from earliest antiquity, or even from protohistory.[14]

The Orthodox and Roman Catholic Churches have been criticized for accepting so many pagan elements. It is a question if these criticisms were always justified. On the one hand, "paganism" could survive only in "Christianized" form, even if at times the Christianization was rather superficial. This policy of assimilating the "paganism" that could not be destroyed was nothing new; the primitive Church had already accepted and assimilated a large part of the pre-Christian sacred calendar. On the other hand, the peasants, because of their own mode of existing in the Cosmos, were not attracted by a "historical" and moral Christianity. The religious experience peculiar to the rural populations was nourished by what could be called a "cosmic Christianity." In other words, the peasants of Europe understood Christianity as a cosmic liturgy. The Christological mystery also involved the destiny of the Cosmos. "All Nature sighs, awaiting the Resurrection" is a central motif not only in the Easter liturgy but also in the religious folklore of Eastern Christianity. Mystical empathy with the cosmic rhythms, which was violently attacked by the Old Testament prophets and barely tolerated by the Church, is central to the religions of rural populations, especially in Southeastern Europe. For this whole section of Christendom "Nature" is not the World of sin but the work of God. After the Incarnation, the World had been re-established in its original glory; this is why Christ and the Church had been imbued with so many cosmic symbols. In the religious folklore of Southeastern Europe the sacraments sanctify Nature too.

For the peasants of Eastern Europe this in no sense implied a "paganization" of Christianity, but, on the contrary, a "Christianization" of the religion of their ancestors. When the time comes for the history of this "popular theology" to be written on the evidence that can be traced in seasonal festivals and religious folklores, it will be realized that "cosmic Christianity" is not a new form of paganism or a pagan-Christian syncretism. Rather it is an original religious creation, in which eschatology and soteriology are given cosmic dimensions. Even more significantly, Christ, while remaining the Pantocrator, comes down to Earth and visits the peasants, just as, in the myths of archaic peoples, the Supreme Being was wont to do before he became a *deus otiosus;* this Christ is not "historical," since popular thought is interested neither in chronology nor in the accuracy of events and the authenticity of historical figures. This does not mean that, for the rural populations, Christ is only a "God" inherited from the old polytheisms. For, on the one hand, there is no contradiction between the Christ image of the Gospels and the Church and the Christ image of religious folklore. The Nativity, the teaching of Jesus, and his miracles, the Crucifixion and the Resurrection are essential themes in this popular Christianity. On the other hand, it is a *Christian spirit*—not a pagan spirit—that impregnates all these folklore creations; they tell of man's salvation by Christ; of faith, hope, and charity; of a World that is "good" because it was created by God the Father and redeemed by the Son; of a human existence that will not be repeated and that is not without meaning; man is free to choose good or evil, but he will not be judged solely by that choice.

It does not lie within the scope of this book to outline this "popular theology." But it is obvious that the cosmic Christianity of the rural populations is dominated by nostalgia for a Nature sanctified by the presence of Jesus. It is, in some sort, a nostalgia for Paradise, the desire to find again a transfigured and invulnerable Nature, safe from the cataclysms brought by wars, devastation, and conquests. It is also the expression of the "ideal" of these agricultural societies, constantly terrorized by allogeneous warrior hordes and exploited by the various classes of more or less autochthonous "masters." It is a passive revolt against the tragedy and injustice of History, in the last analysis against the fact that evil proves to be no longer only an individual decision but, increasingly, a transpersonal structure of the historical World.

But to return to our theme, it is clear that this popular Christianity has kept alive certain categories of mythical thought even down to our day.

Eschatological Mythologies of the Middle Ages

In the Middle Ages we witness an upwelling of mythical thought. All the social classes depend on their mythological traditions. Knights, artisans, clerks, peasants, accept an "origin myth" for their condition and endeavor to imitate an exemplary model. These mythologies have various sources. The Arthurian cycle and the Grail theme incorporate, under a varnish of Christianity, a number of Celtic beliefs, especially those having to do with the Other World. The knights try to follow the example of Lancelot or Parsifal. The trouvères elaborate a whole mythology of woman and Love, making use of Christian elements but going beyond or contradicting Church doctrine.

It is especially in certain historical movements of the Middle Ages that we find the most typical manifestations of mythical thought. Millennialist exaltation and eschatological myths come to the fore in the Crusades, in the movements of a Tanchelm and an Eudes de l'Etoile, in the elevation of Frederick II to the rank of Messiah, and in many other collective messianic, utopian, and prerevolutionary phenomena, which have been brilliantly treated by Norman Cohn in his *The Pursuit of the Millennium*. To dwell for a moment on the mythological aureole of Frederick II: the imperial chancellor, Pietro della Vigna, presents his master as a cosmic Saviour; the whole World was awaiting such a Cosmocrator, and now the flames of evil are extinguished, swords are beaten into plowshares, peace, justice and security are firmly installed. "More than all this—Frederick possesses a unique virtue which binds the elements of the universe together, reconciling heat with cold, the solid with the liquid, all opposites with one another. He is a comic messiah whom land and sea and air unite in adoring. And his coming is a work of divine providence; for the world was sinking toward its end, the Last Judgment was already at hand, when God in his great mercy granted a reprieve and sent this pure ruler to make an age of peace and order and harmony in the Last Days. That these phrases fairly reflected Frederick's own view is shown by the letter which he addressed to his birthplace, Jesi near Ancona; for there he makes it quite clear that he regards his own birth as an event possessing the same significance for mankind as the birth of Christ and Jesi as a second Bethlehem. Probably alone among medieval monarchs, Frederick believed himself to be divine in virtue not of his office but of his inborn nature—nothing less than incarnate God."[15]

The mythology of Frederick II did not disappear with his death, for the simple reason that his death could not be believed: the Emperor must have retired to a distant country, or, according to the most popular legend, he was sleeping under Mount Aetna. But one day he would wake again and return to claim his throne. And in fact, thirty-four years after his death an impostor was able to convince the city of Neuss that he was Frederick II *redivivus*. Even after this pseudo-Frederick was executed at Wetzlar, the myth did not lose its virulence. In the fifteenth century it was still believed that Frederick was alive and would live until the end of the World, in short, that he was the only legitimate Emperor and that there would never be another.

The myth of Frederick II is only a famous example of a far more widespread and persistent phenomenon. In fact, the religious prestige and eschatological function of kings survived in Europe to the seventeenth century. The secularization of the concept of eschatological King did not extinguish the hope, deeply rooted in the collective soul, for a universal renewal brought about by the exemplary Hero in one of his new forms—the Reformer, the Revolutionary, the Martyr (in the name of the freedom of peoples), the Party Leader. The role and mission of the Founders and Leaders of the modern totalitarian movements include a considerable number of eschatological and soteriological elements. Mythical thought transcends and discards some of its earlier expressions, outmoded by History, and adapts itself to the new social conditions and new cultural fashions—but it resists extirpation.

As to the Crusade phenomenon, Alphonse Dupront has well demonstrated its mythical structures and eschatological orientation. "At the center of a Crusade consciousness, in the cleric as in the non-cleric, is the duty to free Jerusalem. . . . What is most strongly expressed in the Crusade is a twofold fulfillment: an accomplishment of the times and an accomplishment of human space. In the sense, for space, that the sign of the accomplishment of the times is the gathering of the nations about the sacred mother city, the center of the world, Jerusalem."[16]

The proof that we are here in the presence of a collective spiritual phenomenon, of an irrational drive, is, among other things, the

Children's Crusades that suddenly began in Northern France and Germany in the year 1212. The spontaneity of these movements appears to be beyond doubt: "No one urging them, either from foreign lands or from their own," says a contemporary witness.[17] Children "having at once two characteristics that were signs of the extraordinary, their extreme youth and their poverty, especially little herd-boys,"[18] took the road, and the poor joined them. There were perhaps thirty thousand of them, and they walked in procession, singing. When asked where they were going, they answered: "To God." According to a contemporary chronicler, "their intention was to cross the sea and do what kings and the mighty had not done, to recapture Christ's Sepulchre."[19] The clergy had opposed this rising of children. The French crusade ended in catastrophe. Reaching Marseilles, they embarked in seven large ships, but two of these ran aground in a storm off Sardinia and all the passengers were drowned. As for the other five ships, the two treacherous shipowners took them to Alexandria, where they sold the children to the Saracen leaders and to slave dealers.

The "German" crusade followed the same pattern. A contemporary chronicle tells that in 1212 "there appeared a boy named Nicolas who gathered around him a multitude of children and women. He affirmed that, by order of an angel, he must go with them to Jerusalem to free the Saviour's cross and that the sea, as formerly for the people of Israel, would let them pass dryshod."[20] They were unarmed. Starting from the region around Cologne, they traveled down the Rhine, crossed the Alps, and reached Northern Italy. Some of them got as far as Genoa and Pisa, but they were turned back. Those who managed to reach Rome were obliged to admit that they were backed by no authority. The Pope disapproved of their project, and they were forced to return. As the chronicler of the *Annales Marbacenses* puts it, "they came back starving and barefoot, one by one and in silence." No one helped them. Another witness writes: "The greater part of them lay dead from hunger in villages, in public places, and no one buried them."[21]

P. Alphandéry and A. Dupront have rightly recognized in these movements the elect role of the child in popular piety. It is at once the myth of the Holy Innocents, the exaltation of the child by Jesus, and the popular reaction against the Crusade of the Barons, the same reaction that appeared in the legends that crystallized around the "Tafurs" of the earliest Crusades.[22] "The reconquest of the Holy Places can no longer be expected except from a miracle—and the miracle can only come about in favor of the purest, of children and the poor."[23]

Survivals of the Eschatological Myth

The failure of the Crusades did not put an end to eschatological hopes. In his *De Monarchia Hispanica* (1600), Tomasso Campanella begged the King of Spain to furnish the money for a new Crusade against the Turkish Empire, and, after the victory, to establish the Universal Monarchy. Thirty-eight years later, in the *Ecloga* addressed to Louis XIII and Anne of Austria to celebrate the birth of the future Louis XIV, Campanella prophesies the *recuperatio Terrae Sanctae*, and, with it, the *renovatio saeculi*. The young king will conquer the whole Earth in a thousand days, laying the monsters low, that is, subduing the kingdoms of the infidels and freeing Greece. Mohammed will be driven out of Europe; Egypt and Ethiopia will again be Christian, the Tartars, the Persians, the Chinese and the whole East will be converted. All peoples will be united in one Christendom and this regenerated Universe will have one Center— Jerusalem. "The Church," Campanella writes, "began at Jerusalem, and to Jerusalem it will return, after circling the world."[24] In his treatise *La prima e la seconda resurrezione*, Campanella no longer sees the conquest of Jerusalem, in the manner of St. Bernard, as a stage on the way to the Celestial Jerusalem but as the establishment of the messianic reign.[25]

It is needless to multiply examples. But it is important to stress the continuity between the medieval eschatological conceptions and the various "philosophies of History" produced by the Enlightenment and the nineteenth century. During the last thirty years it has begun to be realized what an exceptional role was played by the "prophecies" of Gioacchino da Fiore in instigating and articulating all these messianic movements that arose in the thirteenth century and continued, in more or less secularized form, into the nineteenth.[26] Gioacchino's central idea—that is, the imminent entrance of the World into the third age of History, which will be the age of freedom since it will be realized under the sign of the Holy Spirit—had considerable repercussions. This idea ran counter to the theology of History accepted by the Church from the time of St. Augustine. According to the current doctrine, perfection having been achieved on Earth by the Church, there will be no *renovatio* in the future. The only decisive event will be the Second Coming of Christ and the Last Judgment. Gioacchino da Fiore brings back into Christianity the archaic myth of universal regeneration. To be sure, it is no longer a periodic and indefinitely repeatable regeneration. Yet it is none the less true that Gioacchino conceives the third age as the reign of Freedom, under the guidance of the Holy Spirit—which implies transcending historical Christianity and, in the last analysis, abolishing all existing rules and institutions.

We cannot here present the various eschatological movements inspired by Gioacchino. But we must at least refer to some unexpected continuations of the Calabrian prophet's ideas. Thus, for example, Lessing in his *Education of the Human Race* elaborates the thesis of continual and progressive revelation culminating in a third age. To be sure, Lessing thought of this third age as the triumph of reason through education; but it was none the less, he believed, the fulfillment of Christian revelation, and he refers with sympathy and admiration to "certain enthusiasts of the thirteenth and fourteenth centuries," whose only error lay in proclaiming the "new eternal Gospel" too soon.[27] Lessing's ideas aroused some repercussions and, through the disciples of Saint-Simon, he probably influenced Auguste Comte and his doctrine of the three stages. Fichte, Hegel, Schelling were influenced, though for different reasons, by the Gioacchinian myth of an imminent third age that will renew and complete History. Through them this eschatological myth influenced certain Russian writers, especially Krasinsky, with his *Third Kingdom of the Spirit,* and Merejkowsky, author of *The Christianity of the Third Testament.*[28] To be sure, we are now dealing with semiphilosophical ideologies and fantasies and no longer with the eschatological expectation of the reign of the Holy Spirit. But the myth of universal renovation in a more or less imminent future is still discernible in all these theories and fantasies.

"The Myths of the Modern World"

Some forms of "mythical behavior" still survive in our day. This does not mean that they represent "survivals" of an archaic mentality. But certain aspects and functions of mythical thought are constituents of the human being. We have discussed some "myths of the modern world" elsewhere.[29] The problem is complex and absorbing; we cannot hope to exhaust in a few pages what would furnish the material for a large volume. We will confine ourselves to briefly discussing some aspects of "modern mythologies."

We have seen the importance of the "return to the origins" in archaic societies, a return that can be effected in a number of ways. Now, this prestige of the "origin" has also survived in the societies of Europe. When an innovation was to be made, it was conceived, or presented, as a return to the origin. The Reformation began the return to the Bible and dreamed of recovering the experience of the primitive Church, or even of the earliest Christian communities. The French Revolution had its paradigmatic models in the Romans and the Spartans. The inspirers and leaders of the first successful radical revolution in Europe, which marked not merely the end of a regime but the end of a historical cycle, thought of themselves as restoring the ancient virtues praised by Livy and Plutarch.

At the dawn of the modern World the "origin" enjoyed an almost magical prestige. To have a well-established "origin" meant, when all was said and done, to have the advantage of a noble origin. "We find our origin in Rome!" the Romanian intellectuals of the eighteenth and nineteenth centuries proudly repeated. In their case consciousness of Latin descent was accompanied by a kind of mystical participation in the greatness of Rome. Similarly the Hungarian intelligentsia found a justification for the antiquity, nobility, and historical mission of the Magyars in the origin myth of Hunor and Magor and in the heroic saga of Arpad. All through Central and Southeastern Europe at the beginning of the nineteenth century the mirage of "noble origin" aroused nothing short of a passion for national history, especially for its earliest phases. "A people without history" (read: without "historical documents" or without historiography) "is as if it did not exist!" This anxiety is perceptible in all the national historians of Central and Eastern Europe. Such a passion for national historiography was, to be sure, a consequence of the awakening of nationalities in this part of Europe. Then too, it was soon transformed into an instrument of propaganda and political warfare. But the desire to prove the "noble origin" and "antiquity" of one's people dominates Southeastern Europe to such an extent that, with few exceptions, all of the respective historians confined themselves to national history and finally wound up in cultural provincialism.

The passion for "noble origin" also explains the racist myth of "Aryanism" which periodically gains currency in the West, especially in Germany. The socio-political contexts of this myth are too well known to require discussion. What is of concern for our study is the fact that the "Aryan" represented at once the "primordial" Ancestor and the noble "hero," the latter laden with all the virtues that still haunted those who had not managed to reconcile themselves to the ideal of the societies that emerged from the revolutions of 1789 and 1848. The "Aryan" was the exemplary model that must be imitated in order to recover racial "purity," physical strength, nobility, the heroic "ethics" of the glorious and creative "beginnings."

As for Marxist Communism, its eschatological and millennialist structures have been duly noted. We remarked not long ago that Marx had taken over one of the great eschatological myths of the Asianico-Mediterranean world: the redeeming role of the Just Man (in our day, the proletariat), whose sufferings are destined to change the ontological status of the World. "In fact, Marx's classless society, and the consequent disappearance of all historical tensions, find their most exact precedent in the myth of the Golden Age which, according to a number of traditions, lies at the beginning and the end of History. Marx has enriched this venerable myth with a truly messianic Judaeo-Christian idealogy; on the one hand, by the prophetic and soteriological function he ascribes to the proletariat; and, on the other, by the final struggle between Good and Evil, which may well be compared with the apocalyptic conflict between Christ and Antichrist, ending in the decisive victory of the former. It is indeed significant that Marx turns to his own account the Judaeo-Christian eschatological hope of an *absolute* [*end to*] *History*; in that he parts company from the other historical philosophers (Croce, for instance, and Ortega y Gasset), for whom the tensions of history are implicit in the human condition, and therefore can never be completely abolished."[30]

Myths and Mass Media

Recent studies have brought out the mythical structures of the images and behavior patterns imposed on collectivities by mass media. This phenomenon is found especially in the United States.[31] The characters of the comic strips present the modern version of mythological or folklore Heroes. They incarnate the ideal of a large part of society, to such a degree that any change in their typical conduct or, still worse, their death, will bring on veritable crises among their readers; the latter react violently, and protest by sending thousands of telegrams to the authors of the comic strips or the editors of the newspapers in which they appear. A fantastic character, Superman, has become extremely popular, especially because of his double identity; although coming from a planet destroyed by a catastrophe, and possessing prodigious powers, Superman lives on Earth in the modest guise of a journalist, Clark Kent; he is timid, unassertive, dominated by his colleague Lois Lane. This humiliating camouflage of a Hero whose powers are literally unlimited revives a well-known mythical theme. In the last analysis, the myth of Superman satisfies the secret longings of modern man who, though he knows that he is a fallen, limited creature, dreams of one day proving himself an "exceptional person," a "Hero."

Much the same could be said of the detective novel. On the one hand, the reader witnesses the exemplary struggle between Good and Evil, between the Hero (= the Detective) and the criminal (the modern incarnation of the Demon). On the other, through an unconscious process of projection and identification, he takes part in the mystery and the drama and has the feeling that he is personally involved in a paradigmatic—that is, a dangerous, "heroic"—action.

The mythicization of public figures through the mass media, the transformation of a personality into an exemplary image, has also been analyzed. "Lloyd Warner tells us of the creation of such a public figure in the first section of his *The Living and the Dead*. Biggy Muldoon, a Yankee City politician who became a national figure because of his colorful opposition to the Hill Street Aristocracy, had a demagogic public image built up by the press and radio. He was presented as a crusading man of the people attacking entrenched wealth. Then, when the public tired of this image, the mass media obligingly turned Biggy into a villain, a corrupt politician seeking personal profit out of the public necessity. Warner points out that the real Biggy was considerably different from either image but actually was forced to modify his style of action to conform to one image and fight the other."[32]

Mythical behavior can be recognized in the obsession with "success" that is so characteristic of modern society and that expresses an obscure wish to transcend the limits of the human condition; in the exodus to Suburbia, in which we can detect the nostalgia for "primordial perfection"; in the paraphernalia and emotional intensity that characterize what has been called the "cult of the sacred automobile." As Andrew Greeley remarks, "one need merely visit the annual automobile show to realize that it is a highly ritualized religious performance. The colors, the lights, the music, the awe of the worshippers, the presence of the temple priestesses (fashion models), the pomp and splendor, the lavish waste of money, the thronging crowds—all these would represent in any other culture a clearly liturgical service. . . . The cult of the sacred car has its adepts and initiati. No gnostic more eagerly awaited a revelation from an oracle than does an automobile worshipper await the first rumors about the new models. It is at this time of the annual seasonal cycle that the high priests of the cult—the auto dealers—take on a new importance as an anxious public eagerly expects the coming of a new form of salvation."[33]

Myths of the Elite

Less attention has been paid to what could be called the myths of the elite, especially those crystallized around artistic creation and its cultural and social repercussions. These myths, be it said, have succeeded in imposing themselves far beyond the closed corporation of the initiate, principally because of the inferiority complex that now afflicts both the public and official art circles. The aggressive incomprehension of the public, of critics, and of the official representatives of art toward a Rimbaud or a Van Gogh, the disastrous consequences—especially for collectors and museums—produced by indifference toward innovating movements, from impressionism to cubism and surrealism, have been hard lessons for the critics and the public as well as for art dealers, museum directors, and collectors. Today their only fear is not to be advanced enough and hence not to be in time to recognize genius in a work that is at first sight unintelligible. Perhaps never before in history has the artist been so certain that the more daring, iconoclastic, absurd, and inaccessible he is, the more he will be recognized, praised, spoiled, idolatrized. In some countries the result has even been an academicism in reverse, the academicism of the "avant-garde"—to such a point that any artistic experience that makes no concessions to this new conformism is in danger of being stifled or ignored.

The myth of the damned artist, which obsessed the nineteenth century, is outmoded today. Especially in the United States, but also in Western Europe, audacity and defiance have long since ceased to be harmful to an artist. On the contrary, he is asked to conform to his mythical image, that is, to be strange, irreducible, and to "produce something new." It is the absolute triumph of the permanent revolution in art. "Anything goes" is no longer an adequate formulation: now every novelty is considered a stroke of genius beforehand and put on the same plane as the innovations of a Van Gogh or a Picasso, even if the artist only mutilates a poster or signs a sardine tin.

The significance of this cultural phenomenon is the greater because, perhaps for the first time in the history of art, there is no longer any tension between artists, critics, collectors, and the public. They are all in agreement always, and long before a new work is created or an unknown artist discovered. The one thing that matters is not to have to say later that one did not understand the importance of a new artistic experience.

We cannot, of course, here analyze the mythology of the modern elites in all its manifestations. We shall confine ourselves to a few remarks. First of all, we may note the redeeming function of "difficulty," especially as found in works of modern art. If the elite revel in *Finnegans Wake*, or in atonal music, or in *tachisme*, it is also because such works represent closed worlds, hermetic universes that cannot be entered except by overcoming immense difficulties, like the initiatory ordeals of the archaic and traditional societies. On the one hand, one has the experience of an "initiation," an experience that has almost vanished from the modern World; on the other hand, one proclaims to the "others" (i.e., the "mass") that one belongs to a select minority—not, as once, to an aristocracy (for modern elites lean toward the left), but to a gnosis that has the advantage of being at once spiritual and secular in that it opposes both official values and the traditional churches. Through their cult of extravagant originality, of difficulty, of incomprehensibility, the elites advertise their escape from the banal universe of their parents while at the same time revolting against certain contemporary philosophies of despair.

Basically, being fascinated by the difficulty, not to say the incomprehensibility, of works of art expresses the desire to discover a new, secret, hitherto unknown meaning for the World and human life. One dreams of being "initiated" and thereby made able to understand the occult meaning of all these destructions of artistic languages, these "original" experiences that, at first sight, no longer seem to have anything in common with art. The torn posters, the empty, scorched, slashed canvases, the "art objects" that explode on opening day, the improvised plays in which the actors' speeches are drawn by lot—*all this must have a meaning*, just as certain incomprehensible words in *Finnegans Wake* come to be fraught with many meanings and values and with a strange beauty for the initiate when he discovers that they are derived from modern Greek or Swahili words disfigured by aberrant consonants, and enriched by secret allusions to possible puns when they are spoken aloud and very fast.

To be sure, all the genuine revolutionary experiences of modern art reflect certain aspects of the contemporary spiritual crisis or at least of the crisis in artistic knowledge and creation. But what concerns our investigation is the fact that the "elites" find in the extravagance and unintelligibility of modern works the opportunity for an initiatory gnosis. It is a "new World" being built up from ruins and enigmas, an almost private World, which one would like to keep for oneself and a very few initiates. But the prestige of difficulty and incomprehensibility is such that, very soon, the "public" too is conquered and proclaims its total acceptance of the elite's discoveries.

The destruction of artistic languages was accomplished by cubism, dadaism, and surrealism, by atonality and "musique concrete," by James Joyce, Becket, and Ionesco. Only the epigones are left furiously demolishing what has already been demolished. For the genuine creators are not willing to take their stand on ruins. Everything leads us to believe that the reduction of "artistic Universes" to the primordial state of *materia prima* is only a phase in a more complex process; just as in the cyclic conceptions of the archaic and traditional societies "Chaos," the regression of all forms to the indistinction of the *materia prima*, is followed by a new Creation, which can be homologized with a cosmogony.

We cannot here develop and refine these few observations, for the crisis in the modern arts is only of subsidiary concern to our study. Yet we must dwell for a moment on the situation and the role of literature, especially of epic literature, for it is not unrelated to mythology and mythical behavior. We do not intend to discuss the "origins" of epic literature; it is well known that, like the other literary genres, the epic and the novel continue mythological narrative, though on a different plane and in pursuit of different ends. In both cases it is a question of telling a significant story, of relating a series of dramatic events that took place in a more or less fabulous past. There is no need to go over the long and complex process that transformed some particular "mythological material" into the "subject" of an epic. What we consider important is the fact that in modern societies the prose narrative, especially the novel, has taken the place of the recitation of myths in traditional and popular societies. More than this—it is possible to dissect out the "mythical" structure of certain modern novels, in other words, to show the literary survival of great mythological themes and characters. (This is true especially in regard to the initiatory theme, the theme of the ordeals of the Hero-Redeemer and his battles with monsters, the mythologies of Woman and of Wealth.) From this point of view we could say, then, that the modern passion for the novel expresses the desire to hear the greatest possible number of "mythological stories" desacralized or simply camouflaged under "profane" forms.

No less significant is the fact that people feel the need to read "histories" and narratives that could be called paradigmatic, since they proceed in accordance with a traditional model. Whatever the gravity of the present crisis of the novel, it is none the less true that the need to find one's way into "foreign" Universes and to follow the complications of a "story" seems to be consubstantial with the human condition and hence irreducible. It is a difficult need to define, being at once desire to communicate with "others," with "strangers," and share in their dramas and hopes, and at the same time the need to know what *can have taken place*. It is hard to conceive of a human being who is not fascinated by "narrative," that is, by a recounting of significant events, by what has happened to men endowed with the "twofold reality" of literary characters (for, on the one hand, they reflect the historical and psychological reality of members of a modern society and, on the other, they possess all the magical power of an imaginary creation).

But it is especially the "escape from Time" brought about by reading —most effectively by novel reading—that connects the function of literature with that of mythologies. To be sure, the time that one "lives" when reading a novel is not the time that a member of a traditional society recovers when he listens to a myth. But in both cases alike, one "escapes" from historical and personal time and is submerged in a time that is fabulous and trans-historical. The reader is confronted with a strange, imaginary time, whose rhythms vary indefinitely, for each narrative has its own time that is peculiar to it and to it alone. The novel does not have access to the primordial time of myths, but in so far as he tells a credible story, the novelist employs a time that is *seemingly historical* yet is condensed or prolonged, a time, then, that has at its command all the freedoms of imaginary worlds.

More strongly than any of the other arts, we feel in literature a revolt against historical time, the desire to attain to other temporal rhythms than that in which we are condemned to live and work. One wonders whether the day will come when this desire to transcend one's own time—personal, historical time—and be submerged in a "strange" time, whether ecstatic or imaginary, will be completely rooted out. As long as it persists, we can say that modern man preserves at least some residues of "mythological behavior." Traces of such a mythological behavior can also be deciphered in the desire to rediscover the intensity with which one experienced or knew something *for the first time;* and also in the desire to recover the distant past, the blissful period of the "beginnings."

Here too, as we might expect, there is always the struggle against Time, the hope to be freed from the weight of "dead Time," of the Time that crushes and kills.

NOTES

1. For what follows, see Robert M. Grant, *The Earliest Lives of Jesus* (New York: Harper and Row, 1961), 10ff.

2. Ibid., 15. On Theon, see ibid., 39ff. Cf. also, idem, *The Letter and the Spirit* (London: S.P.C.K., 1957), 120ff., and Jean Pepin, *Mythe et Allégorie. Les origines et les contestations judéo-chrétiennes* (Paris: Editions Montaigne, 1958).

3. Grant, op. cit., 21.

4. Origen, *De principiis*, 4, 2, 9, as cited by Grant, op. cit., 65.

5. Ibid., 66.

6. Origen, *Contra Celsum I*, 42, as cited by Grant, op. cit., 71.

7. Origen, *Contra Celsum II*, 56–59, as cited by Grant, op. cit., 75.

8. Cf. Grant, op. cit., 93.

9. Cf. ibid., 78.

10. See ibid., 115–116, and Jean Daniélou, *Message évangélique et culture hellénistique aux IIe et IIIe siècles* (Paris: Desclée, 1961), 251ff.

11. *Commentary on John*, 20, 20, as cited by Grant, op. cit., 116.

12. Mircea Eliade, *Myths, Dreams and Mysteries* (New York: Harper and Row,

1975 [1960]), 30–31. See also Allan W. Watts, *Myth and Ritual in Christianity* (London and New York: Thames and Hudson, 1953); Olivier Clément, *Transfigurer le Temps* (Neuchâtel-Paris: Delachaux et Niestlé, 1959).

13. Cf. Erwin Goodenough, *Jewish Symbols in the Greco-Roman Period*, Volumes *VII-VIII: Pagan Symbols in Judaism* (New York: Pantheon Books, 1958); Jean Daniélou, *Les symboles chrétiens primitifs* (Paris: Éditions du Seuil, 1961).

14. Leopold Schmidt has shown that the agricultural folklore of Central Europe contains mythological and ritual elements that had vanished from classic Greek mythology even before the times of Homer and Hesiod; cf. Leopold Schmidt, *Gestaltheiligkeit im bäuerlichen Arbeitsmythos* (Vienna: Verlag des Österreichischen Museums für Volkskunde, 1952), esp. 136ff.

15. Norman Cohn, *The Pursuit of the Millennium* (New York: Harper and Row, 1961 [1957]), 104. On the messianic claims of Frederick II, cf. E. Kantorowitz, *Frederick the Second, 1194–1250* (London: Constable and Company, Ltd., 1931), 450ff., 511ff.; Cohn, op. cit., 103ff.

16. Alphonse Dupront, "Croisades et eschatologie" in *Umanesimo e esoterismo. Atti del V Convegno Internazionale di Studi Umanistici, a cura di Enrico Castelli* (Padua: CEDAM, 1960), 177.

17. Paul Alphandéry and Alphonse Dupront, *La Chrétienté et l'idée de Croisade* (Paris: A. Michel, 1959), Vol. II, 118.

18. Ibid., 119.

19. Reinier, as cited by Alphandéry and Dupront, op. cit., 120.

20. *Annales Scheftlariensis*, text cited by Alphandéry and Dupront, op. cit., 123.

21. Texts cited by Alphandéry and Dupront, op. cit., 127.

22. On the "Tafurs," cf. Cohn, op. cit., 45ff.

23. Alphandéry and Dupront, op. cit., 145.

24. Campanella's note to verse 207 of his *Ecloga*, as cited by Dupront, op. cit., 187.

25. Critical edition by Romano Amerio (Rome: CEDAM, 1955), 72; Dupront, op. cit., 189.

26. Ernesto Bonaiuti derserves the greatest credit for having begun the revival of Gioacchinian studies with his edition of the *Tractatus super quatuor Evangelia* (Rome, 1930) and his *Gioacchino da Fiore* (Rome, 1931). Cf. also his two important articles: "Prolegomeni alla storia di Gioacchino da Fiore," *Ricerche Religiose* IV (1928), and "Il misticismo di Gioacchino da Fiore," *Ricerche Religiose* V (1929), reprinted in the posthumous volume *Saggi di Storia del Cristianesimo* (Vicenza, 1957), 327–382. See also Ernst Benz, "Die Kategorien der religiösen Geschichtsdeutung Joachims," *Zeitschrift für Kirchengeschichte* (1931), 24–111, and idem, *Ecclesia Spiritualis* (Stuttgart: W. Kohlhammer, 1934).

27. Cf. Karl Lowith, *Meaning in History* (Chicago: The University of Chicago Press, 1949), 208.

28. Lowith, op. cit., 210, draws attention to the fact that this last work inspired *Das dritte Reich* by the Russo-German author H. Moeller van der Bruck. Cf. also Jakob Taubes, *Abendländische Eschatologien* (Bern: A. Francke, 1947), who compares Hegel's philosophy of history with Gioacchino da Fiore's.

29. Cf. Eliade, op. cit., 23–38.

30. Ibid., 25–26.

31. Cf. for example, Coulton Waugh, *The Comics* (New York: Macmillan Company, 1947); Stephen Becker, *Comic Art in America* (New York: Simon and Schuster, 1960); Umberto Eco, "Il Mito di Superman" in *Demitizzazione e Imagine, a cura di Enrico Castelli* (Padua: CERAM, 1962), 131–148.

32. Andrew Greeley, "Myths, Symbols and Rituals in the Modern World," *The Critic* Vol. XX, No. 3 (December 1961/January 1962), 19.

33. Ibid., 24.

Part II:

Art and the Sacred

II / 1

Divinities: Art and the Divine

THE FACT THAT ORIGINALLY all art was "sacred" should not be allowed to obscure the distinction that has always existed between activities in which this sacred quality is merely implicit (for instance, the manufacture of utensils according to a model that had been revealed by a divine being in mythical times) and those activities designed specifically to proclaim, meditate upon, and worship a sacred power or being (for instance, the creation of an altar, religious symbols, or the statue of a god). In this latter activity man is directly concerned with a sacred concept and seeks to give it form and definition. Through the mediation of artistic expression the attributes of a religious abstraction are revealed, so to speak, for it is presented in a visible form. Hence, it may be said that sacred art seeks to represent the invisible by means of the visible. This intent is especially true of more highly developed cultures, in which philosophical speculation has evolved a systematic treatment of the nature and attributes of divinity. Thus in India after the period of the Upanishads (Skr., *Upaniṣad*), artists and philosophers were aware of the fact that a work of art gives form (Skr., *rūpa*) to what is in itself beyond form (Skr., *arūpa, para-rūpa*).

Even in archaic and "folk" cultures, lacking any philosophical system and vocabulary, the function of sacred art was the same: it translated religious experience and a metaphysical conception of the world and of human existence into a concrete, representational form. This translation was not considered wholly the work of man: the divinity also participated by revealing himself to man and allowing himself to be perceived in form or figure. Every religious expression in art represents, therefore, an encounter between man and the divine. Such encounters may be, on the one hand, a personal religious experience; or on the other, a religious perception of the world, the discovery that the world is a divine work, the creation of the gods.

"Divinities: Art and the Divine" was first published in English in the *Encyclopedia of World Art* (London and New York: McGraw-Hill, 1961), Volume 4, Columns 382–387 and is reprinted by permission.

The first form of encounter or experience presupposes the consent of the deity in letting himself be grasped as a "form" or "figure"; that is, these artistic images of the deity are to be considered the immediate consequences of divine dispensation. In India, for example, Shankara writes: "The Supreme Lord may if he wishes assume a corporeal form consisting of maya (Skr., *māya*), as a favor to his devout worshipers" (*Brahmasūtra-bhāṣya*, I, 1, 20). The popular worship of idols and cult objects is interpreted by Vishnuite theologians as proof of the god's compassion in manifesting himself to men, in letting himself be perceived by the senses, even at the risk of being transformed into an idol and of being confused with the material objects that he had sanctified with his presence.

The great paradox common to all religions is that God in showing Himself to mankind is free to take any form whatsoever but that, by this very assertion of His freedom, He "limits Himself" and reduces Himself to a mere fragment of the whole which He represents. In effect, God's freedom to reveal Himself to men brings with it the risk of being interpreted in the opposite sense—especially of being taken as evidence of anthropomorphism, that is, of a dependence upon the human imagination or intelligence. All the varieties of idolatry, as well as all the arguments against the existence of God, ultimately derive from the initial paradox that divine revelation is accessible only within the context of human experience. Nevertheless, once this paradox has been accepted, every manifestation of divinity—however humble or contradictory it may be—deserves to be considered for its own sake, not discarded for reasons extrinsic to the religious experience.

The mystery of the Incarnation, which is the ultimate form of God's self-revelation, led William of Ockham to write: "Est articulus fidei quod Deus assumpsit naturam humanam. Pari ratione potest assumere lapidem aut lignum." ("It is an article of the Faith that God took on the nature of a human being. By this same token He can take on that of a stone or of a piece of wood.") Aside from any theological considerations, Ockham's conception of divine freedom provides a context within which the so-called "primitive" religions may be viewed simply as a series of paradoxical, frequently even grotesque, "revelations." In archaic stages of culture it is believed that the divine may be manifested both in natural objects (stones, plants, etc.) and in various sectors of the universe (heavens, stars, bodies of water, etc.); in fact, a large part of the history of archaic religions may be reduced to such cosmic revelations, that is, to the worship of the sacred as directly manifest in the universe. Without pursuing the details of this sacred dialectic, one may remark that the sacred is manifested in a variety of aspects and in the most archaic religions as well as in the more complex; and that in manifesting itself it becomes limited and altered. If one may speak of any continuity in the religious history of mankind, it lies in the simple fact that from the most ancient times the divine has been revealed to the religious man by means of "something other" than itself. This characteristic may be ascribed to the Christian mystery of the Incarnation.

The various formulas that men have used to express this encounter with the divine are by no means homologous; when their structures and characteristics are examined, one becomes aware of the diversity of religious situations that these represent. On the one hand, there are manifestations that disclose the sacred significance of a part of the cosmos (the sky, the earth, etc.) or of a natural object (a tree or stone, etc.); on the other hand, there are manifestations which reveal a divine "form" or "figure" and which are in the strictest sense epiphanies and theophanies. In the former case, the religious man is confronted with the sacred character of the cosmos; that is, he discovers that the world has a sacred significance in its very structure. In the latter experience he discovers something more, for he finds himself before a supernatural being that has a form and a biography or mythology, a divine history.

To cite only a single instance, the heavens have transcendent and sacred implications. Rising infinitely, they are immutable and over-powering; they intimate that such loftiness is a dimension inaccessible to human beings, and hence an attribute of divinity. This celestial imagery leads man to understand existentially that the sacred is some-thing totally different from himself, that it belongs to a different order of being and is thus, in philosophical terms, transcendent. The student of comparative religions also finds many cosmic deities, even among archaic cultures such as those of the hunters and trappers of Australia, Tierra del Fuego, etc. Although these celestial gods display certain cosmic attributes (they inhabit the heavens, manifest their presence through meteorological phenomena, dispense rain, have the stars as their eyes, etc.), they embody something more: a personality and a his-tory. In this respect such cosmic deities are closer to man than was the purely abstract awareness of celestial sacredness, but they differ from him in being considered the omnipotent and omniscient creators of the universe and of man. If they have not become *dei otiosi*, they are still benevolent and terrifying at the same time, for their actions are essen-tially unpredictable. They do not resemble man; yet they have a shape and a personality that render them more accessible and intelligible than the abstract magico-sacred forces which men find everywhere in the cosmos. And there clings to them still the memory of a distant time when the gods descended from the skies and met with men on earth. For the most part these supreme beings are not represented by means of images; or if so, the images are created only during the secret initiation rituals, to be shown to the neophytes and then carefully destroyed (as in the case of Daramulun, the supreme being of the Yuin, in Australia).

Artistic endeavor inspired by divine subject matter seeks to demonstrate the nature of the gods and their creations. It is an effort to depict both their "form" and their "works." The forms of the gods are not necessarily anthropomorphic: they may be inspired by any sort of morphology, concrete or imaginary; but their depiction—or suggestion—is always a question of forms, even when these are reduced to the most elementary geometric shapes. More important for artistic purposes is the desire to show what these gods have created. This impulse was often one of the sources of inspiration for architecture since it was thought that altars and sanctuaries represent an *imago mundi*, a miniature cosmos— and the cosmos is the supreme example of the work of the gods.

Even certain prehistoric rock carvings seem to show supernatural beings enacting parts of their histories, now obscure to us: a magical gesture, a dance, a ritual, or some act essential for prolonging life (in general, there are more easily comprehensible references to hunting, to the gathering of the harvest, or to sexuality). It is not always possible to decipher the religious connotation of these figures or to determine whether they represent gods, demons, or wizard-priests; but by representing magico-religious ceremonies they indicate directly or indirectly what supernatural beings have done as an aid or example to mankind. In fact, the "history" of what the gods have accomplished and of the consequence of their creative act—the world—has furnished the subject matter for a large part of the world's art. The acts of the gods, like those of the heroes, are illustrated in a great variety of motifs, genres, and techniques in the art of the ancient Near East and Mediterranean, as well as in India, Indonesia, and pre-Columbian Central America. Even when a divine history is not being recounted directly, one may assume that forms and iconographic systems which tend to reveal some aspect of the world or of the fundamental interplay between cosmic life and human existence are intimately related to the personality and creative activity of the gods. This relationship is true in ancient China, where the *t'ao-t'ieh*—already found on the ritual bronzes of Shang and Chou—whatever its precise interpretation may be, is illustrative of the sacred aspects of the cosmos. It alludes to the structure of the world in a less symbolic form than does the sacred diagram *t'ai-chi t'u*, which unites the two opposed principles of *yin* and *yang* that form the very essence of life. Apparently these graphic forms either refer to the sacred character of the cosmos, and therefore indirectly to cosmogonic divinity, or else they constitute an aniconic representation of the divinity. China was, in fact, to create divine images only as a result of Buddhist influence, shortly after the beginning of the Christian era.

At this point there arises the complex problem of the relationships between divinities and their symbols. It should not be forgotten that, in some parts of the ancient Near East, in India, and elsewhere, symbols precede any actual figures of the gods. For instance, in Mesopotamia one finds a number of vegetable symbols, the lunar crescent, the sun, lightning, or geometrical designs, which are independent of the deities and which precede their appearance on monuments. Many of these symbols were assimilated by those divinities who later dominated the religious life of Mesopotamia. One cannot discount the possibility that a symbol had belonged to a prehistoric deity who disappeared from worship and that it was later assimilated by another deity. Such cosmic symbols have a magico-religious potency sufficient to preserve their autonomy even when they are incorporated into the personality of a god. Furthermore, it is known that some Mesopotamian divinities had no anthropomorphic form: for example the celestial god Anu and the god of the earth Enlil were represented simply by a horned tiara resting on a throne. Hence it is possible that religious symbols at times took the place of the gods themselves. Subsequently, when the divinities were represented in anthropomorphic form, the symbols that had formerly replaced them became their attributes (lightning, the bull, the stag, or the eagle in the case of Teshub, the Hittite weather god; the lotus flower for Ea, a water god).

Symbols never wholly vanish from art and religious iconography, even when anthropomorphism reaches the perfection of classical Greece. Lightning, the winged disk, the ear of corn, and many other symbols indicate that a particular statue is not of a human being but of a divinity. The supernatural character of the image is seen still more clearly when the divinity is presented in theriomorphic, phytomorphic, or fantastic forms. Formal elements drawn from the animal and vegetable worlds or from the realm of the imagination clearly show that the divinity who exhibits them enjoys a mode of being different from the human and controls magico-religious forces inaccessible to men. The theriomorphic elements of a divine image testify that the divinity shares the secrets and magic of the animal world and partakes of all its fertility and creative potential, manifest and hidden. The same mystery of a paradoxical unity that transcends the various manifestations of the divine is suggested by the formal elements taken from the vegetable world. The phytomorphic and dendromorphic aspects of divinities indicate their polymorphism, their possibility of existing simultaneously on a number of different levels, and their control over the sources of the earth's fertility. The integration of theriomorphic and phytomorphic elements in sculptural representations of divinities expresses something more than the mere manifestation of the cosmic sacredness of the animal or vegetable worlds. Such symbols touch upon secrets that are more abstruse, and sometimes even terrifying, since they allude to incomprehensible bonds between the most important gods and certain animals or plants—as though these gods in a part of their lives unknown to men had led a secret existence, disguised as beasts and plants.

These complex and polymorphic gods appear in the agricultural religions and are especially dominant in the urban civilizations of the ancient Near East, the Mediterranean, and India. They have a richer, more dramatic mythology than do the ancient gods of the heavens, the lords of animals, and the goddesses of earlier civilizations. The artistic creation of antique cultures has been especially stimulated and enriched by these gods. In Egypt, Mesopotamia, and Greece they were responsible for inspiring the artist to translate into concrete forms their cosmogonic power, unlimited force, and combative drive, as well as the characteristics that distinguish them from humans, their majesty and the inexorability of their decisions. Still more striking are the iconographic elements taken from the realm of fantasy and dream: the monstrous, grotesque, and demonic figures or the many-headed divine beings that have multiple arms and bodies covered with eyes. Obviously there is a structural difference between the first group of purely fantastic creations and the second, in which the essential factor is the multiplicity of members (heads, arms, eyes); nevertheless, all these figures not only manifest the irreducible quality of the gods—the fact that they do not belong to the world of humans—but underline their strangeness, their extravagance, and their freedom to assume any form whatsoever. Among primitive peoples the worship of the dead and the presence of masked societies have favored the creation of monstrous figures, representing various personifications of some legendary ancestor who is simultaneously considered the first mortal to have died and the lord of the underworld. The imaginary world from which these terrifying forms derive is at the same time the world of dreams and that of the dead. Sometimes these two worlds are in communication, for the dead return in dreams, and during sleep the soul wanders in the realm of the dead.

In one way or another, all divine, semidivine, or demonic images with a monstrous and terrifying aspect either belong to funerary mythologies or have at least some connection with death. This is not to say that all the deities of death have a fantastic form or a sinister aspect and are intended to cause fear. Throughout the mythology and iconography of

Persephone, but above all during the Hellenistic period, the Mediterranean and Roman worlds produced certain images that show death as a deep sleep, a return to the maternal womb, a ritual passage toward a blessed world, or an upward journey through stellar space. In the primitive world, however, in India as well as in Tibet and southeast Asia, the divinities having a terrifying aspect are more or less directly connected with death, even when their principal function is not funerary. Although Śiva and Kālī-Durgā are not funerary divinities, their iconographic representation clearly shows that the continual destruction and re-creation of the universe inexorably implies death, even if this death is sometimes viewed as a spiritual experience: that is, to die in one's profane, unenlightened human condition in order to proceed to a superior level of being, that of liberty or immortality.

The iconographic representation of divine beings with numerous members is clearly different from that of the terrifying divinities. The multiplicity of members expresses by means of an artistic convention the fact that one is dealing not with a human being but with a god. Many-headedness signifies that a god is capable of looking in different directions at the same time, that he is all-seeing and consequently omniscient. The three-headed god is found on seals from Mohenjo-daro and two-headedness is seen in Mesopotamian and Greek art (Argus, for instance). Three-headed divinities are quite frequently shown on Thracian and Celtic monuments, while polycephalic divinities were illustrated in the statuary of the pagan Slavs. Mut, Horus, and Bes are shown in Egypt as covered with eyes, like Argus. In India, the multiplication of arms is expressive of divine omnipotence, especially in the divinities that control the rhythms of the universe (Śiva, Kālī). Mahayana Buddhism led to the diffusion in Tibet, China, and Japan of iconographic figure types with innumerable arms and with hands sometimes covered with eyes (Tārā, in Tibet; Kwannon, in Japan).

When Greek art reached its formal perfection in the classical period, and the gods—long since anthropomorphic in their forms—came to be represented as types exemplary of human beauty, artistic genius still managed to retain the divine quality in the structure of the image itself. Perfect serenity, a mysterious smile, and wide-open eyes, all serve to indicate that one is dealing with personages who transcend human modes of being. Symbols, which have by now become attributes of the gods, complete these divine images: they are there to remind one that mysteries, potencies, and absolute autonomy are an integral part of the personality of a god. A similar technique was developed, as a consequence of Greek influences, in Buddhist statuary. The iconography of the Buddha expresses the blessedness and serenity of the individual who

1. Head of Apollo, Greco-Roman Period

2. Head of the Buddha, 9th century

3. Icon of Christ as Pantocrator, 6th century

has experienced the supreme enlightenment and who has been transported from his human condition.

The creativity of the artist was nowhere so fully tested as in classical Greece, Buddhist Asia, and Christian Europe. Although approached from different points of view, the central problem was the same: how to project a personal concept of divinity by means of an image that as far as possible was to resemble the human figure. The Greeks sought to exalt bodily beauty, without trying to disfigure it. For the Buddhists the problem was less difficult, since Buddha had been and remained human despite his having become superior to the gods. Essentially it was a question of expressing through iconography the fact that the human condition may be radically altered as a consequence of spiritual illumination.

For the Christian artist the problem of representing divinity has been and still is practically insoluble for no means has yet been found to demonstrate in convincing pictorial form that Christ is God, other than introducing some symbolic element such as the halo. It is for this reason that the masterpieces of Christian art almost never show Christ preaching his message (although there were in Early Christian times attempts to show Christ as the Logos in the figure of a philosopher, as in the sarcophagus in S. Ambrogio, Milan), but show instead the crucified or resurrected Christ, Christ in Majesty, or Christ as judge and ruler of the Universe, since all these epiphanies of Christ could be expressed in comprehensible form. Such restriction of subject matter reflects the difficulty of expressing by artistic means the mystery of the Incarnation, the simple fact that God concealed Himself in human flesh and thereby made Himself no longer recognizable as God.

Masks: Mythical and Ritual Origins

CEREMONIAL NAKEDNESS greatly increases the magico-religious power of woman, and the chief attribute of the Great Mother is her nakedness. In her body, by her body, the goddess reveals the mystery of inexhaustible creation on all levels of life in the cosmos. Every woman shares the essence and the import of the goddess in this archetypal nakedness. The ancient concept involved here has never wholly disappeared, even in very highly evolved religions. For the Hindus, for example, every nude woman incarnates *prakrti*, nature, matter, the primordial substance, and the prototype of woman.

Man, on the contrary, increases his magico-religious possibilities by hiding his face and concealing his body. When he puts on a mask, he ceases to be himself; at least, he seemingly, if not actually, becomes another. This amounts to saying that, at least after a certain period in history, a man knows himself as a man precisely by changing himself into something other than himself. By wearing a mask he becomes what he is resolved to be: *homo religiosus* and *zoon politikon*. Such behavior has a good deal of bearing on the history of culture.

There are three general kinds of masks with three different purposes: ritual masks, war masks, and masks for spectacles. However, all masks are ritual in origin. War masks are fashioned to frighten and paralyze the enemy; they represent terrifying monstrous faces. Their magical function is unmistakable; it derives from the practice of painting the head and body, the earliest known magico-religious disguise. The cultural origin and function of dance and spectacle masks are plain enough.

Ritual use of masks is extremely varied, but two important classes of masks may be distinguished: those worn by the living and the masks of the dead.

It is worth stressing the almost world-wide diffusion, the antiquity,

"Masks:: Mythical and Ritual Origins" first appeared in English in the *Encyclopedia of World Art* (London and New York: McGraw-Hill, 1964), Volume 9, Columns 520–525, and is here reprinted by permission

and the continuity of masks. There are masks attested as early as paleolithic times; in Europe they have a history of more than 30,000 years, and there are villages where masks are to this day worn in ritual. Paleolithic hunters' masks represent wild beasts. The cultural heirs of neolithic man, the modern European peasantry, use, together with masks of stags, wolves, and bears, also masks of domestic animals and (these probably of urban origin) human faces. Certainly the religious role of the mask was different for paleolithic hunters from what it was for neolithic farmers. Still, the cultural role of stag masks and bear masks in central and eastern Europe is a continuation of traditions originating in the religious ideas of paleolithic man.

Some fifty-five paleolithic representations of men in animal disguises are known. From Teyjat in Dordogne there are antlers carved with three figures disguised as chamois; and from Lourdes comes a slate plaque showing a man in deerskin, antlers, and a long horse's tail. But the religious function of the mask in paleolithic hunting cultures is most plainly revealed by the great "sorcerer" of the Trois-Frères cave. Thirty inches high, deeply carved in the rock, the sorcerer dominates the many animal figures on the walls. He has a stag's head topped with immense antlers, an owl's face, ears like a wolf's, a long goat's beard, uplifted arms ending in bear paws, and a long horse's tail.

This sorcerer may represent a human being or perhaps a supernatural being, a hunters' god in the guise of a paleolithic sorcerer. A. C. Blanc has compared him to a Melanesian spirit with fish in the place of its head, hands, and feet. This Melanesian spirit is protector both of sea creatures and of fishermen; he fills nets but can also do harm. Whatever the Trois-Frères figure represents, it is certain that paleolithic sorcerer-priests used animal disguises like this for the purpose of raising themselves to a superhuman state.

There are many modern examples of magico-religious transformation brought about by wearing a mask. The Eskimos believe that the wearer is mysteriously impregnated with the spirit represented by the mask: to put on the mask representing a totem is to become that totem. Certain aspects of shamanism contribute to a better understanding of the function of the Trois-Frères sorcerer. In their trances Siberian shamans wear costumes with animal motifs, among others. Along with bird motifs (of an obvious symbolism) appear deer and reindeer antlers. The costumes of Altaic and Tungusic shamans include furs and hides and ribbons and scarves representing serpents. The shaman possesses, among other powers, the ability to identify himself with an animal or magically to transform himself into an animal. In certain places, the shaman represents the Lord of the Beasts, playing an important role in the community hunt.

True masks are rather rare among Siberian shamans, but among the Eskimos, especially in Alaska, where the influence of American Indian cultures is strong, the shamans do use masks. However, shamanic dress is in itself and in origin a mask. Mask or dress, the function is the same: to proclaim the incarnation of a mythological figure—a god, ancestor, or mystic animal. The mask effects the transubstantiation of the shaman, transforming him before everyone's eyes into the supernatural being he is impersonating.

A similar transformation takes place in the ceremonies of certain mask societies, but the magico-religious experience involved here is different from the shaman's or from the paleolithic hunter's. In this case it is bound up with a community rite of ancestor worship. The masks represent the ancestors; by wearing masks the members of the secret society personify the ancestors. By means of masks, the dead return to life. It is no longer the mask-wearers who perform the rite but the mythico-ritual beings whom they have become. For the dead are mythico-ritual beings absorbed into the mythical First Ancestor, the first man to know death. In other words, when members of the secret society wear masks, they act out a myth of beginnings: how in days primordial the Ancestor met his death—changed his state and became "other"—and afterward revealed to the people the mysteries of death and resurrection through the dramatic ceremonies of initiation. All mask societies are based on origin myths. Therefore the mythical event that gave birth to the secret society is periodically reenacted in its ceremonies.

It is likely that mythico-ritual ceremonies involving the ritual presence of ancestors (represented by masked initiates in the guise of wild beasts) were common among primitive men on a cultural par with paleolithic hunters. In some African initiation ceremonies the officiants are clad in lion and leopard skins, complete with claws, and the circumcision knives are furnished with hooks. Circumcision symbolizes the destruction of the genitals by the animal patron of the initiation. The officiants are sometimes called "lions," and circumcision is expressed by the verb "kill." Afterward the neophytes are themselves "masked," that is, dressed in leopard or lion skins. In other words, they are assimilated to the divine essence of the initiation animal and hence are reborn in him.

The masks—the ancestors—terrify women and the uninitiated and impose severe tests on the neophytes during their initiation. For example, the cruelties of the Duk-duk society of New Britain are well known. The maskers harass, attack, and sometimes kill those whom they meet in their way. The behavior of wild beasts is the model of certain men's

4. Raven Mask, Kwakiutl, British Columbia

5. Pre-Columbian Mask

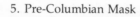

6. Gyodo Mask,
Processional Mask of a Bosatsu

7. Ligbe Mask, Ghana

societies. The members enjoy a predatory privilege that associates them with the carnivores. In the secret brotherhoods of the Japanese and of the Germanic tribes of antiquity, the masks, the indescribable uproar, and the barking of dogs (ritually become "wolves") testify to the ancestors' presence, the return of the dead. Because of the terror they inspire, masked brotherhoods sometimes come to have a certain political power. Some carnivorous animal—such as the wolf in central Asia and in Europe, the leopard in Africa—constitutes the model both of the perfect hunter and formidable warrior and of the invincible conqueror and absolute master. It is through masks that this power is constituted and maintained.

Initiation into this sort of secret society necessarily involves, however, the disclosure of the purely human nature of the wearers of the masks. In Ubangi country, this revelation has a dramatic character. An old man, costumed and masked, comes out of the bush, runs and leaps upon the freshly circumcised neophytes, lashes them with a whip, and then disappears. At the close of the rites, the neophytes, encouraged by the leader of the initiation, seize the masked one, take away his whip, unmask him, and recognize the face of an old man of the village. From then on, they know. They have learned not only that the masked one is a human being but how to go about striking terror into the uninitiated. They have learned the secret of incarnating the spirits of the dead by smearing themselves with paint and wearing masks. This knowledge does not do away with the sense of mystery, for even while knowing the nature of his mask, the member of a secret brotherhood continues to look upon the masks of superior members as truly supernatural beings. Moreover, the mask-wearer finally becomes fascinated with his own mask and by the fear that it elicits. "He no longer knows himself, a monstrous cry escapes his throat, the cry of a beast or a god, a superhuman outcry, a pure emanation of battle force, of creative passion, of boundless magic power by which he believes himself—by which he is, in this moment—possessed."[1]

The morphology of terror-producing masks is extremely rich. Principal sources of inspiration are the world of nightmares, death myths, demonology, and images relating to the process by which a cadaver is transformed into a skeleton. All these images of terror express the otherness of the dead, the different ways of becoming "other" (cadaver, skeleton, ghost, demon). The masks used in the "devil dances" (Tibet, China, Ceylon) are related both to the ritual for expelling demons (souls of the dead) and to that of initiation. In Tibet masks represent certain demonic beings that the soul meets after death. By attending the ritual dances, onlookers learn to overcome their fear of the death journey; they are prepared for encounters beyond the grave.

Sometimes masks represent superhuman beings not in *concreto* but in spirit. The best-known examples are the Zuñi kachina masks. The kachinas are spirits of the dead, more or less identified with ancestors. According to myth, they periodically used to return to visit the living; and whenever they took their leave, women followed them. The kachinas then decided to come no longer in person but in spirit. They commanded that masks be made resembling the ones they wore themselves in the other world and declared that they would be present in spirit in these masks. The masked dances are a re-creation of mythical times; they reproduce certain deeds performed by the kachinas at the dawn of time. The masks are neither theriomorphic nor terrifying. They are geometrical faces, abstractions. The geometrical design expresses the remote, the nonhuman, the transcendent. This is to say that the kachinas are exemplars, archetypes existing in another world, who, while remaining in touch with our own, transcend it.

The periodic visit of the kachinas has a religious function: they bring rain and bless the harvest. Among farming peoples, masked processions are believed to have a beneficent influence on cattle and crops. The Slavic and Balkan *kolyadi* are groups of young people, sometimes masked, who visit houses, singing and dancing, during the Twelve Days of Christmas. Their songs (*kolyadki*) invoke the harvest's abundance and the cattle's increase. But the association with the spirits of the dead is plain: if they enter a house in which the family has lately lost a member, the *kolyedari* bring news of the departed. In fact, some Bulgarian masks simulate a death's head. The *kolyedari* and their counterparts in other parts of central Europe are masked, carry trappings shaped like goats or horses, and make noise with bells or other instruments. Their masks are theriomorphic (stags, goats, foxes, eagles, and so on) or represent various figures from Christian folklore (the Devil, for example). The procession takes place during the 12 days between Christmas and Epiphany or during carnival.

These masked processions carry animal effigies curiously vestigial of Dionysiac processions, and in so far as elements of cults of the dead and of agricultural religion are present in the Dionysiac tradition, this resemblance in folk custom is easily explainable. But the mask is still more closely linked with the cult of Dionysos, for it played a leading role in the origin of tragedy. In this case the mask is anthropomorphous, but the human element is transfigured by the mask's very structure; the rigidity, the fixity, and immobility of feature do not belong to an ordinary man; only gods or the dead present such immobility of expression, while still being able to speak, to communicate their desires and their thoughts. The context here is that of another cultural sphere, the expression of another level of consciousness. Despite its anthropomorphism, the Greek mask, too, depicts an archetype, an exemplar. The play— whether tragedy or comedy—reenacts a fabulous deed performed by type characters in paradigmatic situations. The actor temporarily loses his identity: he becomes another, he *is* the character he enacts. Masks used in Japanese drama have a like function: they help to transcend earthly space and time and lead the audience into a world where it is not men who move, but types.

Gold funerary masks are attested from as long ago as the 2d millennium B.C. in the Cretan-Mycenaean age. Perhaps they should be thought of as portraits, specifically death portraits, since the fine gold leaf was surely molded on the dead man's face. The Romans molded faces in wax and painted them in natural colors; these were used during the rites for the dead and were preserved later. But long before molds were employed to preserve a likeness of the dead, there were funerary masks. They are found in gold, silver, bronze, or terra cotta, from Mesopotamia and Phoenicia to England, in the valley of the Danube, and in the Crimea. The idea is everywhere the same: the preservation of the dead person. The means and meaning of the preservation vary from culture to culture. In the Minusinsk region (the Tashtyk culture), plaster masks were made to preserve the individuality of the dead man, along with his soul substance (derived from the ancestors), which was retained in his bones or ashes.

Some death masks were, in fact, supplementary to mummification and later became a substitution for it. In front of or upon the case in which a body was mummified, the ancient Peruvians placed a rude wooden image, fashioned while a man was still alive and usually painted and adorned with human hair or a headdress. In Melanesia the skull itself served as a mask during the sacred dances. Obviously, in this case, it was no longer a matter of making a death mask, a portrait or representation of the dead. The skull itself represented the departed and preserved the essentials. Closer to the idea of a portrait mask are Etruscan funerary urns in the shape of a human face, a variant of the anthropomorphous urn. The attempt was to preserve the identity of the man's ashes, or, more exactly, to connect them with the face that was shown to his fellows in his lifetime.

Masks, then, are always, in one way or another, bound up with the idea of time. Whatever sort of mask is worn, the wearer transcends earthly time. Whether ritual, funerary, or for any spectacle, the mask is an instrument of ecstasy. He who wears one is no longer himself, since he is projected beyond his personal temporal identity. He becomes "other," even when the mask is his own portrait.

The mask's capacity for existence on another time level perhaps explains its dual function: alienation of the personality (ritual and theater masks) and preservation of the personality (death masks and portraits). Both cases exemplify a reactivation of past time: primordial time in the case of ritual and spectacle masks; historic and personal time in the case of death masks and portraits. Primordial mythological time, reactualized by ritual and spectacle masks, can be *lived*, but only by means of changing the personality and becoming "other." On the other hand, death masks and portraits reactualize historic time, which is not only past but dead, for no one can relive the inner life of anyone else. In either case, the time implied by the mask is ecstatic time, removed from the here and now. Whatever its type, every mask proclaims the presence of some being who does not belong to the everyday world.

NOTE

1. G. Buraud, *Les Masques* (Paris: Hachette, 1948), 101.

II / 3

Reflections on Indian Art

Notes on Indian Art

INDIAN ART, in contrast with that of Japan, for example, which quickly conquered the affections of Occidentals—has had to wait a long time to be understood and relished in the West. One finds even now handbooks on the history of Indian art in which the authors confess from the first page that they *like almost nothing* of the art works whose literary history they have chronicled (Vincent Smith, for instance). Some find it grotesque, barbarian, inhuman; others judge it hybrid and inert; some complain of a lack of proportion, perspective, naturalness; others believe in the contribution of Greek sculptors who taught Indian masters how to sculpture a human body in a lifelike way.

It seems to me that this difficulty of appreciating Indian art is due primarily to a mistaken way of looking at it. The one who, standing before an Indian sculpture, will seek to find the same "nature" he is accustomed to find in European graphics, or who will contemplate the work without making the necessary effort of *abstraction* (without realizing from the outset that before being a work of art, an Indian specimen is a work of creation, and that it is necessary to discover its metaphysical validity), not only will not understand anything about it, but he will also find a series of arguments to prove inertia, dullness, monotony, and lack of creative genius in Indian art. He will end by saying that India, being the land where spirit and philosophy have permeated the whole race more than any other place, is capable of metaphysics—but sterile with respect to art.

Now, the interesting thing is that precisely because India is a country of metaphysics—of the purest and most abstract effort to attain love,

"Reflections on Indian Art" was originally published in Romanian as "Notes on Indian Art" in *Cuvântul* 8 (October 12, 1932), 2685, 1–2; and "Notes on Indian Iconography" in *Cuvântul* 8 (October 20, 1932), 2693, 1–2. These essays also appeared in *Insula lui Ethanasius* (Bucharest: Fundația Regale pentru Literatură și Artă, 1943), 309–319. They are translated from the Romanian by Mac Linscott Ricketts.

understanding, and harmony with life—precisely for the reason it has created an art that is original, vital, and pure.

Indian art never made compromises with the flat beauty of picture post cards—because it had back of it metaphysics. The Indian artist never tried to copy nature because, being a philosopher (in the Indian sense of the word: a pure and harmonious man), he could *be* nature, and thus he could create in parallel with nature, imitating only the organic impulse, the thirst for life and growth, the caprice of discovering new forms and new delights, while not imitating directly the *creations* of nature, forms already achieved and thus, in a sense, dead. Whereas the European artist imitated the creations of nature and tried to reproduce its forms—passing them through his soul in order to give them a new emotional potential—the Indian artist imitated the *gesture* of nature and created on his own account, using however a different space and different forms from natural ones.

The European offers an aesthetic thrill; the Indian offers more: a sentiment full of harmony with nature, of equality with and love for all her innumerable creations.

It was logical moreover, that things should happen this way. A "natural" landscape is possible only in the intuition of a man (or a culture) who has separated from nature and is trying to approach it and reintegrate himself in it. To want to describe or suggest aspects of nature is a sign of dissociation of nature from consciousness (the case of Europe). But India still is *living in* nature; thus, she does not observe it, but *realizes* it. The Indian artist in his work of creation coincides with nature—and his works are nothing but new forms, rich and living, of the same nature which creates flowers, lakes, and monsters.

* * *

In analyzing an Indian masterpiece of plastic art, what impresses one from the first is the organic continuum of forms, their undulating rhythm, sweet and full. The plastic European organism (especially in Greek and Renaissance art) accentuates the principal features, those of self definition, isolation, and victory (the muscles, the specification and perfection of surfaces, etc.). Life is manifested aggressively here, through its planes of resistance against the medium, with the hostility of the individual and the mineral. There is a rock-like resistance in these perfect bodies, these perfect muscles—a resistance whose spiritual geology, however, was never written. But India represents life in plastic art in a different way. It expresses the organic continuum, the circulation of the vital juices, a rhythm of forms and volumes devoid of effort and hesitations, a rhythm that betrays an inner energy of circulation without

8. Sleeping Buddha, Ajanta Caves

9. Detail of the Gateway,
   Stupa at Sanchi

obstacles, nourishing muscles and bones, but making them disappear beneath fuller and more harmonious undulations of life.

Look at the arms and fingers in the frescoes from the Ajanta cave. They are arms with an amazing dynamics: round, live, but seemingly floating in an infinity beyond and on this side of the plane of the painting, continuing in the same harmonious motion and shouting their joy to be floating freely, without tension of the muscles, without leverage of the bones. No other painting in the world has created shoulders, arms, and fingers more perfect in their organic life, in their gesture of full and free existence.

No matter how you have looked at an Indian painting, you must return again and again to view it in its wholeness, in its organic movement. Each example *flows*—you sense it pervaded by life, even to the most insignificant corner—and you *cannot look at it fragmentarily*, you cannot isloate one gesture from another and evaluate it independently. It all escapes you if you have not perceived this continuum of plastic life, if you have not intuited this vital current, the sap which passes through each line and links it to another and yet another, as in an organic circuit.

We should have to go into greater depth, to the dual roots of primitive art, in order to understand the whole *Weltanschauung* of Indian graphics, to understand the substance of that organic "fabric" laden with magic power, which we find always in the plastic space of any example of Indian art. Perhaps we shall try to analyze this on another occasion.[1] Here we limit ourselves to an analysis of space in Indian art.

It is true that Indian art does not know perspective, but visualizes a scene from an analytic and qualitative viewpoint. The detail is always found in its place, but it is not represented in perspective—rather, in conformity with its particular *function*. The bed, seat, or umbrella, for instance, are shown as seen from above, the tree in profile, and the footprints also from above. The function of these details, their real value, have priority over their *images*. Indian art does not know "the image," the projection of the object onto a plane of perspective. It always seeks and represents the object as such, in a space of its own; it does not copy the image of the object from exterior space, which is a quantitative space having a physical equilibrium and a harmony of volume and perspective.

Plastic proportions do not correspond to natural proportions. The latter are exterior, quantitative; they appertain to physics, not aesthetics. Indian aesthetics respects quality, spirit, interior life, and gesture—not volume. That is why, on Buddhist bas-reliefs, elephants are small, so small they stand on lotuses, while Māyā, the Buddha's mother, is huge. Māyā predominates; the elephants have come only to prostrate themselves, to worship. Therefore, the elephants will stand on lotuses, will be like butterflies or bees, while Māyā will be represented in her true spiritual value.

Indian art, identifying the function of the artist with life, creates according to its values—which are spiritual, not physical—on its own plane, which is qualitative, not quantitative.

Space no longer appertains to diurnal experience, but to the sensibility of purity, to spiritual faith. In order to be realized, only the artist's power of visualization is necessary; in order to be felt, only the emotion of the viewer has to be involved. The diurnal space of the world of phenomena, of dead images, does not count. The dimension of power gives way to the moral dimension.

Indian plastic art is surprisingly alive and flowing. But in order to understand its life, an effort of abstraction, of breaking away from the everyday, of ascension and purification is required.

Notes on Indian Iconography

LET US FOCUS on one aspect of Indian graphic creation, iconography: that is, on a creative activity in which the artist has no initiative, in which he finds the problems and their solutions long since formulated, in which he conforms to a well-established hieratic canon and expresses neither his personal emotions nor the beauty of nature. It is what is called orthodox or classical art (shastrīya), which does not create works of art, but spiritual models, images to be interiorized through meditation; its action upon man does not conduce to aesthetic feeling, but to a sentiment of reconciliation and perfection, the point of departure for a spiritual ascent which far transcends profane art.

That is why, in order to be able to achieve in matter the model indicated in the iconographic treatise, the craftsman must lead a pure and serene life, and before setting to work he must clarify his vision through meditation and Yoga. He does not create natural phenomena in space; his colors and lines are not those of profane intuition; his beauty will not reflect anthropomorphic beauty. His work as a master craftsman is itself a contemplation, an imitation of the models to which he gives form. His total submission to the canon is the purest ascesis.

Ascesis does not always entail suffering of the flesh and victory of the spirit. Ascesis exists in any renunciation of personal initiative, in any lucid abandonment of the spirit in order to be shaped by a superhuman will manifested in static, hieratic gestures. The Indian craftsman in his work of reflecting on the hieratic gesture employs the practice of Yoga. "Yoga" means both "restraint" and "union": restraint of ordinary activities, of the mental dynamics of everyday, and union with the divinity chosen for one's meditation (*ishtadevata*).

The texts are quite specific in this regard. Shukrāchārya writes: "Let the imager establish images in temples by meditation on deities who are the objects of his devotion. For the successful achievement of this yoga the lineaments of the image are described in books to be dwelt upon in detail. In no other way, not even by the direct and immediate vision of an actual object, is it possible to be so absorbed in contemplation, as thus in the making of images."[2]

The mental concentration on the image of the divinity which is to be reflected in the material is not practiced by the craftsman only. It is indispensable also for the devotee, the one who contemplates the image after it has been installed in the temple or the shrine. Any approach to the divinity made through images (because there is also a direct approach, without images, and it is considered superior) cannot be accomplished without a preliminary interiorization of the image, that is, without its being "meditated" and "transposed" onto an interior plane of vision. These elementary things were forotten by those European savants and missionaries who hastened to speak of Indian "idols" and "idolatry." The truth of the matter is that there is no such thing as an "idol" in the Indian religious experience.

Images of the gods are only the support for meditation, the objective point of departure for a meditative experience which is refracted in the consciousness of the devotee. The image is a pretext, a vehicle which leads into another life—a life more harmonious, joyous and free. The offerings brought to the "idol" are nothing but a gesture of giving and renunciation—of renunciation in that the devotee renounces his right of initiative and practices a ritual imposed by *dogma*, i.e., by a law which transcends him and subjugates him. The offering, being the first step toward de-individualization, produces instantly a refreshing of the consciousness, a liberation from individualism, and makes possible an approach to other states of consciousness, another life.

Thus, Indian iconography represents a series of potencies which must be actualized, scenes which must be dramatized and experienced through a life of their own on another plane than that of diurnal consciousness; that which is hieratic and algebraic in their gesture and techtonics must be dynamized, quickened, and lived by a sincere effort of interiorization and a desire for holiness. Indian statues and images must not be understood symbolically. Their gesture betrays the same invitation always: be like us! When an Indian meditates on an iconographic theme, he does nothing but follow the indication of the gesture —not through an external imitation, but by seeking the essence, the experiential and concrete fruit of the gesture.

10. Dancing Krishna,
13th–14th century

11. Shiva Nataraja, Lord
of the Dance,
11th century

Every iconographic theme is at the same time a liturgical theme. That is why meditation by contemplation of images is never done alone, but is always accompanied by a mental or oral liturgy (the repetition of *mantras*), in order to provoke a state of consciousness liberated from mental dynamics, from what is transitory and illusory in human consciousness, and to obtain a state of perfect coincidence with the divinity. The iconographic gesture, therefore, is nothing but a stimulus to an *experience*, to a life untainted by passion. The hieratic gesture corresponds on the divine plane to the desire for holiness on the human plane. The devotee approaches the image with the desire for liberation, for transcending the illusory life which he leads. Meditation, interiorization, imitation of the divinity—these are the corollaries of any iconographic theme. The concrete point between two worlds. The gesture which calls for imitation and experiencing. The spiritual fruit which is untranslatable for the one who has not himself attempted this ascension through meditation.

Indian iconography in its totality is nothing but an endless series of human dramas of ascents toward perfection—ascents guided by the desire for the holiness (freedom and pity for all creatures) of man. That is why every iconographic theme—being connected with a certain meditation, a certain experience—has its own separate key. It is what Europeans call the "symbolism" of Indian iconography. Actually, it is nothing but its algebraic formulation—that is, in terms that are sacred and easily understood by those who know the alphabet of this language.

In both Hinduism and Buddhism—to speak only of the main religious currents of India—each divinity (in Buddhism the various hypostases of the Buddha became in time separate divinities) has its own special color, gesture, and symbol. And not only that, but in each ritual—i.e., in each schema of meditation, of experimentation—the color changes and combines, the gesture is modified, the symbols are varied. As a result, iconography knows an infinite number of nuances, each indicating a certain step, a state well established on the spiritual ladder of ascent. The drama of liberation is experienced through an infinite series of acts and scenes. But note carefully: the iconography is only the algebra of this drama, the hieratic formulation of the states of the soul which must be experienced before becoming perfectly harmonious, perfectly free, perfectly serene. You cannot ascend to the top of the ladder. At the most, what is sought is not freedom, but harmony with the transcendent, with dogma, with supernatural power. This holds true for the vast majority of the Indian people. It is they whom we ordinarily call . . . idolators.

NOTES

1. Since I have never returned to this matter of the dual origins of primitive art, I recall in brief the observations of Hoernes, from which all the subsequent speculations have set out. The art of agricultural peoples is a geometrical one in which account is taken only of relationships, while the human individual is neglected to such an extent that sometimes the human form decomposes into geometric figures. On the other hand, the art of nomadic peoples who live by hunting is based on the naturalistic drawing of animals, a drawing which takes account only of the individual and which represents him without any relationship to the surroundings. The man of agricultural and matriarchal cultures represents the Cosmos as a *fabric* in which the individual plays no real role. The Cosmos of the nomad and the hunter, on the contrary, is disintegrated into atoms. Naturally, in the art of any complex culture such as that of India, the two modes of representing the Cosmos are present to a more or less organic degree (1939).

2. Cited by Ananda K. Coomaraswamy in *The Dance of Shiva* (New York: Noonday Press, 1957), 26.

II/4

The Sacred and the Modern Artist

The Quest for the Unrecognizable Sacred

EVER SINCE 1880, when Nietzsche first proclaimed it, people have been talking a great deal about the "death of God." Martin Buber asked recently whether this is a question of a genuine "death" or simply of the eclipse of God—the fact that God is no longer in evidence, that he is no longer responding to the prayers and invocations of man. Nevertheless, it does not seem that his rather optimistic interpretation of Nietzsche's verdict is able to assuage all doubts. Certain contemporary theologians have recognized that it is necessary to accept (and even to assume) the "death of God," and are trying to think and to build on the basis of this fact.

A theology based on the "death of God" can give rise to exciting debates, but for our purposes it is only of subsidiary interest. We have made allusion to it to recall the fact that the modern artist encounters a similar problem. There is a certain symmetry between the perspective of the philosopher and theologian, and that of the modern artist; for the one as for the other the "death of God" signifies above all the impossibility of expressing a religious experience in traditional religious language: in medieval language for example, or in that of the Counter-Reformation. From a certain point of view, the "death of God" would rather seem to be the destruction of an idol. To acknowledge the death of God would thus be equivalent to admitting that one had been taken in, that he had been worshiping just a god and not the living God of Judaeo-Christianity.

Be that as it may, it is evident that, for more than a century, the West has not been creating a "religious art" in the traditional sense of the term,

"The Sacred and the Modern Artist" was first published as "Sur la permanence du sacré dans l'art contemporain," XXᵉ Siècle 26 (1964), 3–10. The English translation first appeared in Criterion 4 (1965), 22–24; and was reprinted in Art, Creativity and the Sacred: An Anthology in Religion and Art, edited by Diane Apostolos-Cappadona (New York: The Crossroad Publishing Company, Inc., 1984), 179–183. It is reprinted here by permission.

has not been creating a "religious art" in the traditional sense of the term, that is to say, an art reflecting "classic" religious conceptions. In other words, artists are no longer willing to worship "idols"; they are no longer interested in traditional religious imagery and symbolism.

This is not to say that the "sacred" has completely disappeared in modern art. But it has become *unrecognizable;* it is camouflaged in forms, purposes and meanings which are apparently "profane." The sacred is not *obvious,* as it was for example in the art of the Middle Ages. One does not recognize it *immediately* and *easily,* because it is no longer expressed in a conventional religious language.

To be sure, this is not a conscious and voluntary camouflage. Contemporary artists are by no means believers who, embarrassed by the archaism or the inadequacies of their faith, do not have the courage to avow it and who thus try to disguise their religious beliefs in creations which appear to be profane at first glance. When an artist recognizes that he is a Christian, he does not dissimulate his faith; he proclaims it according to his own means in his work as, for example, Rouault has. Nor is it difficult to identify the biblical religiosity and the messianic nostalgia of Chagall even in his first period, when he peopled his paintings with severed heads and bodies flying upside down. The ass, a messianic animal, *par excellence,* the "eye of God" and the angels were there to remind us that the universe of Chagall had nothing in common with the everyday world—that it was in fact a sacred and mysterious world such as that which is revealed during childhood. But the great majority of artists do not seem to have "faith" in the traditional sense of the word. They are not consciously "religious." Nonetheless we maintain that the sacred, although unrecognizable, is present in their works.

Let us hasten to add that this is a question of a phenomenon which is generally characteristic of modern man, or more specifically of man in Western society: he wants to be, and declares himself to be areligious— completely rid of the sacred. On the level of everyday consciousness, he is perhaps right; but he continues to participate in the sacred through his dreams and his daydreams, through certain attitudes (his "love of nature," for example), through his distractions (reading, theater), through his nostalgias and his impulses. That is to say, modern man has "forgotten" religion, but the sacred survives, buried in his unconscious. One might speak, in Judaeo-Christian terms, of a "second fall." According to the biblical tradition, man lost after the fall the possibility of "encountering" and "understanding" God; but he kept enough intelligence to rediscover the traces of God in nature and in his own consciousness. After the "second fall" (which corresponds to the death of God as proclaimed by Nietzsche) modern man has lost the possibility of experiencing the sacred at the conscious level, but he continues to be nourished and guided by his unconscious. And, as certain psychologists never stop telling us, the unconscious is "religious" in the sense that it is constituted of impulses and images charged with sacrality.

We are not about to develop these few remarks about the religious situation of modern man here. But if what we are saying is true of Western man in general, it is *a fortiori* still more true of the artist. And this is for the simple reason that the artist does not act passively either in regard to the Cosmos or in regard to the unconscious. Without telling us, perhaps without knowing it, the artist penetrates—at times dangerously—into the depths of the world and his own psyche. From cubism to tachism, we are witnessing a desperate effort on the part of the artist to free himself of the "surface" of things and to penetrate into matter in order to lay bare its ultimate structures. To abolish form and volume, to descend into the interior of substance while revealing its secret or larval modalities—these are not, according to the artist, operations undertaken for the purpose of some sort of objective knowledge; they are ventures provoked by his desire to grasp the deepest meaning of his plastic universe.

In certain instances, the artist's approach to his material recovers and recapitulates a religiosity of an extremely archaic variety that disappeared from the Western world thousands of years ago. Such, for example, is Brancusi's attitude towards stone, an attitude comparable to the solicitude, the fear, and the veneration addressed by a neolithic man towards certain stones that constituted hierophanies—that is to say, that revealed simultaneously the sacred and ultimate, irreducible reality.

The two specific characteristics of modern art, namely the destruction of traditional forms and the fascination for the formless, for the elementary modes of matter, are susceptible to religious interpretation. The hierophanization of matter, that is to say the discovery of the sacred manifested through the substance itself, characterizes that which has been called "cosmic religiosity," that type of religious experience which dominated the world before the advent of Judaism and which is still alive in "primitive" and Asiatic societies. To be sure, this cosmic religiosity was forgotten in the West in the wake of the triumph of Christianity. Emptied of every religious value or meaning, nature could become the "object" *par excellence* of scientific investigation. From a certain viewpoint, Western science can be called the immediate heir of Judaeo-Christianity. It was the prophets, the apostles, and their successors the missionaries who convinced the Western world that a rock (which certain people have considered to be sacred) was only a rock, that the planets and the stars were only cosmic *objects*—that is to say, that they were not (and could not be) either gods or angels or demons. It is as a result of this long process of the desacralization of Nature that the Westerner has managed to *see* a natural object where his ancestors saw hierophanies, sacred presences.

But the contemporary artist seems to be going beyond his objectivizing scientific perspective. Nothing could convince Brancusi that a rock was only a fragment of inert matter; like his Carpathian ancestors, like all neolithic men, he sensed a presence in the rock, a power, an "intention" that one can only call "sacred." But what is particularly significant is the fascination for the infrastructures of matter and for the embryonic modes of life. In effect we might say that for the past three generations we have been witnessing a series of "destructions" of the world (that is to say, of the traditional artistic universe) undertaken courageously and at times savagely for the purpose of recreating or recovering another, new, and "pure" universe, uncorrupted by time and history. We have analyzed elsewhere the secret significance of this will to demolish formal worlds made empty and banal by the usage of time and to reduce them to their elementary modes, and ultimately to their original *materia prima*.[1] This fascination for the elementary modes of matter betrays a desire to deliver oneself from the weight of mortal form, the nostalgia to immerse oneself in an auroral world. The public has evidently been particularly struck by the iconoclastic and anarchistic furor of contemporary artists. But in these vast demolitions one can always read like a watermark the hope of creating a new universe, more viable because it is more true, that is, more adequate to the actual situation of man.

However, one of the characteristics of "cosmic religion" both among the primitives and among the people of the Ancient Near East is precisely this need for periodically annihilating the world, through the medium of ritual, in order to be able to recreate it. The annual reiteration of the cosmogony implies a provisory reactualization of chaos, a symbolic regression of the world to a state of virtuality. Simply because it has been going on, the world has wilted, it has lost its freshness, its purity and its original creative power. One cannot "repair" the world; one must annihilate it in order to recreate it.

There is no question of homologizing this primitive mythico-ritual scenario to modern artistic experiences. But it is not without interest for us to note a certain convergence existing between, on the one hand, repeated efforts at destroying traditional artistic language and attraction towards the elementary modes of life and matter and, on the other hand, the archaic conceptions which we have tried to evoke. From a structural point of view, the attitude of the artist in regard to the cosmos and to life recalls to a certain extent the ideology implicit in "cosmic religion."

It may be, furthermore, that the fascination for matter may be only a precursory sign of a new philosophical and religious orientation. Teilhard de Chardin, for example, proposes to "carry Christ . . . to the heart of the realities reputed to be the most dangerous, the most naturalistic, the most pagan." For the Father wanted to be "the evangelist of Christ in the universe."

NOTE

1. Cf. Mircea Eliade, *Myth and Reality* (New York: Harper and Row, 1963).

II / 5

A Dialogue with Marc Chagall

Why Have We Become So Anxious?
by Marc Chagall

I HAVE COME AMONG YOU, not for the first time, because it seems to me that the idea of this association is of great interest. Had I followed the course of reason I should perhaps have remained at my last, for my art is my life because I dare to hope that I am not working only for myself.

It is good to find that, in these times, there are those who meet to exchange their ideas concerning the ultimate goals of existence. What could be more moving in our community here on earth than to listen closely to a human heart, to hear in it the throbbings of a world, its sighs and its dreams?

During the hundreds and thousands of years that have preceded us it was much easier morally for a man to live. He had a moral foundation of one kind or another, very deeply embedded, fitting exactly into his conception of life. We see this engraved with great clarity in the works of distant eras.

Yet with the passing of the years, increasingly, those older conceptions have revealed their impotence to animate human beings and fill their inner lives, to give them the strength they need, not only for creative work but simply to live.

In speaking of this I am not overcome by sadness for I am not a pessimist. There are no powers capable of dragooning me to lose my faith in the human person, because I believe in the grandeur of all nature. I also know that human will and human conduct are often the result of cosmic forces set in motion by this same nature and by the march of history and the pace of destiny.

"Why Have We Become So Anxious?" by Marc Chagall is based on remarks made in 1963 before the Committee on Social Thought at Meridian House in Washington, D.C. It was translated by Edmund S. Glenn and first appeared, along with "Beauty and Faith" by Mircea Eliade, in *Bridges of Understanding*, edited by John U. Nef (New York: University Publishers, 1964), 112–123. Both are reprinted here by permission.

Yet, in spite of this faith, how can we prevent ourselves from asking and repeating the question, *Why have we become so anxious in recent times?*

The more audaciously man has freed himself from his so-called chains, the more he feels alone, lost in the multitude, the prisoner of his destiny.

But, as is always true of me, I want to draw closer to Art. I want to speak to you of that.

With the coming of impressionism, a window opened for us. A rainbow began to glow on the horizon. Yet while the world appeared in different and more intense colors, it seems to me that, in general, it became narrower than, for example, the naturalistic world of Courbet, just as the naturalism of Courbet had become, in its turn, narrower than the world of romanticism introduced with Delacroix—and, again, just as the world of Delacroix had been more declamatory and confined than the neoclassical world of David and of Ingres. At this point I shall stop. . . .

After impressionism came the world of cubism which introduced us into the geometrical tunnels of reality, just as later, abstractionism led into the world of atoms and of matter.

So we have the pitch and the dimensions of a continually contracting scene. In such a sequence as this, one has the impression that as one moves forward the scope of art progressively shrinks. Where are we headed?

Let us try to discover what is authentic in our lives.

The world belongs to us from the moment we are born, and we have the impression of being armed from the beginning.

For about two thousand years we have been nourished by a reserve of energy which has sustained us and given content to life. But during the past hundred years this reserve has broken up and its elements have begun to disintegrate.

God, perspective, color, the Bible, form, lines, traditions, the so-called humanisms, love, caring, the family, the school, education, the prophets, and Christ Himself have fallen to pieces.

Perhaps I too at times have been beset by doubts. I painted pictures upside down. I cut off heads and hacked my subjects to bits, left floating in the air in my pictures. I did this on behalf of a different perspective, of a different kind of composition, of a different formula.

And little by little our world seems to be a smaller world on which we small ones swarm, clinging to the smallest elements in our nature, until we submerge ourselves in the tiny pieces of nature, even in the atom.

Doesn't this so-called scientific gift of nature, by emptying the soul, limit the source of poetry? Doesn't it deprive man of even the physical opportunities for calm and quiet? And doesn't all this deprive his system of any sense of moral direction connected with his life and his creative work?

In the course of recent years, I have often spoken of the so-called chemistry of authentic color, and of matter, as providing the measure of authenticity. An especially sharp eye can recognize that an authentic color, like authentic matter, inevitably contains all possible techniques. It has also a moral and a philosophical content.

If there is a moral crisis, it is a crisis of color, of matter, of blood and its parts, of words and sounds, and all the rest of the elements with which one constructs a work of art as well as a life. For even if a canvas is covered with mountains of color, whether or not it is possible to distinguish an object—even if there are lots of words and sounds—these do not necessarily make the work authentic.

To my mind, Cimabue's combination of color and matter in itself marked a turning point in the art of the Byzantine period. Just as somewhat later Giotto's color was no less authentic—and I would emphasize this word in relation to the chemistry of which I have spoken—because that marked another artistic and moral turning point, as is true of Masaccio and some others. . . .

I should repeat that it is not a new conception of the world, it is nothing literary or symbolic that brings about this change. It is blood itself, a certain chemical process in nature, in things, and even in human awareness. This new *authenticity* is seen in all sides of life.

What gives birth to this so-called chemical change? How is she reared? How does she live? I ask these questions because she is the source of art, of a true view of the world and of life itself.

She is born and lives and is sustained by love and by a genuine simplicity, like nature itself; she cannot endure wickedness, nor hatred, nor indifference.

If we are moved to the depths of our souls by the Bible, for example, this is because above all, even chemically, it is the greatest work of art in the world, containing the highest ideal concerning life on earth. May another authentic chemistry of genius appear, and may humanity follow her as a new conception of the world and a fresh gleam of life.

I make no pretense that these few words of mine can reveal the other, the most diversified values which our history contains. But I do believe that those persons are mistaken who think this chemistry can be found in scientific laboratories or in factories, or that she can be taught in the studios or by theories of art.

No, she is inside us; in our hands, in our soul. She is innate though also influenced by education.

In order to deal in something more than generalities, to be concrete, I want now to tell you what it is I am doing. I think I shall continue the biblical series I have begun, destined henceforth for a building which is neither a chapel nor a museum but a place where all who are seeking this new, spiritual, plastic content of which I have spoken can find a home.

I feel that there are among us persons who are seeking this. Some are perhaps here today, and tomorrow there may be others. . . .

While I pretend to no philosophical calling, I cannot fail to feel what today is strangling art and culture and sometimes life itself.

In fact, in this epoch, which is marked by a continual weakening in the intensity of religious belief—into the causes for which I do not care to enter—we cannot fail to see how, during the same period, the art of the nineteenth and twentieth centuries appears as a feeble reflection of scientific discoveries. Whereas, up to and including the epoch of the Renaissance, art reflected the religious spirit, or at least illustrated the intense religious feeling of the times. I cannot refrain from saying that so-called scientific art, or the art of pleasure-seeking, like that of cooking, is not a vital value. It can, little by little, fade away.

They say that a good man may be a bad artist. But he isn't and will never be an artist who is not a great and therefore a "good" man.

I know that in our times certain people discredit nature. After Cézanne, Monet, Gauguin, there seems to be no genius to reflect it.

It is a kind of convention now to avoid nature as much as possible. This convention evokes in me the impression I receive from those persons who never want to look you in the eyes; they frighten me and I avert my eyes from them.

There are certain revolutionary people who wish, by means of science, to introduce order into the economic and social life of our world. But, as time passes, all theories that have a scientific character come into partial collision with other theories.

Changes in the social order, as in Art, are perhaps more trustworthy if they come from our soul as well as from our intelligence. If men would read more deeply the words of the prophets, they could find in them some keys to life.

Are there not revolutionary methods other than those in the shadow of which we have been living?

Is there not a foundation for Art other than that offered by the decorative art which exists only to please, or by the art of experience, and by that pitiless art whose purpose is to shock us?

It is childish to repeat the truth, which has been known so long: In all its aspects the world can be saved only by love. Without love, it will die little by little.

12. "I and the Village" by Marc Chagall

If the theoretical and scientific sources of art and of life of which I have spoken could be subordinated to love, their results might become valid and more just. In connection with Art I have often spoken of the color which is Love.

In our atomic era we seem to be approaching certain frontiers. What are they? We shrink back on the edge of the precipice of universal destruction. It has taken me a long life to recognize the role of evil, and to understand how much easier it is to scale Mont Blanc than to transform the human being.

I delight in thinking of the youth in whom our hopes for an echo are focused, and also in thinking that among you who listen and you who read what we say there may be those who share our anxiety and concern.

And I like to dream that this call will be more than the cry of a voice in the desert.

Beauty and Faith
by Mircea Eliade

"WHY HAVE WE BECOME SO anxious in recent times?" Chagall asks himself. And he sees the chief cause of our collective anxiety in the disintegration of the values which have guided western societies for two thousand years [*a disintegration to which Bourbon Busset has also drawn our attention*]. This process of disintegration has taken many forms. Naturally, Chagall, who is above all a painter, observes the disintegration of traditional values mainly in the recent history of painting. And in that sphere obviously we are witnessing artistic experiments which aim to explode and to destroy the traditional plastic universe.

This is not the place to discuss the causes and profound significance of this will to destroy. Chagall himself recognizes in his declaration that during a certain phase of his career he was tempted, like others, to destroy the "natural" cosmos and replace it with a topsy-turvy world in which he cut off the heads of his subjects to leave them floating in the air. But, what is most rare in our time, Chagall resisted the temptation to demolish altogether the world of his masters and his ancestors.

Perhaps alone among the great masters who are still alive, Chagall has not succumbed to the general fascination which slaughter has for our contemporaries. Even when he distorts and paints objects upside down, he never really wanted to build another world from scratch. Even in his distortions, there is a love of the "natural" cosmos, expressed especially in the ways he creates his animals.

Yet his refusal to follow the experiments of the cubists and their successors has not been accompanied by an acceptance of any traditional artistic universe, such as, for example, naturalism, romanticism, or impressionism. In refusing to transform living Nature into abstract forms and geometrical spheres, he has not yielded either to the tendency of some of his predecessors to deprive the cosmos of its holy aura in search of the realistic. [*Did not Paul Valéry once suggest that the character of an artist is revealed "by the nature of his refusals?" Chagall has made the right refusals.*]

He has done more. For him the sacred has not been discredited; on the contrary, he has rediscovered the mystery and the holiness of Nature. This is one of the most characteristic traits of his genuis. Nature as studied by the scientists and reproduced by the photographers doesn't interest him. The Nature created by Chagall is primeval and maternal—a place where man, the animal, and the angel live together peacefully under the eye of God, or beneath a great moon such as appeared when the world was first created. For Chagall the archetype of the animal is the donkey—and it is well known that the donkey is *par excellence* the animal of the Messiah.

Chagall's Nature is rich in images and symbols of Paradise. In fact, the friendship between man and the animal world is a paradisiacal symptom—and Chagall loves to illustrate this friendship by the omnipresence of the donkey. We know that before the Fall, man lived in peace with the animals and understood their language. It was only after he was expelled from Paradise that Adam became the animals' enemy and forgot their language. And so we may say that the Nature of Chagall is transfigured by memory of and nostalgia for Paradise. The engaged couple which reappears in his paintings, the angels who float about the villages, are also paradisiacal images.

Chagall's world, this maternal and primeval Nature, inhabited by engaged couples, donkeys, and angels, is the mythological and sacred world of childhood. We are less in the presence of a nostalgic memory than of a past revisited and re-created. The mystery of the world is revealed in childhood, but is generally forgotten afterwards. For maturity abolishes mystery, and removes the holy from the cosmos and from human existence. Chagall has known how to recapture these revelations of childhood. They are most certainly of a religious order—even though the artist is not always conscious of this fact.

That is why the work of Chagall has such a great importance for us. Chagall takes his place among the very few contemporary artists who have recovered the holiness that is present in the world and in human life. Thereby he takes his place among the few who have rediscovered happiness. Such happiness has been lost by almost the entire western intelligentsia following this past half-century of crisis and torment. The work of Chagall shows us that it can be recovered.

Brancusi and Mythology

I HAVE RECENTLY BEEN REREADING the fascinating documents that make up the controversy surrounding Brancusi: did he remain a "Carpathian peasant" despite having lived for half a century in Paris, at the very heart of all the innovations and revolutions of modern art? Or, on the contrary—as the American critic Sidney Geist thinks, for example—did Brancusi become what he was as the result of influences exerted on him by the School of Paris and the discovery of exotic art forms—above all, the discovery of African masks and sculpture?

As I read these documents, I looked at the photographs, reproduced by Ionel Jianou in his monograph (Paris: Arted, 1963), showing Brancusi in his studio on the Impasse Ronsin, his bed, his stove. It is difficult not to recognize in them the "style" of a peasant dwelling. And yet there is something else there too: one is seeing Brancusi's *abode*, his very own "world," which he had forged all by himself, with his own hands, one might almost say. It is not a replica of any preexisting model, whether "Romanian peasant dwelling" or "avant-garde Parisian artist's studio."

And then, one only needs to take a really good look at that stove. Not only because the need to have a peasant stove tells us a lot about the way of life Brancusi chose to retain in Paris, but also because the symbolism of the stove or hearth can illuminate a certain secret of Brancusi's genius.

There is, indubitably, this fact—a paradoxical one for many critics—that Brancusi seems to have rediscovered a "Romanian" source of inspiration after his encounter with certain "primitive" archaic artistic creations.

Now this "paradox" constitutes one of the favorite themes of folk wisdom. I shall limit myself to a single example here: the story of Rabbi

"Brancusi and Mythology" was originally published as "Brâncuși et les mythologies" in *Témoingages sur Brâncuși*, edited by Petru Comarnescu, Mircea Eliade and Ionel Jianou (Paris: ARTED, Editions d'Art, 1967), 9–19. This English translation by Derek Coltman first appeared in *Ordeal by Labyrinth* by Mircea Eliade (Chicago: The University of Chicago Press, 1982), 193–201, and is reprinted by permission.

Eisik of Cracow, which the Indianist Heinrich Zimmer took from Martin Buber's *Tales of the Hasidim*. This pious rabbi, Eisik of Cracow, had a dream telling him to go to Prague, where, beneath the great bridge leading to the royal castle, he would find a buried treasure. The dream recurred three times, and the rabbi resolved to make the journey. He arrived in Prague and found the bridge, but it was guarded night and day by sentries, so that Eisik didn't dare to dig beneath it. His constant prowling finally drew the attention of the captain of the guard, who asked him in a friendly way if he had lost something. The rabbi, a simple man, recounted his dream. The officer burst out laughing: "Really, my poor chap," he said to the rabbi, "you haven't actually worn out all that shoe leather coming here simply on account of a dream, have you? What rational person would believe in a dream?" The officer too had heard a voice in a dream: "It went on about Cracow, telling me to go there and look for a great treasure in the house of a rabbi called Eisik, Eisik son of Jekel. I was supposed to find this treasure hidden in a dusty recess behind the stove." But the officer put no faith in dream voices; the officer was a rational man. The rabbi bowed very low, thanked him and hurried back to Cracow. He searched in the walled-up recess behind his stove and uncovered the treasure that put an end to his poverty.

"And so," Heinrich Zimmer comments, "the real treasure, the treasure that brings our wretchedness and our ordeals to an end, is never far away. We must never go looking for it in distant lands, for it lies buried in the most secret recesses of our own house; in other words, of our own being. It is behind the stove, the life- and heat-giving center that governs our existence, the heart of our hearth, if only we know how to dig for it. But then there is the strange and constant fact that it is only after a pious journey to a distant region, in a strange land, a new country, that the meaning of the inner voice guiding our search can be revealed to us. And added to that strange and constant fact there is another: that the person who reveals the meaning of our mysterious inner voyage to us must himself be a stranger, of another faith and another race."

To return to our subject: even if we accept Sidney Geist's view—in particular, that the influence exerted by the School of Paris was decisive in Brancusi's formation and that "the influence of Romanian folk art was nonexistent"—the fact remains that Brancusi's masterpieces are an extension of the world of Romanian folk mythology and its plastic forms and sometimes even have Romanian names, as in the case of the *Maïastra*, for example. In other words, Geist's "influences" must have produced a kind of anamnesis that led ineluctably to a process of self-discovery. Brancusi's encounters with the creations of the Parisian avant-garde and

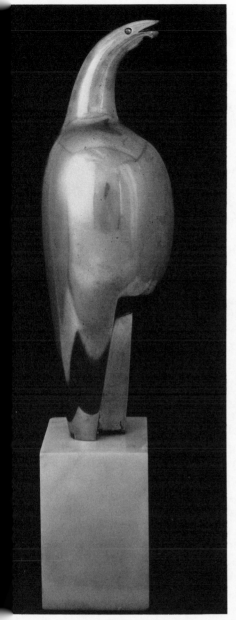

3. "Maiastra" by Constantin Brancusi

14. "Bird in Space" by Constantin Brancusi

those of the archaic world (Africa) triggered a process of "interiorization," a journey back toward a world that was both secret and unfor-
gettable because it was simultaneously that of childhood and that of the
imagination. Perhaps it was indeed *after* he had realized the importance
of certain modern creations that Brancusi rediscovered the artistic richness of his own peasant tradition; that he divined, in short, the creative
possibilities of that tradition. In either case, however, what Brancusi
certainly did not do, having made that discovery, was to settle down to
producing "Romanian folk art." He didn't imitate already-existing forms;
he didn't make copies of traditional folk artworks. On the contrary, he
understood that the source of all those forms—those of his own country's
folk art as well as those of Balkan and Mediterranean protohistory and
of "primitive" African or Oceanian art—was very deeply buried in the
past; and he understood equally that this primordial source bore no relation to the "classical" history of sculpture in which he had been situated,
like all his contemporaries, during his youth in Bucharest, Munich,
and Paris.

Brancusi's genius stems from the fact that he knew where to look for
the true "source" of the forms he felt himself capable of creating. Instead
of reproducing the plastic worlds of Romanian or African folk art, he set
himself to "interiorizing," as it were, his own vital experience. So that
he succeeded in rediscovering the "presence-in-the-world" specific to
archaic man, whether Lower Paleolithic hunter or Mediterranean,
Carpatho-Danubian, or African Neolithic cultivator. If people have been
able to perceive in Brancusi's work not only a structural and morphological solidarity with Romanian folk art but also analogies with Black
African art and with the sculpture of Mediterranean and Balkan prehistory, that is because all those plastic universes can be regarded as
culturally homologous: their sources are all to be found in the Lower
Paleolithic and the Neolithic. In other words, thanks to the process of
"interiorization," already referred to, and the anamnesis that followed it,
Brancusi succeeded in "seeing the world" in the same way as the creators
of prehistoric, ethnic, or folk-art masterpieces. He rediscovered, in a
way, the presence-in-the-world that enabled those anonymous artists to
create their own plastic universe within a space that had nothing whatever to do with, for example, the space of classical Greek art.

All this does not, of course, "explain" Brancusi's genius or his work.
It is not enough to rediscover the presence-in-the-world of a Neolithic
peasant to be able to create like an artist of that period. But drawing
attention to this process of "interiorization" does help us to understand,
first, Brancusi's startling originality and, second, why certain of his

works appear to be structurally akin to peasant, ethnic, or prehistoric artistic productions.

Brancusi's attitude toward his materials, and especially toward stone, may possibly help us one day to understand something about the mentality of prehistoric man. For Brancusi addressed himself to certain stones with the awed and ecstatic reverence of someone for whom such an object was the manifestation of a sacred power and was thus, in itself, a sacred mystery.

We shall never know in what imaginative universe Brancusi was moving during his long polishing process. But that prolonged intimacy with the stone undoubtedly favored the "material reveries" so brilliantly analyzed by Gaston Bachelard. It was a sort of immersion in a deeply buried world where stone, the most "material" form of matter we have, revealed itself as a thing of mystery, since it embodies and conceals sacrality, energy, and chance. In discovering "matter" as a source and locus of epiphanies and religious meanings, Brancusi was able to rediscover, or divine, the emotions and the inspiration of the artist of archaic times.

Moreover, "interiorization" and "immersion" in the depths both formed part of the early twentieth-century *Zeitgeist*. Freud had just developed his technique for exploring the deeps of the unconscious; Jung believed in the possibility of penetrating even more deeply, down to what he called the collective unconscious; the speleologist Emile Racovitza was in the process of identifying "living fossils" among the subterranean fauna, organic forms made all the more precious by the fact that they are no longer fossilizable; Lévy-Bruhl was isolating his "primitive mentality," an archaic, prelogical phase in the development of human thought.

All these researches and discoveries had one thing in common: they were revealing values, states, or forms of behavior hitherto unknown to science, either because they had previously been inaccessible to research or, above all, because they had offered nothing of interest to the rationalistic mentality of the second half of the nineteenth century. All these researches implied some sort of *descensus ad inferos* and, as a consequence, the discovery of phases of life, experience, and thought that preceded the formation of those systems of meaning known and studied up till then, the systems that one might term "classical," since they were all, in one way or another, connected with the establishment of reason as the sole principle capable of apprehending reality.

Brancusi was eminently a *contemporary* of this tendency toward "interiorization" and exploration of the "depths," a *contemporary* of this passionate interest in the primitive, prehistoric, and prerational stage of

15. "Endless Column" by Constantin Brancusi

human creativity. Having grasped the central "secret"—that it is not the creations of ethnic or folk art in themselves that will enable us to renew and enrich modern art but rather the discovery of their "sources"— Brancusi threw himself into an endless quest that was terminated only by his death. He returned indefatigably to certain themes, as though obsessed by their mystery or their artistic possibilities, which he never completely succeeded in realizing. For example, he worked for nineteen years on the *Colonne sans fin* and for twenty-eight on the *Birds* cycle. Ionel Jianou, in his *Catalogue raisonné*, lists five versions of the *Colonne sans fin* in oak plus one in plaster and steel, all made between 1918 and 1937. As for the *Birds* cycle, Brancusi completed twenty-nine versions of that between 1912 and 1940, some in polished bronze, some in marble of various colors, some in plaster. It is true, of course, that the constant reiteration of a particular central motif is also found in the work of other artists, ancient and modern. But such a method is characteristic above all of folk and ethnographic arts, in which the exemplary models must be indefinitely reworked and "imitated" for reasons that have nothing to do with "lack of imagination" or the artist's "personality."

It is significant that, in the *Colonne sans fin*, Brancusi should have rediscovered a Romanian folkore motif, the "pillar of the sky" (*columna cerului*), which is an extension of a mythological theme already shown to exist in prehistory, as well as being fairly widespread throughout the world. The "pillar of the sky" supports the heavenly vault. In other words, it is an *axis mundi*, the numerous variants of which are well known: Irminsul, the world pillar of the ancient Germans, the cosmic pillars of the North Asian peoples, the central mountain, the cosmic tree, and so on. The symbolism of the *axis mundi* is complex: the axis supports the sky and is also the means of communication between heaven and earth. When he is close to an *axis mundi*, which is regarded as the center of the world, man can communicate with the heavenly powers. The concept of the *axis mundi* as a stone column supporting the world very probably reflects beliefs characteristic of megalithic culture (four to three thousand years B.C.). But the symbolism and mythology of the sky pillar extend beyond the boundaries of megalithic culture.

In Romanian folklore, at all events, the "pillar of the sky" represents an archaic, pre-Christian belief but one that quickly became Christianized, since it is found in the ritual Christmas songs, or *colinde*. Brancusi would undoubtedly have heard about the sky pillar in the village where he was born, or in the Carpathians, where he served his apprenticeship as a shepherd. The image certainly obsessed him, for, as we shall see, it formed part of the symbolism of ascension, of flight, of transcendence. It is worth noting that Brancusi did not choose the "pure" form of the column—which could signify nothing more than the support, the "prop" of heaven—but a form consisting of repeated rhomboids, which make it akin to a tree or to a notched pole. In other words, Brancusi succeeded in bringing out the inherent symbolism of ascension, since one's imaginative response is a desire to climb this "tree of heaven." Ionel Jianou points out that the rhomboidal shapes "represent a decorative motif taken from the pillars of peasant architecture." And the symbolism of the pillar in peasant houses likewise derives from the "symbolic field" of the *axis mundi*. In many archaic dwellings the central pillar does in fact serve as a means of communication with the heavens, with the sky.

However, it is not the ascension to heaven of the archaic and primitive cosmologies that obsesses Brancusi but the sensation of flight out into infinite space. He calls his column "endless" not only because such a column could never reach a structural conclusion but above all because it hurls itself out into a space that must always remain without limits, since it is based on the ecstatic experience of absolute freedom. It is the same space in which his *Birds* fly. Brancusi has discarded everything from the old symbolism of the sky pillar except its central element: ascension as a transcendence of the human condition. But he successfully revealed to his contemporaries that what concerned him was an ecstatic ascension stripped of all mysticism. One need only allow oneself to be "carried away," lifted, by the power of the work to recover the forgotten bliss of an existence freed from any and every system of conditionings.

The theme of his *Birds* series, which began in 1912 with the first version of the *Maïastra,* is even more revealing. Taking a well-known motif from Romanian folklore as his starting point, Brancusi worked his way through a long process of "interiorization" toward a simultaneously archaic and universal exemplary theme. The Maïastra—or, more specifically, the Paserea Maïastra (literally "The Magic Bird")—is a fabulous bird that assists the Prince Charming (*Fat-Frumos*) of Romanian folktales in his combats and ordeals. In another narrative cycle the Maïastra succeeds in stealing the three golden apples that a magic apple tree produces every year. Only a king's son can wound or capture it. In some variants, once wounded or snared, the magic bird reverts to its true shape as a fairy. In his first version (1912–17) it is as though Brancusi wished to suggest this mystery in its double nature by emphasizing the Maïastra's femininity. Fairly soon, however, his interest becomes concentrated on the mystery of the bird's flight. Ionel Jianou has collated various statements made by Brancusi himself on this point: "I wanted the *Maïastra* to raise its head aloft without expressing either pride or defiance by that movement. That was the most difficult problem, and it was only after a long struggle that I succeeded in integrating that movement into the soaring movement of the bird's flight." The Maïastra, which in folklore is practically invulnerable—the Prince alone can wound it—then becomes Bird in Space. In other words, it is now its "magical flight" that Brancusi wants to express in stone. The first version of the Maïastra as Bird in Space dates from 1919, the last from 1940. In the end, as Jianou writes, Brancusi succeeded in "transforming his amorphous material into an ellipse with translucent surface, of a purity so dazzling that it irradiates the light around it and embodies, in its irresistible upward impulse, the very essence of flight."

Moreover, Brancusi himself said: "I have been searching a whole lifetime for only one thing: the essence of flight. . . . Flight, what happiness!" He did not need to read books to find out that flight is an equivalent of happiness because it symbolizes ascent, transcendence, a farewell to our human condition. Flight proclaims that *weight has been abolished*, that an ontological mutation has taken place within man's very being. Myths, tales, and legends relating to heroes or magicians who can move freely between earth and heaven are found everywhere in the world. A whole cluster of symbols bearing on the life of the spirit, and above all on ecstatic experiences and the powers of the mind, relies on images of birds, wings, and flight. The symbolism of flight expresses an escape from the universe of everyday experience, and the double intentionality of that escape is obvious: it is at the same time *transcendence* and *freedom* that one obtains by "flight."

This is not the place to repeat the analyses that I have offered elsewhere; but it is possible to show that on the different interdependent levels of dream, active imagination, mythological and folk creation, rituals, metaphysical speculation, and ecstatic experience, the symbolism of ascension always signifies the shattering of a "petrified" or "blocked" situation, the bursting-open of a "ceiling," a sudden possibility of transition to another mode of being and, ultimately, the freedom to "move," or, in other words, to change situations, to abolish a system of conditionings. It is significant that Brancusi was obsessed throughout his life with what he called "the essence of flight." But it is extraordinary that he succeeded in expressing that soaring, upward impulse by using the very archetype of *heaviness*, that ultimate form of "matter"—stone. One might almost say that he performed a transmutation of "matter" or, more precisely, that he brought about a *coincidentia oppositorum*, since he achieved in one and the same object a coincidence of matter and flight, of weight and its negation.

Part III:

Sites of the Sacred

III / 1

Sacred Architecture and Symbolism

SIGNIFICANTLY AFTER 1925, studies on architectonic symbolism multiplied and assumed a great import. It suffices to indicate the research of Ananda K. Coomaraswamy,[1] the monumental *Barabudur* of Paul Mus,[2] the sumptuous publications of Giuseppi Tucci,[3] the studies of Walter Andrae,[4] and, finally, those of Stella Kramrisch,[5] Carl Hentze,[6] and Hans Sedlmayr.[7] A common trait characterizes these studies: methodology. Instead of looking for "explanations" following the principles of empirical science, that is to say in applying the reductive method, these authors endeavoured to present the symbolism of religious movements as it had been recorded by diverse traditional cultures, without prejudging eventual contradictions or apparent absurdities. For example, should a Hindu affirm that his house is in the "Center of the World," one accepts his belief as a living truth and, consequently, a spiritual reality; it is no longer submitted to a test of scientific reduction in order to demystify it, by observing that if all Indian houses were proclaimed to be in "the Center of the World," there must exist an infinity of such centers, which is obviously absurd. On the contrary, in the face of such beliefs, western scholars inferred the only possible conclusion: namely, that the sacred space in which the "Center of the World" is inscribed has nothing to do with the profane space of geometry; it has another structure and responds to another experience.

The problem became more delicate when it no longer included any oral or written evidence specifying the meaning attached to the symbolism of a religious monument. In a number of cases, the original significance had been profoundly modified. It even happens that after

"Sacred Architecture and Symbolism" was originally published as "Architecture sacrée et symbolisme" in *Mircea Eliade,* edited by Constantin Tacou (Paris: L'Herne, *Cahiers de l'Herne #33* 1978), 141–156. That French essay was a revision of "Centre du monde, temple, maison," which was first published in *Le symbolisme cosmique des monuments religieux,* edited by Guiseppi Tucci (Rome: Istituto Italiano par il Medio ed Estremo Oriente, 1957), 57–82. It is translated from the French by Diane Apostolos-Cappadona and Frederica Adelman.

historic catastrophes and cultural syncopes, the original significance of a sacred monument has been completely lost. The exegesis founded solely upon the analyses of symbolic structures ran the risk of being suspect; one could always think that, not backed by the written and oral historical evidence, advanced interpretation only represented the personal point of view of the researcher, which would remain unverified as long as an autochthonic memory did not confirm it.

Happily, the discoveries of depth psychology were such as to reassure even the most skeptical inquirer. One could demonstrate that the function and import of a symbol were not exhausted on the plane of diurnal life and conscious activity. It makes no difference that one individual bears in mind that the image of a green tree can symbolize cosmic renewal, or that the staircase climbed in a dream signifies the passage from one mode of being to another, and announces a break in levels. One single important fact is that the presence of such images in dreams or in daydreams of an individual translate into psychic processes homologable to a "renewal" or to a "passage." In other words, the symbol delivers its message and fulfills its function when its significance escapes the *conscious* level.

These precisions furnished by depth psychology seem important to us.[8] The ethnologist, the historian of religions, the specialist of religious symbolism often address their documents a little like the psychologist before the memories and dreams of his patient: the client was not nor is any longer conscious of the significance of lived images; it remains that they acted upon his being, that they determined his conduct. Likewise when it is a question of interpreting a religious symbolism witnessed in a primitive society, the historian of religions must not only take into consideration all that the autochthones can say about this symbol, he must also question the structure of the symbol and what it reveals by itself. If, as we will soon see, a tent or a hut are provided with an upper opening to allow the smoke to escape, if in addition their owners believe that the Polar Star marks a similar opening in the celestial tent, we are justified in concluding that the tent or the hut exists symbolically as the "Center of the World," even if their inhabitants are no longer conscious *today* of this symbolism. What is of primary significance is the demeanor of religious man, and his demeanor is better revealed by the symbols and myths which he cherishes than by the explanations which he can be led to provide.

These few preliminary remarks immediately introduce us to our subject. To understand the symbolism of temples and human dwellings, is, above all, to understand the religious value of space; in other words, to know the structure and function of sacred space. Such symbolisms, such rituals, transform space in which is inscribed a temple or a palace simultaneously into an *imago mundi* and into a Center of the World.

At first view, it seems evident to us that a sanctuary represents the sacred zone *par excellence*. Let us specify however that it is not always the sanctuary which consecrates the space; many times, it is just the opposite; the sacrality of the place precedes the construction of the sanctuary. But in one case as in the other, we are concerned with a sacred space, that is to say a territory qualitatively different from the surrounding cosmic environment, a zone which is singled out and is detached within the profane space. Thus we find at the origin of all types of sanctuary space, from the most modest to the most sumptuous, the idea of sacred space encircled by an enormous, chaotic, little-known zone of profane space. Chaotic zone precisely because it is not organized; little-known zone as it knows neither its limits or its structure. Profane space is clearly opposite to sacred space because this latter has some precise limits, it is perfectly structured, it is as we say "centered," concentrated."

How does any space transform itself into sacred space? Simply because a sacrality is manifested there. The answer may seem to us too elementary, almost infantile. It is in effect quite difficult to understand. Since a manifestation of the Sacred, a hierophany, bears for the consciousness of archaic peoples a rupture in the homogeneity of space. In more familiar terms, we would say that the manifestation of the Sacred in any space whatsoever implies for one who believes in the authenticity of this hierophany the presence of transcendent reality. It is useless to add that the terms "reality" and "transcendence" do not exist in the vocabularies of archaic peoples. But for our purpose, it is not the vocabulary which matters, it is the demeanor. However the comportment of man belonging to archaic societies is established upon the opposition of the Sacred and the Profane. The Sacred is that something altogether other to the Profane. Consequently, it does not belong to the profane world, it comes from somewhere else, it transcends this world. It is for this reason that the Sacred *is* the real *par excellence*. A manifestation of the Sacred is always a revelation of *being*.

Sacred Space

To summarize what we have just said, sacred space constitutes itself following a rupture of levels which make possible the communication with the trans-world, transcendent realities. Whence the enormous importance of sacred space in the life of all peoples: because it is in such a space that man is able to communicate with the other world, the world of divine beings or ancestors. Every consecrated space represents an opening towards the beyond, towards the transcendent. It even seems that until a certain era, man could not live without such openings toward the transcendent, without a sure means of communication with the other world, inhabited by the gods. We will see that this "opening" has sometimes been signified in a concrete manner, for example, in the form of a hole, in the actual body of the sanctuary or dwelling.

We say a space can be consecrated by a hierophany, but man may also construct a sacred space by effecting certain rituals.⁹ We will not recall the innumerable examples where a divine apparition or a hierophany consecrates the place and imposes the construction of a sanctuary. Numerous times, there is no need of a theophany or a hierophany (properly called): any sign suffices to indicate the sacrality of a place; one pursues a wild beast and at the place where it is overpowered, a sanctuary is built; or, one frees a domestic animal, for example a bull, after several days, it is located and sacrificed on the spot. Afterwards an altar will be erected and a village will be built around the altar.

But it is particularly the symbolisms and rituals concerning the *construction* of a sacred space which interest us. We said that the sacred space is the place where communication is possible between this world and the other world, from the heights or from the depths, the world of the gods or the world of the dead. And then soon enough the image of the three cosmic zones is imposed, generally: Heaven, Earth, Underworld; the communication between these three zones implies a break in the levels. In other words, the sacred space of the temple makes possible the passage from one level to another; first and foremost, the passage from Earth to Heaven. Let us note that the communication between the cosmic planes also comprises a rupture of the ontological order: the passage from one mode of being to another, the passage from a profane state to a sacred state or from Life to Death. The symbolic concepts of communication and connection between the three cosmic stages is manifested in the names of certain Mesopotamian temples and royal cities, which are precisely called (like Nipur, Larsa, Babylonia), "the connection between Heaven and Earth." Babylonia was Bâb-ilâni, a "door of the gods," because it is from there that the gods descended to the Earth. On the other hand, the temple or the sacred city also made the liason with subterranean regions. Babylonia was built on *bâb-apsî*, "the Door of *Apsû-apsû*," designating the Waters of Chaos before Creation. One encounters the same tradition among the Hebrews: the high rock of the Temple of Jerusalem penetrated deeply into the *tehôm* (Hebrew equivalent of *apsû*).¹⁰

The point of intersection between the three cosmic zones, the temple or the sacred city constituted by consequence a "Center of the World," because it is through there that the axis of the Universe, the *Axis*

Mundi, passes. The rock upon which the Temple of Jerusalem was built was considered as being the *umbilicus terrae.* The Irish pilgrim, Nicholas of Thvera, who had visited Jerusalem in the twelfth-century, wrote of the Holy Sepulchre: "There is the Center of the World: there, on the day of the summer solstice, the sunlight fell perpendicular from the sky." A cosmological idea of indubitable archaism, and which survived into the late Middle Ages: on medieval maps, Jerusalem was always situated in the Center of the World. But this image was continually re-evaluated on the different levels of Christian experience. Abélard wrote that the ". . . soul of the world is found at the middle of the world: consequently, Jerusalem from whence comes Salvation is found at the Center of the World."[11]

Such speculations of a theological and philosophical order prolonged these simpler and older beliefs. Adam having been buried at the very place where he had been created, that is to say in Jerusalem, was redeemed by the Saviour's blood on Golgotha.[12]

Universalis Columna

As one would expect the *Axis Mundi* was imagined many times in the form of a pillar which held up Heaven. When Alexander asked the Galatians what they feared the most in the world, they responded that they feared nothing except the collapse of Heaven (Arrian, *Anabasis,* I, IV, 7). Saints Patrick and Brigid have handed down to us other accounts relating to Celtic ideas of the pillar which held up the Earth.[13] Similar beliefs were evidenced among the Germans: the *Chronicum Laurissense breve* written around 800 reports that Charlemagne on the occasion of one of his wars against the Saxons (772) had the temple in the town of Erisburg and the sacred woods of their renowned "Irmensul" demolished (*fanum et lucum corum famosun Irminsul*). Rodolph of Fulda (c. 860) specifies that this famous column is the ". . . . Column of the Universe holding up almost all things" (*universalis columna quasi sustinens omnia*).[14]

Moreover, this cosmological image is widespread. One finds it among the Romans (Horace, *Odes,* III, 3); in Vedic India (*Rig Veda,* I, 1051 X, 89, 4, etc.), where it is a question of the *skambha,* the cosmic pillar;[15] but also among the inhabitants of the Canary Islands[16] and in cultures as distant as the Kwakiutl (British Columbia) and the Nad'a of Flore (Indonesia). The Kwakiutl believe that a copper pole pierces through the three cosmic levels: the "Gate of the World on High" is located where the pole is embedded. The visible image of this cosmic image is the Milky Way in the Heavens. On Earth, it is incarnate in the sacred post of the cultic house called by the initiates "the post of cannibals": it is a cedar trunk of 10 to 12 meters in length to which one addresses prayers before felling it,[17] and of which more than one half sticks out through the roof of the cultic house (a roof which is cracked for this purpose; see below for the ritual importance and symbolism of the "cracked roof"). The pillar plays an important role in the ceremonies; it is that which confers a cosmic structure to the cultic house. In the ritual songs, the house is called "Our World" and the novices proclaim: "I am at the Center of the World [. . .] I am near the Pillar of the World, etc."[18]

A similar assimilation of the Cosmic Pillar to the sacred pole and the cultic houses of the Universe occurs among the Nad'a of Flore. The sacrificial pole is called "Pole of Heaven" and is reputed to hold up Heaven. Among the Nage, a people located to the east of Nad'a, it is clearly expressed: the pole impedes Heaven from falling onto the Earth.[19]

The Cosmic Mountains

Other symbols reinforce this identification of the temple as "the Center of the World." There is above all the homologation of the temple and the royal city with the cosmic mountain. The Mesopotamian temples are called "Mount of the House," "Mount of the Tempests," "House of the Mount of All Lands," etc. But in several traditions, the Cosmos is shaped like a mountain whose peak touches Heaven: above, where the Heavens and the Earth are reunited, is the "Center of the World." This cosmic mountain may be identified with a real mountain, or it can be mythic, but it is aways placed at the center of the world. This is the case of Mount Meru in the Indian cosmo-mythology; it is also the case of real mountains, like Gerizim in Palestine which was called the "navel of the Earth," or Golgotha for the Judeo-Christian traditions. Consequently, the sanctuaries are symbolically assimilated with the Cosmic Mountains. Examples abound: the Mesopotamian *ziggurat* is properly called a cosmic mountain, its levels symbolizing the seven heavenly planets. Likewise, the Temple of Barabudur, a true *imago mundi*, is built in the form of a mountain.[20]

Following these traditions, the "Center" is not only the summit of the cosmic mountain, whose peak is the highest in the world, but also, we might say the "oldest": because it is the point whence creation began. It even happens that cosmological traditions express creation emanating from a "Center" in terms which could be said to be borrowed from embryology. "The Most Holy created the world like an embryo. Just as the embryo grows from the navel, likewise God began to create the world through the navel and from there it spread out in all directions." *Yoma* affirms: ". . . the world had been created beginning with Zion."[21]

Rabbi ben Gurion said of the rock of Jerusalem that ". . . it was called the Foundation Stone of the Earth, which is to say the Earth's umbilicus, because it is from there that the entire Earth unfurled."[22]

The creation of man, a replica of the cosmology, had taken place likewise in the Center of the World. Following the Mesopotamian tradition, man had been fashioned from "the navel of the Earth," there where one finds the "link between Heaven and Earth: Ahura Mazda created Gayomart, primordial man, at the Center of the World. The paradise where Adam was created from mud was at the center of the Cosmos, of course. Paradise was the "navel of the Earth," and following a Syrian tradition was established on the highest mountain of all. Apocalyptic Judaism and the *Midrash* specify that Adam was made in Jerusalem, therefore at the Center of the World.[25]

It is important to make apparent the coherent and perfectly articulated character of all those beliefs relating to the sacrality of the "Center." It is not a matter of isolated ideas, but of a set of ideas which make a "system." In citing as we have done examples having such or such an aspect of the "Center," one loses sight of the general structure of a symbol. But all these aspects are interdependent, and demand to be integrated to make the theoretical symbol on which they depend stand out. To limit ourselves to only one example, it would be easy to show how in the Iranian tradition, the land of Iran is simultaneously the "Center of the World" and the *imago mundi* because it is there that the cosmic mountain touches Heaven, there the first man was created, and there also at the very heart of this privileged territory and "in the middle of Time," the prophet Zarathustra was born. In effect, the Iranian tradition conceived of the Cosmos in the form of a six-spoked wheel with a large hole in the middle like a navel.[24] The Iranian country (*airyanem vaejah*) is the Center and the heart of the world.[25] Following the Sassinid tradition, Shiz, the city where Zarathustra was born, finds itself in the Center of the Universe.[26] A Pahlavi text specifies that Zarathustra lived in the "middle of Time," that is to say 6,000 years after the creation of man and 6,000 years before the resurrection. Just as the heart is found in the middle of the body, "the land of Iran is more precious than all other countries because it is situated in the middle of the world."[27] It is for this that Shiz, the "Jerusalem" of the Iranians, was also regarded as the original site of royal power.[28] The throne of Khosrau II figured symbolically as just that: it represented the Universe.[29] The idea, moreover, was not uniquely Iranian, it belongs to the *Weltanschauung* of the ancient Near East: the royal cities were the image of the Cosmos, and the King, *cosmocrat*, was the *Axis Mundi*, the Pillar incarnate.[30]

Architecture and Cosmogony

As noted earlier, the cosmogonic significance of the Center is that all creation, be it a cosmogony or an anthropogony, takes places or begins in a center. Moreover, the circumstances could not be otherwise, if one recalls that the Center is precisely the place where a rupture of the levels occurs, where the space becomes sacred, thus *real par excellence*. A creation implies a superabundance of reality, in other words, an eruption of the Sacred into the world. It follows that all construction or fabrication has the cosmogony as an exemplary model. The creation of the world became the archetype of each creative human activity, whatever its plane of reference. In Vedic India, a territory was legally taken into possession by the erection of a fire-altar dedicated to Agni. But such a construction was only a microscopic imitation of the Creation. In effect, following the *Çatapatha Brâhmana*, the water with which the clay is mixed represents the Primordial Waters, the clay that forms the base of the fire-altar is the Earth; the sidewalls represent the atmosphere, etc.[31] In raising the altar, the cosmogony is repeated; in this fashion, the territory that one comes to occupy passes from the chaotic state into the organized state; it is "cosmocized."

We can cite a great number of examples illustrating the idea of taking a territory into possession, of the installation of a village or of the construction of a cultic house representing the symbolic repetition of the cosmogony. The circle or the square built by emanating from a Center is an *imago mundi*. Just as the visible Universe unfolds from a Center and extends towards the four cardinal points, the village is built around a crossing. In Bali, as well as in certain regions of Asia, when a new village is to be built a natural crossing where two roads cross perpendicularly is sought.[32] The division of the village into four sections corresponds to the division of the Universe into four horizons. In the middle of the village, a plaza is often left empty: there a cultic house will be raised much later, the roof of which symbolically represents Heaven (in certain cases, Heaven is indicated by the crown of a tree or by the image of a mountain).[33] On the same perpendicular axis at the other extremity is the World of the Dead symbolized by certain animals (serpent, crocodile, etc.) or by the ideograms of Shadows.[34] The cosmic symbolism of the village is repeated in the structure of the sanctuary or of the cultic house. At Waropen in New Guinea, the "house of men" is in the middle of the village; its roof represents the heavenly canopy, the four walls correspond to the four directions of space. At Ceram, the sacred stone of the village symbolizes Heaven; and the four stone columns which hold it up incarnate the four pillars which hold up Heaven.[35] Similar examples are encountered in North America.

It is not a surprise to encounter analogous ideas in ancient Italy and among the ancient Germans: in sum, it is a matter of an archaic and widespread idea. To build a temple or a city is equivalent to reiterating the "construction" of the Universe; by departing from the center, the four horizons project into the four cardinal directions.[36] The Roman *mundus* was a circular hole in the ground, divided into four, it was simultaneously the image of the Cosmos and the exemplary model of a human dwelling. It has been suggested that the *Roma quadrata* can be reasonably understood not as having the form of a square but as being divided into four.[37] The *mundus* was evidently assimilated to the *omphalos*, to the navel of the Earth: the city was situated in the middle of the *orbis terrarum*.[38] We can show that the same ideas explain the structure of German villages.[39] In these extremely varied cultural contexts, we will always find the same cosmological schema and the same ritual scenario: installation in a territory is equivalent to the establishment of a world.

In India, we will encounter the same symbolism for the construction of a house. Before placing the first stone, the astrologer indicates the point in the foundation which is found above the serpent who supports the world. The master mason hews a post and embeds it in the ground exactly at the designated spot in order to fasten the serpent's head. A foundation stone is then laid down on top of the post. Thus, the corner-stone is located at the "Center of the World."[40] On the other hand, the act of laying the foundation repeats the cosmogonic act because driving the post into the serpent's head and "fastening" it is an imitation of the primordial gesture of Soma or of Indra, when the latter, as recorded in the *Rig Veda*, ". . . struck the Serpent in its den" (VI, 17, 19), when his lightning bolt ". . . cut off his head" (I, 52, 10). The serpent symbolizes chaos, the amorphous, the un-manifested. The decapitation is equivalent to an act of creation, the passage from the formless and the amorphous into the formed.

In this last example, note that it is no longer a matter of the construction of a temple or of a sacred city, but of the building of a simple dwelling. The two themes which preoccupy us, that is to say the repetition of the cosmogony and the symbolism of the Center, are not exclusive to sacred architecture: the same rituals and symbols are present when it is a matter of building a dwelling which to our modern eyes is "profane." But it is evident that we deceive ourselves; it is consecrated by its very architectonic structure exactly like a temple. This poses a considerable problem: does the symbolism of human habitation derive from

16. Holy City of Jerusalem,
Mold for Eucharistic Bread,
7th–8th century

17. Great Pyramid

19. Machu Picchu

18. Temple of Barabudur, 6th century

the symbolism of the sanctuary or vice versa? We will endeavour to answer this question later.

Templum-Tempus

For a moment, it remains for us to elucidate another important aspect of the symbolism of temples. If the sanctuary is built in the "Center of the World" and the ritual construction imitates the cosmogony, if consequently the sanctuary as the replica of the Cosmos becomes an *imago mundi*—we ought to expect to find in this structure also temporal symbolism. Since the Cosmos is a living organism, it then implies natural cyclic time, that is to say circular time which constitutes the year. In effect, we encounter this temporal symbolism in certain traditions. For example, look at what Flavius Josephus (*Ant. Jud.*, III, 7, 7) reports concerning the symbolism of the Temple of Jerusalem: the three parts of the sanctuary correspond to the three cosmic regions (the courtyard representing the "sea," that is to say the inferior regions; the Holy House figuring the Earth; and the Holy of Holies, Heaven); the twelve loaves of bread which are found on the table are the twelve months of the year; the seventy-branch candelabra represents the *decans* (that is to say the zodiac division of the seven planets into tens). In building the temple, not only was the world constructed but cosmic time was also constructed.

It is to Hermann Usener's credit to have been the first to explain the etymological relationship between *templum* and *tempus* in interpreting these two terms through the idea of "intersection" or "crossing."[41] Some more recent research again specified this discovery: *templum* designates a spatial "turning" and *tempus* a "turning" in a spatial-temporal horizon.[42]

The temporal symbolism of a sacred construction is also evidenced in ancient India. Following the fortunate formula of Paul Mus,[43] the Vedic Altar is understood to be time materialized. The Çatapatha Brâhmana (X, 5, 4, 10) clearly states: ". . . that Fire-altar also is the Year—the nights are its enclosing-stones, and there are three hundred and sixty of these, because there are three hundred and sixty nights in the year; and the days are its Yagushmati bricks, for there are three hundred and sixty of these, and three hundred and sixty days in the year." On the other hand, the Year is Prajâpati. Therefore, the construction of each new Vedic altar not only repeats the cosmogony and reanimates Prajâpati, but also builds the "Year," that is to say regenerates time by "creating" it anew.[44]

Let us add that such cosmogonic-temporal conceptions do not constitute an exclusive adjunct of evolved civilizations: one encounters them already in the archaic stages of culture. In order to give only one example: the sacred initiatory hut of certain Algonquin (Odjibwa, etc.) and Sioux (Dakota, Omaha, Winnebago, etc.) tribes also represent the Universe. Its roof represents the celestial canopy, the floor represents the Earth, the four walls the four directions of cosmic space. The ritual construction of the space is emphasized by a triple symbolism: the four doors, the four windows, and the four colors signifying the four cardinal points.[45] The construction of this sacred hut repeats the cosmogony because this small house represents the World.[46] But, the Dakotas affirm that "the Year is a circle around the World,"[47] that is to say around the initiatory hut. They understand the Year as a course across the four cardinal directions.[48] For the Lenapes, who also identify the sacred hut with the Cosmos, the Creator is reputed to live in the summit of the celestial cupola, his hand on the central pillar analogous to the *Axis Mundi*. During the celebration which is called the "Creation of the World," a dance takes place inside the hut, thus in the center of the Universe, and the dancers revolve around this central pillar.[49] We could cite other ceremonies comprising analogous symbolism; for example, that of the Karok, the Yurok and the Hupa tribes of California called the "Renewal of the World," and where the ritual repetition of the cosmogony implies immediately the symbolism of the Center of the World, the construction of space and the renewal of cosmic time.[50]

The spatio-temporal symbolism is also illumined by the vocabulary. The Yakuts use the word "world" in the sense of "year"; they say "the world has died" which is to say "one year has elapsed." For the Yuki, the "year" is expressed by the words "Earth" or "World." Like the Yakuts, they say "the Earth has died" when the year has ended.[51] Among the Cree also, the "world" designates "the year" and the Salteaux interchange the Earth and the year.[52]

Symbolism and History

This mention of North American cases introduces us immediately to the problem that we had put aside earlier, that of the origin and history of all these cosmological-architectural symbolisms of the Centers of the World, of the sanctuaries and dwellings. The problem is extremely difficult; although we do not pretend to present it in all its complexity nor to resolve it. Just as the other elements of culture, mythology, social and economic structure, material civilization, the cosmological ideas and their applications in architectural symbolism have a history; they circulated from one culture to another and have been inevitably subjected to alterations, enrichments or impoverishments; in a word, they have been diversely assimilated and reevaluated by the peoples which received them. For example, Karl Lehman showed the diffusion of celestial symbolism of sacred monuments in the West from Antiquity to the Middle Ages. In his erudite study, "The 'Dome of Heaven' in Asia," Alexander Coburn Soper extended the inquiry into Asia.[53] According to the latter, the symbolism of the celestial dome as it had been expressed by western architects is diffused into the first millennium of the Christian era into India and into all of Asia throughout the Pacific. Let us specify that Soper[54] was solely preoccupied with the diffusion of the architectural formulae and techniques elaborated and perfected in the West, and which according to him are too complex to have been discovered independently in various places in the world. But Soper does not discuss the elementary architectural forms which for example in China and India had preceded western influence. In supposing that one accepts Soper's thesis entirely, it is certain that recent influences of Western origin have consisted especially in a transmission of perfected architectonic recipes; we are not authorized to conclude that the symbolism of the celestial dome evidenced in the Asian religious monuments is the result of western ideas and techniques. It suffices to re-read Coomaraswamy's *The Symbolism of the Dome* to be convinced that such symbolism was amply elaborated in India well before the first millennium of our era.[55]

This example is instructive: it indicates how an external contribution brought by history superimposes itself on a foundation of autochthonic beliefs and gives birth to new expressions. The most illustrious example is the temple of Barabudur. Paul Mus showed how this monument represents a summary of Indian thought even though in the final analysis his architectural formula goes back to a Mesopotamian cosmological schema. Even the Indian concept of seven or nine planetary heavens is most probably of Babylonian origin. But these facts specified, another problem arises: before the Mesopotamian influences probably manifested themselves, didn't India and Indonesia know the symbolism of the Center of the World and the cosmological schema of three levels? The response can only be affirmative. In effect, we recognize the symbolism of a cosmic mountain or of a central tree uniting the three cosmic zones, not only in ancient India and in Indonesia, but also among certain archaic populations where the Indo-Mesopotamian influences are difficult to comprehend; for example, among the Semang Pygmies of the Malay Peninsula.[56] We were able to show that the cosmic tripartition particular to the ancient Tibetan religion, Bon, long preceded Indian influences.[57] The triad and symbolic number three are moreover widely evidenced in ancient China and throughout Eurasia.[58] And as we will soon see, the symbolism of the Center of the World plays an important role among the Australians.

On the other hand, we encounter an analogous situation in central and northern Asia. We now know that the cosmological schema of southern origins had been diffused even into Arctic Siberia. The central and northern Asiatic conception of seven, nine or sixteen heavens derives from the Mesopotamian idea of seven planetary heavens.[59] But the symbolism of the Center of the World and the entire mythico-ritual complex of sacred space and the communication between Earth and Heaven preceded in central and northern Asia the Indo-Mesopotamian influences. These influences which were apparent in successive waves during several millennia, superimposed themselves on a more ancient and more elementary complex cultural autochthon. In effect in all central and northern Asia, we remark on the very structure of the human dwelling as the symbolism of the Tree or of the Pillar which unites the three cosmic zones. The house is an *imago mundi*. Heaven is conceived as an immense tent upheld by a central pillar; in other words, the tent's stake or the central post of a house are assimilated to the pillar of the world and are designated by the same name.[60] The central pillar is a characteristic element of a dwelling of primitive Arctic, North American and North Asian peoples. It has an important ritual role: it is at the foot of this pillar where sacrifices took place in honor of the supreme celestial Being and where prayers reserved for him were addressed.[61] The same symbolism is conserved among the pastoral herders of central Asia but here as the conical roofed dwelling with a central pillar is replaced by the yurt, the mythico-ritual function of the pillar is devolved to the smokehole.[62] One encounters moreover the sacred pillar erected in the middle of the dwelling among the Hamite and Hamitoide shepherd peoples.[63]

This set of facts proves that the symbolism of the Center of the World is older than known cosmologies elaborated in the ancient Near East. The very expression "Center of the World" is literally retrieved and charged with similar symbolism in the ritual of the Kwakiutl[64] and in certain Zuni myths.[65] Finally in a recent study,[66] E. de Martino very clearly interpreted the mythico-ritual complex of the sacred pole (*kauwa-auwa*) among one Arunta tribe, the Achilpa. According to their traditions, the divine being Numbakula had "cosmocized" the territory of the future Achilpa in mythical time, created their ancestors and established their institutions. Numbakula fashioned the sacred pole from the trunk of an Indian rubber tree, and after anointing it with blood, climbed it and disappeared into Heaven. E. de Martino showed that the organization of territory is equivalent to a "cosmocization" starting with an irradiation out from the Center and that the *kauwa-auwa* pole represents a cosmic axis, its ritual role confirms this interpretation perfectly. During their wanderings, the Achilpa always carry the sacred pole with them and choose the direction to follow by its slant. While continually moving about, the Achilpa are never allowed to be far from the "Center of the World"; they are always "centered" and in communication with the Heavens where Numbakula had disappeared. When the pole is broken, this is a catastrophe; in a way, it is the "end of the world," a regression into chaos. Spencer and Gillen record a myth in which the sacred pole being broken, the entire tribe became prey to anxiety, its members wandered for some time and finally they sat down on the ground and allowed themselves to die.[67]

This last example admirably illustrates simultaneously the cosmological function of the Center and its soteriological role; since it is due to the ritual pole, the veritable *axis mundi* that the Achilpa feel they are able to communicate with the celestial domain. To organize a territory, to "cosmocize" it, is equivalent in the final instance to consecrating it. And so, at the root of all such complex symbolism of temples and sanctuaries is found the primary experience of sacred space, of a space where a rupture of levels occurs.

To Create One's Own Universe

We will return to the consequences which derive from these conclusions. For the moment, consider that to inhabit a territory, that is to say to take up one's abode, to build a home, always implies a vital decision which engages the existence of the entire community. To be "situated" in a landscape, to organize it, to inhabit it, are actions which presuppose an existential choice: *the choice of the "universe" that one is prepared to assume by "creating" it.* We saw above that every human establishment includes the fixing of a center and the projection of horizons, that is to say the "cosmocization" of a territory, its transformation into a "universe," a replica of the exemplary Universe, created and inhabited by the gods. Every human installation, whether it is a matter of taking possession of an entire country or of the building of a simple dwelling, thus repeats the cosmogony. We learn elsewhere that the cosmogonic myth is generally the model of all myths and rites relating to a "technique," a "work," a "creation."

But if it is always indispensable to symbolically repeat the cosmogony, to "cosmocize" the space where one has chosen to live, the cultural history of archaic humanity knows several ways of effecting this cosmocization. For our purpose, it is sufficient for us to distinguish two styles corresponding moreover to two cultural styles and to two historical stages: (1) a "cosmocization" of a territory by the symbolism of the Center of the World, an operation which evidently imitates the cosmogony, but a cosmogony reduced to the simple projection of a Center to assure the communication with the above; and, (2) the "cosmocization" which implies a more dramatic repetition of the cosmogony. In effect, beginning with a certain type of culture, the cosmogonic myth explains creation by the execution of a primordial giant (Ymir, Purusha, P'an-ku); his organs give birth to different cosmic regions. According to other groups of myths, it is not only the Cosmos which is born following the immolation of the primordial Being, and of his own substance, it is also the alimentary plants, the human races or the different social classes. These types of myths are interesting to our subject because it is they which in the last instance justify the sacrifices of construction. In effect, we know that to endure, a "construction" (house, technical work and also spiritual work) must be animated; which is to say, to receive a life and a soul at the same moment. The "transfer" of the soul is only possible by means of a blood sacrifice. The history of religions, ethnology and folklore know innumerable forms of *Bauopfer* which is to say the blood or symbolic sacrifices for the benefit of a construction. We have studied elsewhere this mythico-ritual complex;[68] for our purpose, it suffices to say that it is interdependent with the cosmogonic myths which put into relief the immolation of the primordial Being. In the perspective of cultural history, the mythico-ritual complex of the *Bauopfer* forms an integrating part of the *Weltanschauung* of the paleo-cultivators (the *Urpflangen* in German ethnological terminology).

Let us remember the following fact: the installation in a territory just like the construction of a house incorporates a preliminary "cosmocization," this could be symbolic (fixing of the Center) or ritualistic (founding sacrifices as replicas of the primordial cosmogonic dismemberment). Whatever is the modality by which "inhabited chaos" becomes a "Cosmos," the sought-after end is the same: to consecrate the space, to homologize it to the space inhabited by the gods or to make it susceptible to communicate with this transcendent space. But each of these operations implies for the human being a very serious vital decision: *one cannot settle in the world without assuming the responsibility to create it.* And as man always endeavours to imitate the divine models, he is obliged in certain cultural horizons to repeat periodically an original tragedy (in the example which we just described the murder and dismemberment of a primordial Being). But even in leaving aside the blood sacrifices of a founding (of a village, sanctuary or house), it is always the choice and consecration of a space that engage the entire human being: to live in one's own world, it is necessary to create it whatever the price that one must pay to bring about this creation and to make it endure.

House—Human Body

We said above that at the base of the symbolism of temples, we find the primary experience of sacred space. Several important consequences proceed from this fact. Consider first that the symbolism of temples as the "Center of the World" is an ulterior elaboration of the cosmological symbolism of human habitation. As we have just seen, every Arctic house, every tent and every yurt of northern Asia is conceived as situated in the Center of the World: the central pole or smoke-hole signifies the *axis mundi*. We could then say that archaic man endeavoured to live continuously in a consecrated space, in a Universe kept "open" by the communications between the cosmic levels. From a certain stage of culture, the human dwelling imitates the divine dwelling.

A second consequence would be as follows: since the cosmocized territory and the human dwelling are immediately answers to the Cosmos and divine dwelling, the channel remains open for the ulterior homologizations between the Cosmos, the house (or the temple) and the human body. In effect, we find similar homologizations in all the high cultures of Asia, but they are already evidenced at the level of archaic cultures. Moreover, the Cosmos-house-human body homologization gave rise to philosophic speculations still present in India, and which continued in the West until the Renaissance.[69] We will not emphasize these multiple homologizations which precisely constitute one of the most characteristic notes of Indian thought. It is especially Jainism which presents the Cosmos in the form of a human being, but this cosmological anthropomorphy is a specific note in all of India.[70] Let us add at once that it is a question of an archaic idea: its roots plunge into the mythologies which explain the birth of the Cosmos from a primordial giant. Indian religious thought has abundantly used this traditional homologization of Cosmos-Human body, and we understand why the human body, like the Cosmos, is in the final instance an existential situation, a conditional system that one assumes. In the rituals implying a subtle physiology of the yogic structure, the spinal cord is assimilated to the cosmic pillar (*skambha*) or to Mount Meru, breaths are identified as the winds, the navel or the heart as the "Center of the World," etc.[71] But the homologization is also made between the human body and the complex ritual of its entirety: the sacrificial site, the sacrificial tools and gestures are assimilated with the diverse organs and physiological functions. It is due to such a system of homologization that the organic activities, and in the first place sexual experience, have been sanctified and, especially in the Tantric era, used as a means of deliverance.[72] The human body, ritually homologized with the Cosmos or the Vedic altar (*imago mundi*), was assimilated further to a house. A hatha yoga text speaks of the body as "a house with one column and nine doors" (*Goraksa Çataka*, 14).

All this is the same as saying that in consciously placing oneself in the exemplary situation by which one is in some way predestined, man is "cosmocized"; in other words, he reproduces on a human scale the system of reciprocal conditions and the rhythm which characterizes and constitutes a "world," which in sum defines the entire Universe. The homologization also plays on the contrary sense: the temple or the house are in turn considered like a human body. The "eye" of the dome is a common term in several architectural traditions.[73] But it is necessary to emphasize one fact: each of these equivalent images—Cosmos, house, human body—present or are capable of receiving an "opening," making possible the passage into another world. The upper orifice of an Indian tower has among other names that of *brâhmarandhra*.[74] But we know that this term designates the "opening" which is located at the top of the skull and that it plays a capital role in the yogic-tantric techniques:[75] it is also through there that the soul escapes at the moment of death. Let us recall the custom of breaking the skull of the dead yogi in order to facilitate the soul's departure.[76]

This Indian custom has its parallel in the abundantly widespread beliefs of Europe and Asia that the soul of the deceased leaves by the smoke-hole or through the roof, and notably through that part of the roof which is found above the "sacred angle"[77] (of the sanctified space which in certain types of Eurasian habitations corresponds to the central pillar and consequently plays the role of the "Center of the World"); in case of prolonged agony, several boards in the roof are removed or else it is smashed.[78] The significance of this custom is obvious: the soul will detach itself more easily from the body if the other image of the Human body-Cosmos, which is the house, is broken in its upper part.

It is remarkable that the Indian mystical vocabulary has conserved the homologization human body-house, and notably the assimilation of the skull to the roof or to the cupola. The fundamental mystical experience, that is to say the surpassing of the human condition is expressed by a double image: the breaking of the roof and the ascent into the sky. The Buddhist texts speak of Arhats who ". . . soar into the sky by breaking through the roof of the palace";[79] who ". . . soaring by their own will, break and pass through the roof of the house and disappear into the trees,"[80] the Arhat Moggallava, ". . . breaking the cupola, rushed into the sky."[81] These imaged formulae are susceptible to a double interpretation: on the plane of subtle physiology and mystical experience, it is a matter of an "ecstasy" and thus of the flight of the soul by the *brâhma-randhra;* on the metaphysical plane, it is a matter of the abolition of the conditioned world. But these two significations of the "flight" of the Arhats express the rupture of the ontological level and the passage from one mode of being to another, or, more exactly the passage from conditioned existence to an unconditioned mode of being, that is to say perfect freedom.

In the majority of archaic ideologies, the image of "flight" signifies access to a mode of a superhuman being (god, magician, "spirit"), in the final instance the freedom to move by will, thus an appropriation of the condition of the spirit.[82] For Indian thought, the Arhat who ". . . breaks the roof of the house, and soars into the sky illustrates in an imaged manner that he has transcended the Cosmos and has acceded to a paradoxical, indeed unthinkable, mode of being, that is of absolute freedom (whatever name that one gives it: *nirvâna, assansrita, samâdhi, sahaja,* etc.). On the mythological level, the exemplary gesture of the transcension of the world by a violent act of rupture is that of the Buddha proclaiming that he has "broken" the Cosmic Egg, "the shell of ignorance," and that he has obtained "the blessed, the universal dignity of Buddha."[83]

These last examples have opportunely demonstrated to us the importance and perpetuity of archaic symbols relative to human habitation. By continually modifying their values, by enriching themselves with new significances, and by being integrated into more and more articulated systems of thought, these archaic symbols have nevertheless conserved a certain unity of structure. The ideas of the "Center of the World," of the *Axis Mundi,* of the communication between the cosmic levels, of the ontological rupture, etc., have been unequally experienced and diversely valued by different cultures; useful studies could be undertaken on these differences, and to extricate the relations which exist between certain cultural cycles—historic moments or "styles" of civilization—and the triumph of such and such a symbolic expression. But the variations of formulae and the differences of statistical order do not succeed in compromising the unity of structure of this entire class of symbols. Their perpetuity poses a problem that even the historian of religions is not expected to solve: we can ask ourselves, in effect, if such symbols do not express a fundamental existential experience, that notably of the specific situation of man in the Cosmos. At the base of all these symbols, we find the idea of the heterogeneity of space; attested to at all levels of culture, it responds to an original experience, the very experience of the Sacred.

Near the Profane space and in opposition to it, there is Sacred space where the rupture of levels and, consequently, the communication with the trans-human take place.

Along with the experience and notion of Sacred space, we encounter another fundamental idea: every legal and permanent situation implies insertion into a Cosmos, into a perfectly organized Universe, thus imitating the exemplary model, Creation. Inhabited territory, temple, house, human body, as we saw are Cosmoses. But each according to its own mode of being, all these Cosmoses keep an "opening," whichever meaning we attribute to it in the diverse cultures (the "eye" of the temple, the chimney, the smoke-hole, the *brâhmarandha*, etc.). In one way or another, the Cosmos that we inhabit—human body, house, territory, this world—communicates from above with another level which is transcendent to it. It is not the same to ascertain that the members of traditional societies experienced the need to inhabit an "open" Cosmos, the concrete character of the "openings" which we just disclosed in the diverse types of dwellings prove the universality and perpetuity of such a need for communication with the other world.

It happens that in an acosmic religion, like that of India after the Upanishads and Buddhism, the opening towards the superior plane no longer expresses the passage from the human condition to the super-human condition, but transcendence, the abolition of the Cosmos, freedom. The difference between the philosophic significance of the "broken egg" of the Buddha or of the roof cracked by the Arhats—and the symbolism of the passage from the Earth to Heaven along the *Axis Mundi* or by the smoke-hole—is enormous. It remains however that philosophy like Indian mysticism has chosen from preference among the images which could signify the ontological rupture and transcendence this primordial image of bursting the roof. This means that the surpassing of the human condition translates, in an imaged fashion, by the annihilation of the "house," that is to say the personal Cosmos in which we have chosen to live. Every "stable dwelling" where we have "settled" is equivalent to, on the philosophic plane, an existential situation that we have assumed. The image of bursting the roof signifies that we have abolished every "situation," that we have chosen not settling in the world but absolute freedom which, for Indian thought, implies the annihilation of every conditioned world.

NOTES

1. See especially Ananda K. Coomaraswamy, *Elements of Buddhist Iconography* (Cambridge: Harvard University Press, 1935); idem, "Symbolism of the Dome,"

Indian Historical Quarterly XIV (1938), 1–56; and the studies republished in idem, *Figures of Speech or Figures of Thought* (London: Luzac and Company, 1946).

2. Paul Mus, *Barabudur. Esquisse d'une histoire du bouddhisme fondée sur la critique archéologique des textes, I-II* (Hanoi: Impr. d'Extreme Orient, 1935).

3. Guiseppi Tucci, *Mc'ad rten e-ts'a nel Tibet Indiano ed Occidentale. Contributo allo studio dell-arte religiosa tibetana e del suo significato. (Indo-Tebtua,* Vol. I, Rome, 1932); idem, *Il Simbolismo archittectonico dei tempi di Tibet Occidentale (Indo-Tibetica,* Vols. III-IV, Rome, 1938).

4. W. Andrae, *Das Gotteshaus und die Urformim des Bauens im alten Orient* (Berlin: Hans Schoetz and Com., 1930); idem, *Die ionische Saule, Bauform oder Symbol?* (Berlin: Verlag für Kunstwissenchaft, 1933).

5. Stella Kramrisch, *The Hindu Temple,* Volumes I-II (Calcutta: University of Calcutta Press, 1946).

6. Carl Hentze, *Bronzegerät. Kultbauten, Religion im ältesten Chine der Chang-Zeit* (Antwerp: De Sikkel, 1951).

7. Hans Sedlmayr, "Architekur als abbilende Kunst," *Österreichische Akademie der Wissenschaften,* Phil.-hist. Klasse, Sitzungsberichte, 225/3, Vienna (1948); idem, *Die Entstehung der Kathedrale* (Zurich: De Sikkel, 1950).

8. Let us add that it is not a question of applying the methods of depth psychology to the study of the history of religions. We propose to examine elsewhere the relationship between (depth) psychology and the history of religions.

9. See Mircea Eliade, *Patterns in Comparative Religion* (New York: World Publishing, 1970 [1958]), 367ff.

10. One finds several bibliographic indications in Mircea Eliade, *Myth of the Eternal Return or Cosmos and History* (Princeton: Princeton University Press, Bollingen Series 46, 1971 [1959]), 15ff.; cf. also idem, *Images and Symbols* (New York: Sheed and Ward, 1961), 52ff.

11. See the texts and bibliographic references in Lars Ivar Ringbom, *Graltempel und Paradies. Beziehungen zwischen Iran und Europa im Mittelalter* (Stockholm: Walhstrom and Widstrand, 1951), 255ff., 284ff.

12. Cf. Eliade, *Eternal Return,* 16–171; idem, *Patterns,* 375, 377–378.

13. *Irische Texte,* I, 25.

14. Jan de Vries, "La valeur religieuse du mot germanique *irmis,"* *Cahiers du Sud* (1952), 18–27; idem, *Altgermanische Religionsgeschichte,* I (Leipzig: W. de Gruyter and Co., 1935), 186–187.

15. It is to be noted that *brahman* has been assimilated to *skambha,* just as *Urgrund* which holds up the world, both as *cosmic axis* and ontological foundation; cf. Mircea Eliade, *Yoga, Immortality and Freedom* (Princeton: Princeton University Press, Bollingen Series 61, 1973 [1958]), 115. One example among a thousand others of the ulterior philosophic valuation of these very old cosmological schemae and images.

16. Cf. Dominik Wolfel, "Die Religionem dei vorindagermanischen Europa" in *Christus und die Religionem dei Erde,* Vol. I (1951), 163–537, esp. 433.

17. Cf. in ancient India, similar prayers addressed to the tree trunk which will be made into the sacrificial post (*yupa*); Mircea Eliade, *Shamanism* (Princeton: Princeton University Press, Bollingen Series 76, 1974 [1951]), 403ff.

18. See the works of F. Boas, summarized and interpreted by Werner Müller, *Weltbild und Kult der Kwakiutl-Indianer* (Wiesbaden: F. Steiner, 1955), 17–20.

19. Cf. P. Aradt, "Die Megalithenkultur des Nad'a," *Anthropos* 27 (1932), 11–64, esp. 61–62. R. Heine-Geldern noted that the relationship btween *menhir* and ritual pillar in Assam in western Burma and the Celebes Isles, cf. "Die Megalithen Sudostasiens und ihre Bedeutung für die Klärung der Megalithenfrage in Europe und Polynesien," *Anthropos* 23 (1928), 276–315, esp. 283. See also Josef Roder, *Pfahl und Menhir*. Dominik Wolfen believes that, in the protohistoric Mediterranean, the wooden pillar is a megalithic *ersatz* (p. 213).

20. See the references in Eliade, *Eternal Return*, 17ff.

21. Texts cited by A. J. Wensinck, *The Ideas of the Western Semites concerning the Navel of the Earth* (Amsterdam: J. Muller, 1916), 19, 16.

22. Cited by W. Roscher, "Neue Omphalosstudien," *Abh. d. König. Sachs Gesell. Wiss. Phil.-klasse.*, Vol. 31.1 (1915), 16.

23. See the references indicated in Eliade, *Eternal Return*, 16–17.

24. Cf. *Bundahishn*, Ch. V, and the map reproduced by Ringbom, op. cit., 280, fig. 81. See also the illuminating commentary on Henry Corbin, "Terre céleste et Corps de résurrection d'après quelques traditions iraniennes," *Eranos-Jahrbuch* XXII (1954), 97–194, esp. 114ff.

25. *Videvat*, I, 3; Ringbom, op. cit., 292.

26. See the references grouped and interpreted by Ringbom, op. cit., 294ff. and passim.

27. *Saddar*, LXXXI, 4–5; Ringbom, op. cit., 327. Cf. Corbin, op. cit., 153ff.

28. Cf. Ringbom, op. cit., 295ff.; Corbin, op. cit., 123ff.

29. Ringbom, op. cit., 75ff.; H. P. L'Orange, *Studies on the Iconography of Cosmic Kingship in the Ancient World* (Oslo: H. A. Schehoug, 1953), 19ff.

30. Ibid., 13 and passim.

31. *Çatapatha Brâhmana*, I, 9, 2, 299; VI, 5, 1ff.; cf. Eliade, *Eternal Return*, 78ff.

32. C. Tj. Bertling, *Vierzahl, Kreuz und Mandala in Asien* (Amsterdam: 's-Gravenhage, 1954), 11.

33. Ibid., 8.

34. One also finds this complex iconography in China, India, Indonesia and New Guinea, cf. ibid., 8.

35. See the references in Bertling, op. cit., 4–5.

36. Cf. the exegesis of this symbolic complex in Carl Hentze, *Bronzegerät, Religion im ältesten China der Shangzeit*, 198ff. and passim.

37. On the *mundus*, cf. Werner Müller, *Kreis und Kreuz. Untersuchungen zur sakralen Seldlung bei Italiken und Germanen* (Berlin: Widukind Verlag, 1938), 61ff.; on *Roma Quadrata*, ibid., 60, following F. Altheim.

38. W. H. Roscher, according to Müller, *Kreis und Kreuz*, 63.

39. Ibid., 65ff.

40. Cf. the references in Eliade, *Eternal Return*, 19. The site for the fire-altar was determined by turning towards the East and throwing the javelin (*çamyâ*); where the pike entered the earth and remained upright was the "center" (*Pañcavimça Brâhmana*, XXV, 10, 4 and 13, 2); cf. Coomaraswamy, "Symbolism of the Dome," 21, n. 28.

41. Hermann Usener, *Götternamen* (Bonn: F. Cohen, 1929 [1896]), 191ff.

42. Cf. Müller, *Kreis und Kreuz*, 39; see also 33ff.

43. Mus, *Barabudur*, I, 384.

44. On the construct of time, see ibid., II, 733–789.

45. See the materials grouped and interpreted by Werner Müller, *Die blaue Hütte. Zum Sinnbild der Perle bei nordamerikanischen Indianern* (Wiesbaden: F. Steiner, 1954), 60ff.

46. Myths explain and justify this cosmic symbolism: the first initiation had had the entire Universe as its setting; cf. Müller, op. cit., 63.

47. Ibid., 133.

48. Ibid., 134. The spatial-temporal concept of the Universe as the House is formulated by the *Çatapatha Brâhmana* I, 6, 1, 19: "But he alone gains it who knows its doors; for what were he to do with a house who cannot find his way inside?"

49. Ibid., 135.

50. Cf. A. L. Kroeherand, E. W. Gifford, *World Renewal, a Cult System of Native Northwest California* (Berkeley: University of California Press, 1949).

51. A. L. Kroeber, *Handbook of the Indians of California* (Washington, D.C.: U.S. Government Printing Office, 1925), 498, 177.

52. A. I. Hallowell in *American Anthropologist*, n.s., 39 (1937), 665. One will also recall that the Mexican pyramid had 364 steps or 366 niches.

53. "The Dome of Heaven," *The Art Bulletin* XXVII (1945), 1ff.

54. A. C. Soper, "The 'Dome of Heaven' in Asia," *The Art Bulletin* XXIX (1947), 225–248. On the problem of Mediterranean influences on the art of central Asia, see the extensive essay of Mario Bussagli, "L'influsso classico ed iranico sull'arte dell'Asia centrale," *Rivista dell'Istituto Nazionale d'Archeologia e Storia dell'Arte*, Nuova Series, II (1953), 175–262.

55. In any case, it is a matter of the cosmico-architectural symbolism evidenced already in the protohistory of eastern Europe, the Near East and the Caucasus; cf. Ferdinand Bork, *Die Geschichte des Weltbildes* (Leipzig: Eduard Pfeiffer, 1930); Richard Pittoni, "Zum Kulturgeschichtlichen Alter des Blockbaues," *Wiener Zeitschrift für Volkskunde* XXXVI (1930), 75ff.; and Leopold Schmidt, "Die Kittinge, Probleme der Burgenlandischen Blockbauspeicher," *Burgenlandische Heimatblätter* X Heft 3 (1950), 97–116.

56. Eliade, *Shamanism*, 280ff.

57. Helmut Hoffmann, *Quellen zur Geschichte der tibetischen Bon-Religion* (Wiesbaden: Kommission bei F. Steiner, 1950), 139.

58. E. Erkes, "Ein Marchenmotiv bei Lao-Tse," *Sinologica*, III (1952), 100–105.

59. One will find these materials and a discussion in Eliade, *Shamanism*, 326ff.

60. Ibid., 235ff. See also G. Rank, *Die heilige Hinterecke im Hauskuit der Völker*

Nordosteuropas und Nordasiens (Helsinki: FF Communications, Nr. 137, 1949), 91ff., 107ff.; Dominick Schröder, "Zur Religion der Tujen des Sininggebietes, Kukunor," *Anthropos* 48 (1953), 202–259, esp. 210ff.

61. W. Schmidt, "Der heilige Mittelpfahl des Hauses," *Anthropos* 35–36 (1940–1941), 966–969; P. M. Hermanns, "Uiguren und ihre neuentdeckten Nachkommen," *Anthropos* 35–36 (1940–1941), 90ff.; G. Rank, op. cit., 110ff. The pillar (*Axis Mundi*), or the tree deprived of branches (the Cosmic Tree) are conceived as a stairway leading to the sky: shamans climbed it in their celestial journeys; cf. Eliade, *Shamanism*, 125ff. and passim.

62. Ibid., 238ff. See also Rank, op. cit., 222ff. It is by this opening that the shamans escape; cf. Eliade, *Shamanism*, 238.

63. Schmidt, "Der heilige Mittelpfahl," 967. On the subsequent mythico-religious valorizations of the central pillar, cf. Evel Gasparini, *I Riti popolari slavi* (Venice, 1952, Course at the Istituto Universitario di Ca' Foscari), 62ff.; idem, "La cultura lusaziana e i protoslavi," *Ricerche Slavistiche*, I (1952), 88.

64. Cf. Müller, *Weltbild und Kult*, 20.

65. Cf. Elsie C. Parsons, *Pueblo Indian Religion* (Chicago: University of Chicago Press, 1939), 218ff.; myth translated and commented upon by R. Pettazzoni, *Miti e Legende*, III (Turin: Unione tipografico-editrice torinese, 1953), 520ff., esp. 529.

66. E. de Martino, "Angoscia territoriale e riscato culturale nel mito Achilpa delle origine," *Studi e Materiali di Storia delle Religioni*, XXIII (1951–1952), 51–66.

67. Baldwin Spencer and F. J. Gillen, *The Arunta*, I (London: Macmillan and Company, 1927), 388; de Martino, op. cit., 59. On the traditions of the Choctaw Indians concerning the sacred pole and its role in their pilgrimages, cf. Pettazzoni, noted in de Martino's article, p. 60.

68. Cf. Mircea Eliade, "Manole et le monastère d'Arges," *Revue des Etudes Roumaines* 3–4 (1957), 7–28, republished in *Zalmoxis, The Vanishing God* (Chicago: University of Chicago Press, 1972), 164–190.

69. We will return to this problem in a special study. See for the moment, Mircea Eliade, "Cosmical homology and yoga," *Journal of the Indian Society of Oriental Art* (1937), 188–201; idem, *Yoga*, 204ff.

70. Cf. for example, H. von Glasenapp, *Der Jainismus* (Berlin: A. Hager, 1925), Plate #15; W. Kirfel, *Die Kosmographie der Inder* (Bonn and Leipzig: K. Schroeder, 1920).

71. See Eliade, *Yoga*, 104ff., 204ff., etc.

72. Cf. for example the *Brhadâranyaka-Upanishad* VI, 4, 3ff., and the parallel texts on erotic mysticism cited and commented upon in Eliade, *Yoga*, 254ff.

73. Cf. Coomaraswamy, "Symbolism of the Dome," 34ff.

74. Ibid., p. 46, n. 53. This orifice, equivalent to the "eye" of the temple, corresponds to the "hole" (*Axis Mundi*) which marks, at least symbolically, the central pillar to the roof of the construction (Cosmos). In certain *stûpa* the prolongation of the axis from the roof and above the floor is indicated in a concrete manner; see ibid., p. 1. Cf. also Ananda K. Coomaraswamy, "Svayamâtrnna: Janua Coeli," *Zalmoxis* II (1939, published 1941), 1–51.

75. Eliade, *Yoga*, 234ff., 243ff.

76. Cf. ibid., 400. See also Coomaraswamy, "Symbolism of the Dome," 53, n. 60.

77. Rank, op. cit., 45ff.

78. Ibid., 47. The opening allows the soul of the dead to leave and to *return*, during the period when it was not believed to have left the house definitively. At this point the archaic Chinese conception of the urn-house can be recalled; cf. Hentze, *Bronzegerät, Kultbauten, Religion*, 49ff. and passim. Certain funerary houses contain an opening in the roof allowing the soul of the dead person to enter and to leave; see the small earthenware model found in a Korean tomb pictured in Carl Hentze, "Contribution à l'étude de l'origine typologique des bronzes anciens de la Chine," *Sinologica* II (1953), 229–239, figures 2–3.

79. *Jâtaka*, III, 472.

80. *Dhammapada Atthakathâ*, I, 63; Coomaraswamy, "Symbolism of the Dome," 54.

81. *Dhammapada Atthakathâ*, III, 66; *Jâtaka*, IV, 228–229; Coomaraswamy, op. cit., 54. On the ascent of the Arhats, see Eliade, *Shamanism*, 408ff. and idem, *Yoga*, 170ff., 328ff. The apprentice Eskimo shaman, when he experienced *quamaneq* ("illumination" or "flash of lightning") for the first time, it is ". . . as if the house in which he is suddenly rises." Rasmussen as cited by Eliade, *Shamanism*, 61.

82. Cf. Mircea Eliade, "Symbolisme du Vol magique," *Numen* 3 (1956), 1–13.

83. *Suttanibhanga Pârijîka*, I, 1, 4, commented upon by Paul Mus, "La Notion du temps reversible dans la mythologie bouddhique," extracted from *Annuaire de l'école pratique des Hautes Études*, Section des Sciences, 1938–1939, Melun, 1939, 13; see also Mircea Eliade, "Le Temps et l'Éternité dans la pensée indienne," *Eranos-Jahrbuch* XX (1952), 219–252, esp. 238; idem, *Images and Symbols*.

Barabudur, the Symbolic Temple

IT HAS ALWAYS BEEN KNOWN that the great architectonic edifices of "traditional" cultures express a very exacting symbolism. The difficulties begin when one tries to decipher this symbolism, because at that point the poetic intention or the scientific hypothesis of the investigator intrudes, and an attempt is made to reduce, at all costs, the architectonic symbolism to a *sui generis* system interpreted, in most instances, as an "original discovery" of the investigator. Nevertheless, one truth begins to make headway in circles of specialists of all kinds: that the symbolism of ancient constructions—temples, monuments, labyrinths, cities—is closely related to cosmological concepts. On the other hand, so far as we are concerned, a series of researches—the results of which have not yet appeared in print [1937]—have convinced us that in traditional cultures the majority of human gestures had symbolic significance. This assertion should be understood to mean that the activities of the individual, even in the most "profane" intervals of his life, were oriented constantly toward a transhuman reality. Man tries, that is, to integrate himself into an absolute reality which, in the majority of instances, is intuited as a "totality": Universal Life, Cosmos. As such, every human act had, in addition to its intrinsic utility, a symbolic meaning which transfigured it. For instance, an activity so insignificant, so random, as walking or eating was—and still is today in certain Asiatic cultures—a "ritual"; that is, an effort at integration into a supra-individual, supra-biological reality. Also, this integration is made, in our first example, by walking rhythmically, in conformity with the norm of cosmic rhythms (India, China, Austro-Asiatic cultures). Or, with reference to our other example, eating: by the identification of the organs of the human body with certain "powers" (gods of the body in India), which transforms man into a

"Barabudur, the Symbolic Temple" was originally published in *Revista Fundațiilor Regale* IV.9 (1937), 605–617; and reprinted in *Insula lui Euthanasuis* (Bucharest: Fundatia Regale pentru Litteraturā și Artā, 1943), 50–68. It is translated from the Romanian by Mac Linscott Ricketts.

microcosm with the same structure and essence as the Great All, the macrocosm.

Being constantly conscious of this "identity" and "correspondence" of his being with the Cosmos, the man of traditional cultures[1] rarely performed any "meaningless" act, an act of simple biological utility. That is why we stated at the beginning of these notes that symbolism explains not only architectonic constructions of traditional cultures, but it involves also in an absolute way the entire life of those who participate in such a culture. In his unceasing effort at integration—or, more exactly, reintegration—into the Cosmos, the life and deeds of that man were without doubt devoid of any "originality." They were canonical, ritual acts, and for that reason the life of the individual was translucent to and understood by every member of the community (in certain Asiatic communities this is still true today). Since the method of integration was the same on the part of everyone—because it was done in conformity with norms—communication among these people was infinitely easier. They knew and understood each other even before speaking—according to clothing, colors and shapes of precious stones, and the designs in the fabrics worn; according to gestures, manner of walking, etc. In several earlier studies ("Jade," "Mudra"[2]) I have discussed these social aspects of Asiatic symbolism. We plan to return to them in a work of larger proportions, *Symbole, mythe, culture*,[3] in which we shall discuss in particular the metaphysical function of symbol, the generator of myths and the creator of culture. Our work does not fit into the category of modern books on the philosophy of culture because it does not set out from morphological investigation of a particular culture nor does it pursue cultural "styles": rather, it aims at demonstrating the universality of metaphysical traditions and the unity of symbolism in the first human civilizations. A more limited application of this same method is found in our monograph soon to appear, *La Mandragore. Essai sur les origines des légendes.*[4]

These notes here do not, of course, pretend to attack the thorny problem of architectonic symbolism in all its ramifications. We propose only to discuss some of the conclusions reached by a French savant, Paul Mus, who, though today unknown outside a small circle of specialists, will, in a few years hence we are certain, enjoy wide renown. Paul Mus, member of L'École Française de l'Extrême-Orient, author of several studies on Buddhist iconography and the history of Anamese religion, has published recently a monumental work: *Barabudur. Esquisse d'une histoire du Buddhisme fondée sur la critique archéologique des textes.* We do not exaggerate in the least when we state that this gigantic *oeuvre*—which when complete will consist of some two thousand pages, and which has a preface of 302 pages in quarto wherein Mus establishes his method—

will play the fertile role in Indology that has been filled in recent years by the book of the genius Burnouf. But it is not only in Indology that Paul Mus is destined to revolutionize the contemporary viewpoint. *Barabudur* seeks to establish a wholly new and sure foundation for the understanding of the architecture of all Asia and to disclose in a systematic way the cosmological symbolism which every Oriental construction involves. Unfortunately, as Georges Codes admits (he is the director of the French School of the Far East and has written a foreword to this work), few people will be disposed to consult a huge monograph on a Javanese temple for the purpose of reading a new interpretation of Buddhism— *and* a new philosophy of the culture of Further Asia, we would add. It is precisely to attract the attention of nonspecialists—particularly architects, art historians, and historians of religions—that we have written this article. It pleases me even more that Paul Mus, whose erudition is infinite and whose intuition flawless, even when employed in fields other than Orientalism, has demonstrated definitively several conclusions at which we also had arrived in our parallel researches—and he has demonstrated them with a wealth of detail and a precision which we, for our part, could never have attained.

On the subject of Barabudur, the famous Buddhist temple on the island of Java and the most beautiful monument in Asia, whole libraries have been written. Purely technical explanations have been attempted, taking account only of the laws of architecture; endless controversies have been joined over the religious and magical meanings hidden in that colossal monument. Dutch Orientalists and architects have published over the past fifteen years books of great value on Barabudur. The names of Krom, Van Erp, and Stutterheim must be mentioned. The last of these, in a work of 1927, laid the foundation for a true interpretation of the temple: *Barabudur is nothing less than a symbolic representation of the Universe.* From this intuition Paul Mus's investigations start. The beginning of his book consists of a history of the controversy, an exposition of the principal hypotheses, and a critique of methods. Examined in turn are theories of the most illustrious India specialists, art historians, and architects. Then Mus undertakes to discuss the problem. It must be remembered that this gigantic volume is preceded by an *avant-propos* of 302 large pages in which the author establishes the validity of his methodology. In order to justify the symbolic function of the Javanese temple, Mus emphasizes a truth often remarked by Orientalists: that if the Buddha was not represented iconographically for several centuries, it was not due to incapability on the part of Indian artists, but to the fact that a type of representation superior to images was essayed. "That would not have been a defeat of plastic art, but rather the triumph of a magical art."[6] When an iconography of the Buddha was adopted, the symbolism was poor by comparison. The *aniconic symbol* of Enlightenment (the wheel, etc.) was much more powerful, more *pure*, than the statue. Ananda Coomaraswamy also has published evidence for this thesis in his *Elements of Buddhist Iconography*.[7] The conclusion to be drawn from this is that Buddhists, as well as Hindus (and Asians in general) before Buddhism, used symbolism more effectively, precisely because the symbol was more comprehensive and "active" in the magical sense than plastic representation. If the Buddha was indeed considered to be a god (as he was, in fact, immediately after his demise), then his magical "presence" was preserved in anything emanating from him. That is why his *name* had just as much effectiveness as his *doctrine* (his verbal, revealed body) and his *physical remains*. The pronunciation of the Buddha's name, the mental assimilation of his teachings, the touching of his physical remains ("relics" which, according to tradition, were deposited in monuments, *stupas*)—by any of these paths man makes contact with the sacred, absolute body of the Enlightened One.

This being the case, we would suspect from the outset that a grandiose temple like Barabudur must itself be a vehicle to transport the faithful to that supernatural plane where the "touching" of the Buddha is possible. Any work in a traditional culture leads by certain "tracks" (*vestigium pedi*) to the contemplation of the divinity or even to incorporation into him. The first Brahmanical "work of art" was, undoubtedly, the Vedic altar "where the nature of God is reflected but where the sacrificer finds himself also magically incorporated."[8] The journey to divinity in India is made on many paths: ritual (magical), contemplative, mystical. One of the paths most employed down to the present day is meditation on an object so constructed that it "encompasses the doctrine." That object, very simple in appearance, is called a *yantra*. One who meditates on a *yantra* magically assimilates the "doctrine," incorporates it. Mus shows keen insight when he asserts that, from a certain point of view, the Barabudur temple is a *yantra*.[9] The structure is so made that the pilgrim, by walking through it and meditating on each scene depicted in the bas-reliefs in the numerous galleries, assimilates Buddhist doctrine. I must emphasize this point: the temple is a symbolic body of the Buddha, and therefore the believer "learns" or "experiences" Buddhism by visiting the temple just as effectively as by *reading* the Buddha's words or by *meditating* on them. In all these cases there is an approach to the supra-real presence of the Buddha: the temple or *stūpa* is his architectonic body.

Indeed, the *stūpa*—that monument peculiar to Buddhism, which is found in considerable numbers in India, Ceylon, and Burma—is identified with the mystical body of the Buddha.[10] This must be understood, however, according to the mental laws which guide traditional cultures. The *stūpa* is not only a funerary monument, as has been said up to now; the presence of cosmological symbolism gives it a broader meaning.[11] The *stūpa*, like the Vedic altar, is an architectonic image of the world. Its cosmic symbolism is precise: an *imago mundi*. But the *stūpa* may be considered also a funerary monument since—if not in reality, at least in tradition—it contains a relic of the Buddha. Paul Mus calls attention, however, to construction sacrifices of human beings in Asia, sacrifices which—at least in regions studied by him—have the meaning of *animating* the structure. There is need of a *soul*, a *life*, for the new structure to be animated. Perhaps we have here a variant of the legend of Master Manole which, in turn, is only one of numerous examples of "rites of construction" investigated by Lăzar Şăineanu in the case of Balkan peoples.[12]

But the meaning of the Buddhist monument is this: the *stūpa*, being on the one hand an architectonic image of the world while on the other hand the mystical body of the Buddha, a holy relic—it is accorded an *absolute*, supra-temporal life; not only does the brickwork *last* (as in the legend of Master Manole), but it is animated by a sacred life, and it is therefore a world in itself. As Mus says, the *stūpa* is the Buddha's *body* rather than his *tomb*.[13] The monument was not erected to pay homage to relics of the Buddha, but the relics (fictitious, of course) were brought here to animate the monument, Thus, the accent falls not on the funerary character of the *stūpa*, but on its cosmological meaning. The *stūpa*, being the mystical body of the Buddha, is so constructed as to represent symbolically the universe. Moreover, the symbolism is precise: Buddha = cosmos = *stūpa*.[14] On the earthly plane the tomb, which, according to the *Çatapatha Brāhmana* (XIII. 8. 1.1), "will serve either as a dwelling place or as a monument," is assimilated to the dead man himself, so that the grave becomes a sort of "funereal person."[15] All the more does a monument which contains a relic of the Buddha become a "person": that is, it is transformed into a mystical, architectonic body of the Buddha. If we recall, however, that the Buddha himself is imagined as a *"caitya* [small monument] of the world" (in the *Lalitavistara*), it is easy to understand that wherever a relic exists, there is the whole Cosmos. And besides, in the Indian view of things, even the human body is imagined as a Cosmos—with its "horizons," its "winds"—and Mus gives us a penetrating analysis of all the implications of such a concept.[16]

In connection with the double symbolism, funerary and cosmological, of the Buddhist religious monument, one might make an interesting comparison between the *stūpa* and the function of the labyrinth as a postmortem itinerary. C. N. Deedes has attempted an interpretation along these lines,[17] and the analysis could be carried further: for instance, by identifying in the "microcosm" of the human body the whole "mythical map" of the labyrinth.[18]

The symbolic polyvalence of Indian monuments, in particular the *stūpa*, is obvious. On the one hand, a funerary monument; on the other—as we shall show below—a cosmological monument: the *stūpa* encompasses the universe and sustains it. But the *stūpa* has also a "mystical," religious function: it is the Law (*Dharma*) made visible, the mystical, architectonic body of the Buddha.

> The *stūpa* is the cosmic *dharma* rendered visible; as such, it is without other symbolisms, it suffices to insure a contact with the mysterious nature of the Buddha, vanished into Nirvana, but who has graciously left us his Law to take his place. "Whoever beholds the Law beholds me: whoever beholds me beholds the Law," he teaches in effect in the canon. From that high estate of belief, the *stūpa* is made to appear as the Law; it is in the same stroke, to a certain extent, the portrait of the Buddha.[19]

Many investigators have sought to explain the Barabudur temple by means of an architectonic formula involving the *stūpa*; for instance, *stūpa* as *ziggurat*, or *stūpa* as *prāsada* (pyramid). This latter formula is Stutterheim's and it comes very close to the truth. But even the stories and terraces of the Barabudur temple are made in conformity with the norms of ecstatic Buddhist meditation. Let us not forget that the temple, in its polyvalent symbolism, embodies the Law (Dharma) and therefore indicates the path of salvation. The most common soteriological itinerary in Buddhism was ecstatic meditation.[20] Barabudur is so constructed that "spheres" of meditation are realized in stone.

> The Buddhas, at first visible in the niches, then half-hidden under the *stūpa* lattice-work, the inaccessible statue at the level summit—a *marche à illumination*, across a matter less and less substantial, to the anticipated ultimate goal here on earth, a reference to the moment of final extinction, as the finished *stūpa* gives them to understand. The images which are displayed, on the other hand, all along the terraces of galleries, would thus be for the sole purpose of establishing and sustaining the spirit of the lesser ones in their passage through Rupadhatu. A book of stone, as it has been called, but offered for meditation, not for ordinary reading.[21]

The pilgrim does not have a total and direct view of the temple. Viewed from the outside, Barabudur looks like a fortress of stone several stories high. The galleries which lead to the upper terraces are so constructed that the pilgrim sees nothing but the bas-reliefs and statues in

20. Seated Buddha,
    Temple of Barabudur

21. Temple of Barabudur
    (detail)

the niches. The initiation, therefore, is made gradually. Meditating on each scene individually, realizing in order the stages of ecstasy, the pilgrim tours these two and a half kilometers of galleries in unbroken meditation. Moreover, the very physical fatigue of the slow ascent is an *ascesis*. Suffering like a monk, meditating on the "stages of ecstasy" represented iconographically, with his mind purified by *ascesis* and contemplation, the pilgrim realizes as he nears the highest point of the temple that spiritual ascension which the Buddha proclaimed as the only path to salvation. Obviously, the Buddhist path of salvation is long and thorny—and it is admirably formulated in the complex architecture of Barabudur.

> It does not have the appearance of Gothic naves, the symbol of a rapid leap of faith, of a salvation accessible in one life or even, through grace, in an instant, but considered in its massiveness, it represents the interminable ascension which the doctrine apportions among a number of existences. One does not ascend all of a sudden. It is necessary to revolve for a long time in the cycle of birth and to gain the height only gradually.[22]

The temple cannot be "assimilated" from the outside. The statues cannot be seen. Only the initiate who goes through all the galleries discovers gradually the planes of supersensible reality, the grades of meditation expressed iconographically. He discovers them and he assimilates them. The temple is a *closed world*; a microcosm of stone, but a *closed* microcosm.[23] The "world" of ancient cosmologies (Mesopotamia, India, China) was imagined as being like an enclosed vessel. The temple was the *image* of this world; its concrete model was the bubble of air or water, the "cosmic egg." One cannot enter into such a "closed world," of course, except by miracle. Indeed, the gates were considered a "breech," effected by magical means, into the cosmic mountain, i.e., into the temple.

The "closed world," the hollow sphere, has as its center the cosmic pillar separating heaven from the earth, the axis which supports the Universe. This symbol of the axis and the pole, the cosmic pillar, is found in all traditional cultures. It is illustrated especially in the civilizations of Mesopotamia, Indo-Melanesia, and Austro-Asia. The "pillar" supports the world; that is, it separates heaven from earth, just as does the Egyptian god Shu. This pillar is represented in the "Tree of Life," a tradition encountered everywhere.[24] The temple, the Cosmic Mountain, the Pillar, the Tree—all these symbols are equivalent. They support the world, they are the Axis of the Universe, they are the *center* of the world. This is why every sacred city in Asia is considered the *center of the Universe*. (One must always begin from this assumption when he tries to understand Jerusalem, Rome, etc.) The center of the sacred city is constituted by the royal palace, while in the palace, in a certain room, is the throne, the ultimate point, on which sits the sovereign, considered a *chakravartin*, i.e., a "universal monarch." When Buddhism became a state religion it adopted the magico-religious theory of royalty.[25] This explains the double symbolism of the legends of the nativity of the Buddha: the "signs" that were seen on the infant Siddhartha were equivocal: the prince might become either a "universal monarch" (*chakravartin*) or an "enlightened one" (*buddha*).[26]

I stated earlier that the symbolic polyvalence of Buddhist structures, in particular the *stūpa*, does not allow us to accept a single explanation of these monuments, because they manifest diverse symbolisms and fulfill parallel functions. For, example, the *stūpa*, in addition to its funerary and cosmological meanings, has a political value also. To build a *stūpa* in the middle of a region means to devote it to the Buddhist Law (Dharma)[27]—but at the same time to bind it to the sovereign who, being a *chakravartin*, is reckoned to be the "center" of the empire. Each holy city being a "center of the earth," that is, the place where the "cosmic pillar" represented by the temple (the cosmic mountain) is erected, the residents of those cities are considered to be like gods.[28] They dwell at the "navel of the earth" (*omphalos*), in a zone which no longer has anything to do with profane geography, but falls under the criteria of geomancy and "mystical geography." (Examples abound: Jerusalem, Bangkok, Rome; the "rivers" that surround the earth in all traditional cosmologies being almost a reflection of the rivers of Paradise, etc.)

The most important thing to remember out of these too brief notes on holy cities is the fact that the "center" is *constructed*; being constructed, the temple is only an architectonic image of the Universe and Mt. Meru. (The intuition of this magical, polar mountain whose name, Meru, is Indian, was found also among the Mesopotamians and is encountered today in all Asiatic cultures.) The center of the world can be constructed *anywhere*, because one can build anywhere a microcosm in stone or brick. For example, *ziggurats*, those well-known Mesopotamian monuments, represent *artificial mountains*—because to all traditional cultures the cosmos was interpreted as a mountain, while the highest point of the temple, being assimilated to the peak of the magic mountain (Meru), was considered the supreme summit of the cosmic mountain. The construction of the "center" takes place not only in the dimension of "space," but also in that of "time," that is, the temple becomes not only the center of the cosmos, but also the dial marking the "sacred year," i.e., "time." As the *Çatapatha Brāhmaṇa* states, the Vedic altar is time materialized; it is the "year"—the exact assertion that is made about the temple. The construction takes account of the four horizons (space, the Cosmos), but it takes account also of the direction, the order in time of the niches with the bas-reliefs.[29] Thus, all that is *reality* is expressed by the cosmological symbolism of the temple and is, above all, perfectly expressed in that "cosmic clockdial," Barabudur.

These symbols—axis, cosmic pillar, horizons—function with equal validity in both microcosm and macrocosm. It is easy to understand that if the Universe was considered to be a "giant," a "man" (*Purusha*), then cosmic functions are found also in the human body. Indians (and Mesopotamians as well, for that matter) knew a "mystical physiology," that is, a "map" of man drafted in cosmic terms. In our book on Yoga[30] we had occasion to speak about a "mystical physiology" elaborated in terms of ascetic methods, on the basis of contemplative experiences and techniques. Paul Mus, together with Dr. Filliozat,[31] brings out other aspects of these homologies between the human body and the macrocosm. In our book we insisted in particular upon a "mystical physiology" which Indian ascetics created in order to "localize" certain yogic processes and to explain very obscure phenomena of fakirism. Paul Mus investigates older documents in which the homology of microcosm-macrocosm is achieved on another plane: cosmic agents are identified in the human body. The god Indra, for instance, who is considered a "cosmic pillar," who separated day and night, etc., is identified with the human breath (the breath, moreover, was assimilated to the cosmic winds which divide space). "In the human body the breath, consequently, will be a veritable pillar of Indra, which distends the body and makes it, like its cosmic prototype, separate the worlds and put them in opposition."[32] The fundamental homology of the human body with the macrocosm must not be forgotten: the Universe is an enclosed "bubble," a cosmic "sac," just as the human body is a "sac of skin."[33] Bearing in mind all these indications—which are afforded us by architectonic symbolism as well as by mystical physiology, Vedic rituals, etc.—we understand that: "The main point of these symbolisms is the reconstruction of the All-God, Prajāpati, dispersed since creation; the altar will be his person, restored, either under his own name or under that of his 'son' Agni with whom he is at times identified."[34]

We meet here one of the dominants of the whole spiritual life of "primitives": the desire to be integrated into the All, into a Universe which is organic and sacred at the same time, being the body of the god as he was before creation, undivided. The homologation of divine and human life in a culture as original as the Mesopotamian works toward this objective: the reintegration of man into the primordial Cosmos. Moreover, it is not difficult to observe that the majority of symbolisms which we have mentioned in these notes have no other function than to unify, to totalize, to construct a center.[35] Any kind of "consecration" is nothing less than a transcendence of mundane phenomena and the construction of a ritual time and space which participate in eternity and the void (because the ritual space which altars, temples, and so on construct is qualitatively different, being located beyond the world, on a paradisal plane, i.e, devoid of any heterogeneity). Everywhere, back of this architectonic symbolism, we find a tendency toward unity, toward reintegration; because at the same time that classifications are superseded and heterogeneity annuled, "matter" is also abolished,[36] and there begins Absolute Reality (Brahmanism) or Nirvana (Buddhism).

Asiatic mystical architecture in any religious tradition is continually constructing cosmic mountains on which believers climb: on the one hand, in order to assimilate the "sacrality" of the place, the stages of ecstasy represented iconographically (as at Barabudur) and, on the other hand, in order to reach the summit, that is, the center, where passage to transcendent planes is made possible (temples are "gateways"to heaven: Babel, etc.). But even the summit of the temple, that is, the cosmic mountain, has a precise symbolic meaning: here are found the so-called "Pure Lands" of Buddhism.[37] "Pure Land"—that is, level, homogeneous, sacred, "unnatural." Barabudur contains, on the highest terrace, such a terre pure.[38] Initiates who attain this place, circumambulate the terrace, annulling the reality below them, annulling the heterogeneous, the diverse, the disordered, etc. They find themselves now above the world, on a paradisal plane, without diversity or plurality. The object of the Buddhist pilgrim—the transcending of the human condition, the realization of an absolute state—is attained. Man is removed from "life"—that is, from history, from multiplicity and sorrow. He is reintegrated into the absolute All toward which he was aiming, because even the space in which he lives is a "pure land"; it is no longer the heterogeneous space of life, but paradisal, "level" space.

The importance of these cosmological symbolisms which Barabudur encompasses in this, Buddhist Asia's supreme synthesis, does not consist only in the magnificent depth and coherence of the symbolisms, but above all in the fact that they function naturally in the Asiatic folk consciousness. They are not "explained" or "justified," or at any rate the explanation of them is not belabored. They impose themselves naturally on the consciousness of the people; they are "immediate data." This fact verifies an old hypothesis of ours about the analytical possibilities of symbol: in a preliterate culture the symbol, no matter how broad may be the synthesis which gave rise to it, nevertheless expresses, with great precision, an immense number of details which Europeans until recently were justified in believing could only be expressed orally or in writing. Europeans continue to the present day to believe that details cannot be expressed except via speech or writing, ascribing to symbol only a synthetic function. Without ignoring this synthetic function, we have shown in our studies on jade and ritual gestures that symbols can express an enormous number of very precise details, although they express them simultaneously, not successively, as in speech or writing. (For instance, a bracelet made of a certain number of jade stones, of certain colors and shapes, indicates that the girl wearing it belongs to a family that came from the North, that her father is an administrator, that she has three sisters, that she will be engaged in March, that she likes a certain genre of poetry, etc.[39]) This simultaneity of meanings in the symbol is expressed better when we take account of the aim of every symbol: the reintegration of man into the All. But not an abstract All; rather, into a living body which can unite all planes of reality without annihilating them. Barabudur proves that the transcending of the human condition does not mean, as has been believed, the annihilation of life and the Cosmos, but rather the reintegration into the All. Without the tiniest thing in the world being obliterated or being "lost," all things lose their form and significance in that "enclosed seed" which is the Cosmos before the first "division" at Creation.

NOTES

1. By this term we mean any culture, whether ethnographic ("primitive") or literate, which is dominated in its entirety by norms whose religous or cosmological (metaphysical) validity is not doubted by any members of that community.

2. Published in the newspaper *Cuvântul* in February and March, 1932. The article on "Jade" was republished in *Fragmentarium*, Bucharest, 1939, 60–65.

3. This book was never published.

4. This book was never published. Parts of it apppeared in the journal *Zalmoxis*, volumes I and III (1938 and 1941–42). An English version of the former part is found in *Zalmoxis, the Vanishing God* (Chicago and London: University of Chicago Press, 1972), 204–225.

5. Published in *Bulletin de l'École Française de l'Extrême-Orient*. It appeared in 1935, published by Paul Geuthner, volume I comprising 302 + 576 pages in quarto and the first fascicle in volume II in 226 pages in quarto.

6. Paul Mus, op. cit., Avant-propos, 62.

7. Harvard University Press, 1935, 5, etc.

8. Mus, Avant-propos, 73.

9. Ibid., 74.

10. Ibid., 217.

142 SITES OF THE SACRED

11. Ibid., 196.

12. See *Convorbiri literare*, 1888, and "Les rites de la construction d'après la poésie populaire de l'Europe orientale," in *Revue de l'histoire des religions*, 1902. Cf. also P. Caraman, "Considerații critice asupra genezei și răspândirii baladei Meșterului Manole în Balcani," in *Buletinul Institutului de Filologie Româna*, Iași, 1934, Vol. I.

13. Mus, op. cit., 220.

14. Ibid., 218.

15. Ibid., 226.

16. Ibid., 443ff.

17. *The Labyrinth*(London: 1935).

18. Cf. *Zalmoxis*, Vol. I (1938), 237.

19. Mus, op. cit., 248.

20. Cf. Mircea Eliade, *Yoga. Immortality and Freedom* (New York: Pantheon Books, Inc., for the Bollingen Foundation, 1958), 162ff.

21. Mus, *Barabudur*, 68.

22. Ibid., 94.

23. Ibid., 92.

24. See, in addition to the works cited by Mus, the essential monograph of Uno Holmberg, *Der Baum des Lebens* (Helsinki, 1923) and A. K. Coomaraswamy, *Elements of Buddhist Iconography* (Cambridge: Harvard University, 1935), and Mircea Eliade, *Cosmoloie și alchimie babiloniană* (Bucharest, 1937).

25. Mus, op. cit., 251.

26. Ibid., 419.

27. Ibid., 290.

28. Ibid., 352.

29. Ibid., 378, 382, etc.

30. Pp. 227–49.

31. Jean Filliozat, "La force organique et la force cosmique dans la philosophie médicale de l'Inde et dans la Veda," *Revue philosophique* 123 (1933).

32. Mus, op. cit., 454.

33. Ibid., 456.

34. Ibid., 459.

35. Cf. Mircea Eliade, "Cosmical Homology and Yoga," *Journal of the Indian Society of Oriental Art* (1937), 188–203.

36. Mus, op. cit., 465.

37. Ibid., 500.

38. Ibid., 502.

39. Cf. Eliade, "Jade," cited in note 2.

III/3

From the Portuguese Journal, 1941-1944

Vizeu, Portugal

WE PASS THROUGH A GREAT HALL, formerly the episcopal dining room, with wondrous azulejos (glazed tiles): Alexander the Great, Titus, Vespasian; all the same distinct, glossy blue, which one must learn to like.

From the window the whole city presents itself to us, nestled between forested hills. Oaks, pines, and poplars descend almost to the *campo dos touros*, recently built on the outskirts of Vizeu. Houses of an identical red brick, with roof tiles of red or brown. A few white villas, with windows the color of wet granite, looking lost here in the kingdom of nuances of clay.

How beautiful is this street viewed from the foot of the cathedral, which drops off steeply from one wall to the next, propped up here and there by the foundations or corners of houses, turning abruptly and disappearing in a jumble of rooftops far away in the heart of the city.

* * *

The first thing I observe in the cathedral are the Manueline knots affixed to the arches. This detail seems to awaken my interest. I begin to look in a more friendly way at this vast cathedral with its ascetic nudity, which nevertheless is warm, intimate.

The young man with a proletarian face and hair, dressed shabbily, has been gazing for some time at the altar. Now he kneels, with a trace of shyness, and begins to pray.

There are two women also, old women, who undoubtedly observed us enter; they do not let us out of their sight, following us with a callous craftiness all the while they are reciting their prayers and calmly counting their beads.

The abbot shows us the great stairs which lead to the choir. From

"From the Portuguese Journal, 1941-1943" was first published in *Viața ilustrată*, Vol. X.5 (May 1943), 8–11, and reprinted in *Caiete de dor*, 8 (1954), 16–22. It is translated from the Romanian by Mac Linscott Ricketts.

above, in the choir loft, the cathedral acquires more depth and, seemingly, has a different light. Another atmosphere, a less certain space, as if those granite columns had acquired imperceptibly a strange, musical animation.

But the only truly extraordinary features are the choir chairs. The backs and arms of each are decorated with faces and bodies of a rare, unanticipated beauty: demons, chimeras, goats, dragons, fish, heads of the damned. The hand which has rested for so many years on the back has rounded the profile of the devil, giving it an even more sinister expression. How unsettling is that old man's head, with mouth half open in who knows what lewd sighs, with eyes almost on his forehead, situated so high to enable him to see as much and as quickly as possible, now, on the threshold of death. With incomparable courage and genius has the carver animated the hard smooth wood of the chairs with so many stares and grins and monsters. Seated here, of course, were men full of piety, and piously they sang, caressing the horns of the devil beside them, or fingering the stupidly cynical countenance of a guilty monk, or a chimera with a bold tail, or a lizard risen suddenly from out of the wood, or the dragon which for years has striven to detach itself from the chair back and take refuge elsewhere.

No image is like any other. No expression is repeated on any of those faces that stare at you from all sides. By what miracle have these characters out of fairy tales, myths, and beastiaries, from popular farces and monastic legends, come to exist in the choir loft of the Vizeu Cathedral? And what an unbounded spirit of tolerance, and how much understanding and irony on the part of the clerics who saw these wooden images—as tempting as theological virtues—come to life under the master's chisel!

The choir loft is full of surprises, because over each chair, supporting a chain of flowers and seaweed, there bends the body of a woman with waist bare and arched forward. I wonder what these women can possibly signify, whose abdomens remind me of prehistoric idols, the Venus of Willendorf, or any other Eurasian Magna Mater. Useless as far as I could discover were the pair of angel's wings fastened securely to their backs. The protruding curve of the naked abdomen, the breasts of glorious maturity, and, above all, the smile so feminine, so impenetrable, prevent me from perceiving angelic essences in these bodies!

The Museum Grão-Vasco

There are so many art museums about which I have not written in this notebook, yet I cannot bear to forget the museum of the Great Vasco

Fernandes. Perhaps because, although it is entitled modestly a "regional museum," it is one of the most beautiful in Portugal, and undoubtedly would be the most beautiful if the Janelas Verdas in Lisbon did not possess the triptich of Nuno Gonzalves.

To this Vasco Fernandes there are attributed so many canvasses that for a long time modern critics believed it was a matter of a myth. Recently, however, his historical reality was definitively validated. And in this museum—located in a building of the sixteenth century—there have been assembled his principal paintings together with canvasses of other artists of the North and with numerous other precious things, from a marvelous Byzantine pectoral cross to a curious collection of modern water colors and gouaches.

That which troubles me in all Vasco's paintings is not the realism with which he treats his subjects—although this realism, in itself, is full of mystery—but the *ugliness* of his personages. From the Savior in "The Baptism" to the soldiers and the Pharisees in the extraordinary "Calvary," Vasco's countenances reflect the same great, embittered ugliness. There are only two exceptions, to which I shall return. But I approach each painting individually and I find the genius of Vasco being expressed in ugliness, as if it were a predestined spiritual dimension for him. Take, for instance, "Calvary," the great canvas that greets you when you enter the museum. It is, undoubtedly, one of the masterpieces of Portuguese painting—for its boldness, its conception, its skillful execution. But how much ugliness there is in those twenty-five persons! What twisted faces, what opaque grins distort the countenances of the Pharisees [sic] who are casting lots for the Savior's garments; what a bloated profile, like that of a rapacious merchant, has the centurion in the foreground, wrapped in his red mantle, and how much beastial self-satisfaction is in the eyes of all those witnesses to the Passion! From the unrepentant thief writhing on the cross, soldiers with asymmetrical faces bursting with mediocrity and villainy, Longinus on his white horse, the lance almost at the point of leaving his hand—the miracle, evidently, is taking place in his soul; to the holy women in the foreground, crowded around the Lord's Mother who is fainting with melancholy hands clasped—all these images partake of the same ugliness: bitter, sinister, or pathetic, sated with suffering or exhausted by successful efforts. The ugliness of Vasco's personages is not always caricatural or demonical like the faces painted by Bosch or Breughel. In most instances it is only the result of a long, drawn out labor, a lack of grace, an opacity, the callousness which a hard life gives one, the longing for the good life, the craving for power.

The same view has determined also those innumerable other images,

with the exception of St. Sebastian—surrounded by hideous execu-
tioners—and of St. Peter. Almost everyone considers this painting of
St. Peter as Vasco's masterpiece. It is, at any rate, the most popular. The
throne on which the saint is seated looks like the immense baldaquin of
a despot. His imperial mantle falls in rich folds onto a mosaic floor.
Bathed in gold, wearing a sumptuous tiara, holding in his left hand—
which is resting on an open book—the enchanted key to Paradise and
peacefully raising his hand in an apostolic benediction of awful simplicity—St. Peter is represented to us here as a true Cosmocrator.
Seemingly never has a painter lavished more genius, more gold, more
rich colors in order to pay homage to the victory of the Roman Catholic
Church in the august image—a little weary but nonetheless apostolic—of
St. Peter. Everything here shows him as the true ruler of the world, the
Universal Monarch who imposes his laws and ordinances everywhere.
And if I were not tempted by other reflections on this art, so full of
secrets and maritime discoveries, what an excellent excuse this would be
for meditation on the archaic symbolism of Melchizedek, the Priest-
King, the Universal Monarch, the Chakravartin who stands at the center
of the earth and turns the Wheel, and through whom all things are possible and obtain their being.

* * *

Vasco Fernandes, who depicts ordinary people, saints and even
Jesus as he sees them in his fellow citizens, whose faces are marked by
the rigors of Atlantic voyages—is the most bitter of realists. But this
realism, which characterizes the entire contemporary Portuguese school,
also is a creation, together with a great many others, of the spirit of the
era of maritime discoveries. Nothing is further from the graphics of the
Renaissance than this Portuguese style which—perhaps before the
Dutch and in any event independent of them—discovered realism in art.
The canon of classical Mediterranean beauty, with difficulty reactualized
by the Italian Renaissance through humanism and education in the classical taste, was never popularized in Portugal. The age of maritime
discoveries created here a different canon: that of the Atlantic, of the *mar
tenebrosum*. The Manueline style, with all its secrets, with exotic and
maritime influences which strike the eye and disturb, is the most perfect
manifestation of that canon.

But equally interesting and suggestive is the realism of the Portuguese painters of the sixteenth century because all these artists were
contemporaries of the inconceivable efforts expended for crossing the
oceans and discovering new worlds. Many of them lived in the colonies
along the African coast. There they viewed new landscapes, alien faces;

they were introduced into dangerous geographies; they knew a harsh life; at every step they encountered death and the terrible diseases of the Orient; they lived the hard life of seamen . . . and they saw, above all, men scowling, exerting themselves in exhausting efforts, locked in a discouraging struggle with the unknown: men overworked, drained dry, drunk with glory, vice and the sense of power—in a word, *ugly* men. The harshness and beastiality of the faces painted by Vasco Fernandes were those he met everywhere on his contemporaries. He had no chance to glimpse the seraphic, contemplative, Mediterranean beauties of the Italian Renaissance. He had no way of training his spirit to be able to perceive those calm beauties. The brief intervals of Portuguese creativity were always parallel with expeditions.

* * *

Another great painter, contemporary with Grão Vasco: "Maestre do Retabulo da Sé de Viseu," as he is called until his name can be identified, has a whole *oeuvre* collected here. The influences of maritime discoveries are, in the case of this Maestre do Retabulo, also quite evident. One of his best known paintings, "The Adoration of the Magi," portrays a Brazilian Indian as the black king who comes to worship at the Savior's manger. That it is an Indian of Brazil there can be no mistake, since he wears, as he prepares to kneel, a variegated costume, with rings and a string of pearls at his throat, with multicolored feathers around his head, and with a wooden spear in his hand. Undoubtedly, this is the forerunner of exoticism in European painting, the prototype of the "noble savage" which, for over two centuries, was to obsess the imagination of Continental writers and moralists.

Portugal can be proud of being the precursor of exoticism and the whole Romantic literature. Was not Camoens the first European to praise an Indian slave, Barabar, as "the captive who held [him] captive?" The poem "Aquela cattiva," in which the dark color of the skin (*pretidao de amor*) is exalted to the detriment of blond beauty, opened the road to a whole exotic literature, promoted triumphantly by Romanticism. It was not for nothing that Chateaubriand liked "Aquela cattiva," in which he thought he found validated the passion for the non-European, unsophisticated beauty, belonging to geographies which his fervor and that of all the other Romantics assimilated to Paradise.

Thus begin all the currents later to become popular, thus begins every mass fashion and every mass snobbery, whether that of a great poet or of a great painter. The fashion, which began to be popular after 1920, of the bronze, swarthy beauty, the fashion which forced the white Continental youth to "negritize" himself or at least to "bronze" himself by any means possible, is a serious deviation from classical Mediterranean and Nordic canons of beauty which laud blond Hellen and the beautiful maidens with golden hair, Blanchefleur and Margareta. It is true that the mode of swarthy skin invaded Europe simultaneously with Negro music and jazz. But its origins are in Romanticism and in the *pretidao de amor* of Camoens. Several hundreds of years were necessary before it would be accepted by the elite of Europe and America, and be promoted by art, philosophy, and sports on both continents. The "revolt against white skin" is, of course, a complex phenomenon. There can be identified in it also proletarian elements, the revolt against aristocracy and classical canons. But what is the "proletariat" of the admirable dreams of the last century if not *le bon sauvage* of Rousseau multiplied into a collectivity? And is there not some connection between the apology for the "primitive" of the eighteenth and nineteenth centuries, and the messianism elaborated by Socialist doctrinairians in the past hundred years?

Part IV:

Literature and the Sacred

IV/1

Folkloric Themes and Artistic Creations

ANY INTELLIGENT PERSON who investigates the productions of Romanian artists and writers of so-called "folk inspiration" must recognize their general mediocrity. The Brumărescu style in graphic and decorative art, the Rodica style in drama (from Alecsandri to *Chemarea Codrului*), the Mihail Lungeanu style in narrative literature (representing many uncreative elements from Sămănătorism)—all these are well known, and, fortunately the Romanian elite have moved beyond them.

The cause for this lamentable failure is not hard to grasp. "Folk inspiration" was manufactured in a mechanical and exterior way. Folkloric motifs were copied, the rhythm of folk poetry (the *vilă* genre) was reproduced; but all these were *dead forms*. Folk poetry, folk dances, and national costumes—all these are perfect expressions of a certain form of collective life. And as such, being perfect expressions in themselves and the definitive realizations of that life, they cannot serve as the source of inspiration for other artistic realizations, they cannot play the role of *themes*. The "Miorița," perfect as it is, cannot fructify a poetic inspiration. Anything written in the rhythm and vocabulary of the "Miorița" would be a pastiche. In order to create something in the "Miorița style," you would have to pass beyond the forms of folk poetry and seek to adapt yourself to the source from which the "Miorița" sprang. Dan Botta has attempted this poetic technique in "Cantilenă," and he has succeeded.

But what is this source from which popular poetry, graphic art, choreography, and architecture has arisen? What is the living source which nourishes the entirety of folkloric productions? It is the "fantastic presence," an irrational experience, nourished for ages by a certain common life. Precisely this "fantastic presence," this irrational element, was overlooked by those who were inspired by folk art. They "interpreted" folkloric themes, they sought for "symbols" and "characters,"

"Folkloric Themes and Artistic Creations" was first published in *Rampa* XX.5693 (1937), 1; and reprinted in *Insula lui Euthanasius* (Bucharest: Fundatia Regale pentru Litteratură și Artă, 1943), 370–374. It is translated from the Romanian by Mac Linscott Ricketts.

they attempted to be "original" by inverting perspectives and values. They made the dragon into a regular man, they turned Făt Frumos (Prince Charming) into a kindly cynic, and Ileana Consinzeana they converted into a demimonde. They wanted to "interpret" folklore, without being aware of the sterility and superficiality of this operation. Inspiration from folkloric themes has nothing to do with originality. All that a modern artist can do with respect to themes is to deepen them, rediscovering the irrational source which gave them birth. Through interpretation and the search for symbols the irrational character of folklore is lost, and hence also its universal elements.

In other cases, artists and writers have not interfered at all with the folk materials with which they were working. They have simply brought them onto the stage, into books, or into graphic works. The results have been appalling: because they were no longer creations, but pastiches. They were perfect—and therefore dead—folk forms, reproduced under the name of modern authors. Romanian artists and writers were blinded by the brilliance of the many great folk products (the "Miorița," *doina*, dance, costume, decorations) and they tried to imitate them. But one never imitates forms, expressions, and realizations; one imitates, if anything, the technique and the source. Now the source was precisely the "fantastic presence" of which we spoke, and the technique was a magical one of a creation in the depths, of a penetrating into the dark and fertile zones of the folk spirit.

Until Lucian Blaga, there did not exist a single Romanian drama inspired by folklore. And this despite the fact that the Legend of Master Manole had been staged many times. But all those who reworked this legend strove to give it an "original inspiration." Now, what constitutes the pure charm of this theme is the legend itself—don't search for symbols or interpretations! The legend by itself "realizes" that fantastic, irrational presence; it alone, and not symbols thought out by individual effort, introduces us into a folkloric universe in which the inorganic world possesses an animate life and laws identical with those of the inorganic world; where houses and churches are living beings which can last only if a human life is sacrificed to them, so that from its blood and soul they will live forever.

And what ordinarily becomes of Master Manole on the stage? I happened to attend an insipid performance where the poor Master posed problems of conscience to himself (as if his individual conscience constituted the drama of his destiny), and he himself sought to find the "symbolic meaning" of the sacrifice. The author of this play set out from an erroneous assumption: that because the story of Manole is well known, new "angles" and symbols have to be discovered. This is a rationalization which has nothing to do with the legend itself, because it is not the anecdote that counts, but the fantastic presence in the legend as it unfolds. Greek dramas and mysteries were all based on legends known even to children. They evoked an emotional response simply by their dramatic unfolding, because only then was the "fantastic" in them realized. It is like a game that you know, and yet it is new every time you play it, because *experience*, not formal knowledge, constitutes the "fantastic" of the game.

There are certain themes in our folk literature that are extraordinarily rich, from the dramatic point of view. For instance, the Gate, which plays the role in Romanian folk life of a magical structure that watches over all the major acts of an individual's life. The first passing under the gateway means an entrance into life—the real life outside. The gate watches over marriage, and under the gateway the dead man is carried solemnly toward his eternal dwelling place. It is, then, a return to the first world; the circle is closed, and the gate remains in the background with a younger man, to watch over other births, other marriages, other deaths. Think how marvelous it would be to see a play whose action unfolds under the shadow of a gate! The simple presence of the gate would lift the dramatic action well above the plane of everyday consciousness. By means of modern techniques of stage management, the sensation of dreaming, of the supernatural, of the fantastic could easily be realized. And in this collective sensation the words would be more impressive and associations would penetrate more deeply. The individual would participate not only with his diurnal consciousness, but he would participate in the whole drama with all the stages of sleep, all the powers of dreaming, all that subconscious, latent life from which our great works are born and which is present in every decisive act of our lives. . . .

How many folkloric themes lie at hand for the creation of Romanian "fantastic" dramas! The vigil for the dead, children's games (which are remnants of initiatory ceremonies and agricultural rituals), St. Andrew's Eve, the summer solstice, the mystery of the smelting of precious metals—and many more. Each of these themes leads us toward the eternally creative source: the "fantastic presence." Without this presence, any "folk inspiration is a simple pastiche.

I V / 2

Marthe Bibesco and the Meeting of Eastern and Western Literature

[MY DEAR COLLEAGUES,

You have given me a great honor by inviting me to join as prestigious an institution as the Royal Academy of French Language and Literature.[1] However, I must confess that this honor is unmerited. Circumstances being what they were, unpredictable and unalterable, I discovered Paris at the age of thirty-eight after I had already known part of Europe and Asia, and after having lived for three years in India, one year in England, and four years in Portugal. And I had begun to write in French after having published some ten volumes in Romanian, and a number of studies in English and Italian. Certainly as for all Romanians of my generation, French was my second language; but it was rather a language of culture and communication like the *Koine* of the Hellenistic era or the Latin of the Middle Ages. I came too late to France to be able to dream and to imagine in French, in other words to become a writer of the French language. I admire too much the literary genius of my friends Eugene Ionesco and E. M. Cioran to have dared to follow their example. Thus, I was content to write only my philosophic essays, and works on Orientalism and the History of Religions in French. But I have continued to do so even after having accepted the Chair in the History of Religions at the University of Chicago in 1957. It is probably this belief in the unequalled virtues of the French Language, and the faithfulness to a heritage dear to all Romanians, that you my dear colleagues, wished to honor in inviting me to be counted among you.

Sir, I am grateful to you for the flattering portrait which you have just painted. In listening to you, I thought of your fine studies of certain

"Marthe Bibesco and the Meeting of Eastern and Western Literature" was first presented to the Royal Academy of French Language and Literature on 9 February 1977. It was originally published as "Reception de M. Mircea Eliade, Discours" in *Académie Royale de Langue et Littérature Françaises* (Brussels, 1977), 16–26. It is translated from the French by Diane Apostolos-Cappadona and Frederica Adelman.

contemporary writers. How could I have imagined that you would have examined my own books with the same care, and that one day I would have the honor of being welcomed graciously by you into this illustrious company?

You have recalled Father Teilhard de Chardin's effort to surpass the "provincialism" which menaces Western Christianity; in effect, he insisted not only on the universal character of the Church, but also on the "cosmic" vision of Christianity. Teilhard's passionate interest in scientific research revealed the religious value which he accorded Life and the material. The illustrious paleontologist shared the same message as the scriptural tradition: he considered the Cosmos, life and the human race as divine works. Truly, Teilhard was not aware that analogous beliefs were somewhat apparent throughout the world, among archaic peoples as well as in evolved cultures. It is precisely this experience of cosmic sacrality that characterizes the innumerable religions known as "primitive" and "pagan." I dedicated part of my life to the study of these religious forms, both archaic and oriental. I was amply rewarded when I finally understood the fundamental unity of the human spirit, that which allows it to be caught up in the infinite religious creations from the Stone Age to the present day. At this moment in our history characterized by the "planetization" of culture, it seems to me that the History of Religions is called upon to play a privileged role; it can communicate a certain confidence to the activities of the human spirit and even a certain optimistic vision of the future.

You have also evoked my effort to conduct the work of an Orientalist and a Historian of Religions with that of a writer. In effect, I belong to a cultural tradition which did not accept the incompatibility between scientific investigation and literary activity. Several great Romanian scholars, Cantemir, Hasdeu, Iorga, Parvan, had also been accomplished writers; Mihail Eminesco, the most illustrious Romanian poet, was also an original thinker and one of the most erudite among his contemporaries. In my own work, I believe that there exists a structural analogy between scientific work and the literary imagination. It is not necessary to tell you how happy I was to read this statement by the famous American physicist, Jacob Bronowski. "The step by which a new axiom is addressed cannot itself be mechanized. It is a free play of the mind, an invention outside the logical process. This is the central act of imagination in science, and it is, in all respects, like any similar act in literature."]

* * *

A little before her death, it is said of Princess Marthe Bibesco that she was the final witness of "definitive" Europe. In fact, she had known the last Tsar and all the sovereigns of Europe; she counted among her friends King Ferdinand and Queen Marie of Romania as well as the Countess Anna de Noailles, Marcel Proust, Paul Claudel, and Abbé Mungnier; she not only frequented the salons of Parisian writers, but also knew politicians, great military leaders, artists, scholars and princes of the Church throughout Europe, England and the United States. However, Marthe Bibesco was much more than "the final witness of definitive Europe." Rather, she was a mirror of history, and not only contemporary history. Romanian, French, Greek and Italian blood flowed in her veins, and through a long effort of memory, she recalled the story of all the families, the principalities, and the peoples of Europe who had shared in the creativity of her ancestors.

Marthe Bibesco dedicated the last thirty years of her life to preparing a multi-volume work, *La Nymphe Europe*.[2] She confessed to have received inspiration from her ancestors to write "the life of an idea across a family, to search for a lost unity, the pursuit of the Nymph, a word which signifies in Greek a wife." She specifies: "My field of vision extended before me: it was a torn Europe, divided against herself. . . ." Thus, it is in this shattered Europe that she had been condemned to live by "the previsions and the prophecies of her ancestors." But, Princess Bibesco adds, "Before testifying, it was necessary to know my genesis, to place in context this heredity of desperate ones who weighed me down with an almost unbearable force." On one other occasion she returned to the urgent nature of her task: "I drew my ancestry from a family where one and all had written and built, left legible and visible traces of their stay on earth. It was for me to decipher them—since it was not known nor was no longer known—in the present where each generation lived."[3]

When she decided to undertake this gigantic work, Marthe Bibesco was already a celebrated author. Her books, first *Isvor: Country of Willows;*[4] *The Green Parrot;*[5] *The Eight Paradises: Travel Pictures in Persia, Asia Minor, and Constantinople;*[6] *Catharine-Paris;*[7] and *Images d'Épinal,*[8] had simultaneously gained public approval and critical admiration. It is this literary *oeuvre* which constitutes Marthe Bibesco's great merit, and justifies her place in the history of modern French culture. However, I have chosen to concentrate upon a lesser known but equally important aspect of her work in order to learn her interpretation of the European spiritual tradition. As we will see, Princess Bibesco anticipated several discoveries of contemporary historiography, notably the inestimable value of popular cultures, and to dare a barbarism, the redemptive function of European historiography, in the sense that all true historic research leads to the consciousness of the cultural and spiritual unity of Europe.

It is in her book *Isvor: Country of Willows* that Marthe Bibesco reveals the rich and profound religiosity of an archaic civilization, that of the Romanian peasants. As for the redemptive function of European historiography, it would be necessary to await the publication of the other five or six volumes of *La Nymphe Europe* in order to understand all the implications. Happily we have access to three large annotated volumes of her correspondence with Abbé Mungnier, *La Vie d'une amitié*, in which Princess Bibesco constantly refers to the structures and intent of her *magnum opus*. It is moreover in this admirable correspondence that one discovers Princess Bibesco's true personality in all its complexity, and that one is able to grasp the exemplary value of her destiny. Since this descendant of Byzantium and of a Napoleonic general, this practicing Catholic raised in the tradition of the Eastern Church, this rich princess who lived half her life among the poor and the peasants, this linguist who wished to learn all the languages spoken by her ancestors and their adversaries, anticipates in a certain sense an exemplary model for the European of the future.

Later recalling the preparation and the writing of her book on popular Romanian culture, Marthe Bibesco wrote,

> *Isvor* was inspired by daily life in the villages, by the traditional rites observed in a millennium of existences by the peasants of this forested domain of the mountain where I thought that I had come to live forever immediately after my marriage. This book was made from notes which I had taken daily; it does not contain a single story which is untrue, a single invented episode. All of the experiences that are in it truly happened to me; I was deeply attached to these people, to this life where they lived as singularly isolated in time as I myself was in space. And I loved this country; and this people, that I had just discovered. [9]

In fact, Marthe Bibesco had discovered a very old rural civilization, with its roots in the neolithic but enriched by later cultural influences: Greek, Celtic, Romanian and Slavic. *Isvor* can be compared to the texts of certain American anthropologists which became best sellers in the last ten years. The work presents the life of a peasant society in all of its complexity and depth. In pages which have not lost their freshness, Marthe Bibesco evokes with precision, delicacy and intelligence the ritual cycle of a Romanian village, the customs, legends and tasks appropriate to each season. Many times she is struck by their archaicism. With respect to the funerary cake made of baked corn and pounded nuts in honey, Marthe Bibesco adds a note: "The same recipe is given by Fustel de Coulanges in *La Cité Antique* describing the funeral feasts of the Romans." [10] In fact, it refers to a much older ritual, already evidenced in Aegean protohistory.

With the help of her guide and confidente, the old peasant woman

Outza, the Princess discovers the vestiges of an immemorial and secret culture, rarely described by ethnologists and folklorists. I shall cite only one example—that of the Emperor of the Ants to whom the peasant women appealed in order to obtain his protection for their cows. The peasant women made the rounds of all the anthills of their country bringing bread and salt; while kneeling down they said to him:

> Great Emperor of the Ants, I wish you good day! I have come to bring you bread and salt. In exchange, I beg you to hear me and to come to my aide! You whose Empire extends to the borders of the seven provinces, you who go where you wish to go, without worrying about which lands belong to you since no one is strong enough to prevent you from going wherever you wish to go, hear my prayer and grant it! Give my little cow, Florica, the manna spread abundantly in your Empire, that the sweetness and the taste of the grasses goes from her tongue to her flanks, from her flanks to her udder, from her udder to my bowl. Amen! [11]

In discovering this prehistoric heritage and in deciphering daily the deep and secret life of the Romanian peasants, Marthe Bibesco no longer doubts their creative possibilities. She wrote,

> Some day attention will be given to this race, till then unnoticed. Out of this country, long grown silent, will be heard the sounds of songs and music. After a thousand years of existence, this race will be born, and men will be astounded as at a prodigy, to learn at last that this race has already known of the universal knowledge.
>   The rejoicings of these people have remained hidden, and no one has celebrated their misfortunes. There are no books of their mythology, and their history is unknown. Yet these men have possessed, more perhaps than others, the genius of myth. . . . [12]

"Is it possible not to love Romania after *Isvor*?" Rainer Marie Rilke wrote to his Romanian translator, Ian Pilat. The poet was certainly fascinated by the destiny of this people who in the midst of the twentieth-century still conserved its immemorial heritage and mythology, although they had lived for a thousand years under the Terror of History; because in this part of Europe, history is essentially limited to invasions, wars and ruins. However, Marthe Bibesco had predicted the impotence of this terror vainly exerted against a people who in order to survive had decided to ignore history, or, as the great Romanian poet and philosopher Lucian Blaga suggested, "to sabotage it." In effect, Marthe Bibesco wrote,

> Perhaps it is because the whole extent of the country is one great road itself, a path of entry, an immense course which humanity followed in its coming. I love this land for its long memory and for its patient subservience. A dried-up river-bed of the flowing peoples, a disused avenue of the world!

She concludes,

> The migrations are over, the voice of their passing is heard no more. Only these quick-winged birds are to be heard, who make their nests on the ground itself, and fly straight up into the air.[13]

This is the key passage of her book; at the same time it is the secret center of her work. In an article which was particularly dear to her, Jerome and Jean Tharaud wrote:

> Princess Bibesco's friends say that she lives after the fashion of the goddess Persephone six months on earth, six months below. They wish to say by this that she leads six months of Parisian life and then during the other six months she pursues a mysterious existence, which they cannot imagine very well, in the Romanian countryside. The book which she published today, *Isvor: Country of Willows*, will astonish them very much by making them discover that those long months when Persephone disappears from their sight, she frequents the most beautiful world: that of legend and popular reveries.[14]

The comparison with Persephone is correct. The Princess lived six months at the very center of history, and during the other six months she participated in a popular culture, a creation of a people who, to return to Lucian Blaga's expression, had sabotaged history. But Marthe Bibesco passionately loved history. Still very young, she had written *Alexander of Asia*.[15] Moreover in the forested domain, she had discovered that of all the great names of the past, the peasants only recalled that of Alexander. "It is of him that they talk when sitting up at nights, and on the great roads in the time of night carting [. . .] It is his history that the story-tellers are asked for. His is the whole History for those who have no remembrance of their own annals."[16]

However, *this* Alexander is not the genial and enigmatic conqueror who has fascinated the historians for twenty-three centuries, but a mythological hero, and precisely the central personality of the novel *Alexandre de Macédoine*. Written during the Hellenistic Age, this little book had been translated into all the European and Oriental languages, and afterwards was orally circulated through popular culture. At the beginning of the century, we had not yet realized that history knew *two* Alexanders: the real person, the Great Conqueror, and the mythological hero who still haunts the popular imagination from the North Sea and the Atlantic Ocean all the way to the Indian Ocean; moreover, one had not yet understood that the two Alexanders were both equally *true*. If she had known it then, Marthe Bibesco would have particularly loved this detail: in penetrating up to the Punjab, Alexander had not only abolished two Empires and a number of city-states; he had also opened India to European influences. After him, communications between India and the West would never again be completely interrupted. And yet, neither Alexander's name nor the history of his fabulous expedition have been retained by the Indian collective memory: no monument, no inscription, no mention in the works written in Sanskrit, or in the vernacular languages. Following a Persian version, the *Roman d'Alexandre* was translated into several Indian languages several centuries after the invasion; it is due to this legendary tale that the Indians had learned of the catastrophe which had radically changed their historic destiny in 25 B.C. Like the Romanians, the Indians had sabotaged History, they had forgotten or ignored personalities and historic events because they were only interested in permanent values and trans-historical significations.

In her later works, it can be said that Marthe Bibesco strove to reunite through integration these two perspectives: that of history proper, and that of exemplary history, i.e., the creation of mythic thought. If she had rewritten her book on Alexander, she would certainly have used the enormous documentation accumulated in the last quarter century, but she would also have tried to learn the profound significance revealed by the mythology which had transfigured the historic personage of the Macedonian into a demi-god, a favored hero of Romanian folklore.

In any case, Marthe Bibesco came to realize more and more the complexity and the mystery of that which one vaguely calls History (with a capital letter). On the other hand, she was persuaded that the sense and the direction of History are sometimes allowed to get caught up in certain events, even if they are deprived of pomp and immediate resonance; on the other hand, she knew that even the most majestic and most significant historic events were reduced to nothingness if their study and understanding did not restore man to God. On 21 March 1939, she wrote to Abbé Mungnier from London:

> As you had taught me to do, I have written all in my notebook, the same evening as the events, and I recommenced writing this morning [. . .] Last evening, Churchill, his collar awkward in his gilded courtdress, had the air of an angry child or of a clown [. . .] During the intermission, I listened to his words [. . .] which were said with the intention of being overheard. His conclusion was: "We shall have war. The British Empire will go hang . . . and I . . . Well, I feel twenty years younger."[17]

Marthe Bibesco understood the gravity of these few sentences: she now knew that England had accepted the war.

But for Princess Bibesco to decipher the profound significance of these historic events also constituted a spiritual exercise, a meditation of a religious order. On 31 December 1925, she confessed to Abbé Mungnier her passion for all that had happened in this world: "I am intoxicated with History, and I wish to share this intoxication with you, this vanity of vanities, which restores one to God by the shortest path."[18] As Marthe Bibesco was to understand it several years later when she began writing *La Nymphe Europe*, this path certainly was not "the shortest." Known as another *Remembrance of Things Past*, but a *Remembrance* appreciably vaster, this monumental work demanded an enormous effort of memory; because like Proust in his novel, Princess Bibesco was simultaneously the main character and the narrator of her ancestor's story. It was *she*, Marthe, who recollected the dramas, the victories, and the dream experiences of her previous "incarnations"; beginning with her first life on an Aegean island in the twelfth-century. Moreover as she wrote to Abbé Mungnier on 28 March 1935, the vocation of her almost millennial past was divided by taking into account geography and not chronology. "A volume for every country which is found on the map of our old continent," she specified.

We can only deplore the interruption of *La Nymphe Europe*. In judging from her correspondence, it is certain that Princess Bibesco considered *La Nymphe Europe* as her most important book, her *magnum opus*. Not only are the dimensions and perspectives that this work opens on Europe's past imposing but its autobiographical character and spiritual fervour are impressive in its recollection of all her previous lives, that is to say the lives of all her ancestors. Marthe Bibesco forced herself to decipher the significance of these destinies to which she considered herself not only heiress but also as the receptacle in which the memory of a race was conserved. We can imagine her enthusiasm in discovering that her ancestors had been engaged "in the service of one single and same idea under two different aspects, the unity of the Churches, the lost unity of Europe." We then understand her passion for history, and the reason why she accorded a redemptive function to historical research. It is through the effort spent in the study of the past and through the understanding of the profound sense of historic events that one acquires, assessed Marthe Bibesco, the consciousness of the fundamental unity of a tradition; under the circumstances, the European tradition fed, through the millennia, at numerous and complementary springs: Oriental, Mediterranean, Romanian, Celto-Germanic.

Princess Bibesco had succeeded in understanding a considerable number of spiritual values and cultural creations, and had succeeded besides in learning the underlying unity of so many historical events, because she had lived and meditated upon her Christian tradition for a long time. It is due to her faith and to her sacramental life that she understood the role of religion for the individual and the importance of

Christianity for the culture of the European peoples. We were not able to know the *real* Marthe Bibesco before the publication of her correspondence with Abbé Mungnier. Because of her worldwide literary success, Marthe Bibesco was awarded acclaim; but as a result she was also envied and furiously slandered. At the time when she went to the ball with Marcel Proust, there were few who suspected that the Princess still nurtured the hope of retiring to a convent.[19] It is one of the merits of Abbé Mungnier to have persuaded her to remain in the world. And it is moreover to Abbé Mungnier that she dedicated her favorite book, *La Nymphe Europe*.

I have alluded to the exemplary destiny of Princess Bibesco. In effect, she, whose roots were immersed in so many countries, cultures, and parallel Christian traditions, had recognized, after having searched all her life, the lost unity of Europe and waited for the eschatological moment of the unity of the Churches. In her youth, Marthe Bibesco exclaimed: "Nothing can make me an exile in France!" But at the twilight of her life, she had finally understood that no where in Europe was she an exile.

NOTES

1. This text represented the presentation of Mircea Eliade as a member of the Royal Academy of French Language and Literature on 19 February 1977. The opening paragraphs of this text have been retained in the style of a "presentation" as the Editor felt they indicated a series of important insights into Eliade's *oeuvre*.

2. Marthe Bibesco, *La Nymphe Europe* (Paris: Plon, 1960).

3. Marthe Bibesco, *La Vie d'une amitié: Ma correspondence avec l'abbé Mungnier, 1911-1944* (Paris: Plon, 1951), tome 2, 23.

4. Marthe Bibesco, *Isvor: Country of Willows* (London: William Heinemann, Ltd., 1924). Original French edition, *Isvor: le pays des saules* (Paris: Plon-Nourritt, 1923), two volumes.

5. Marthe Bibesco, *The Green Parrot* (New York: Harcourt, 1929). Original French edition, *Le perroquet vert* (Paris: B. Grasset, 1924).

6. Marthe Bibesco, *The Eight Paradises: Travel Pictures in Persia, Asia Minor, and Constantinople* (New York: Dutton, 1923). Original French edition, *Les Huits Paradises: Perse, Asie Minuere, Constantinople* (Paris: Hachette, 1911, 3rd edition).

7. Marthe Bibesco, *Catharine-Paris* (New York: Harcourt, 1928). Original French edition, *Catharine-Paris* (Paris: B. Grasset, 1927).

8. Marthe Bibesco, *Images d'Épinal* (Paris: Plon, 1915).

9. *La Vie d'une amitié*, tome 2, 72.

10. *Isvor*, 47.

11. *Isvor*, tome 1, 225–226. [This passage is not included in the English translation. All other passages quoted from *Isvor* have been quoted from the English translation.]

12. *Isvor*, 105.

13. Ibid., 234.

14. *La Vie d'une amitié*, tome 2, 91.

15. Marthe Bibesco, *Alexander of Asia* (New York: William Heinemann, 1935). Original French edition, *Alexandre Asiatique, ou l'histoire du plus grand bonheur possible* (NP, 1912).

16. *Isvor*, 182.

17. *La Vie d'une amitié*, tome 3, 398–399.

18. Ibid., tome 2, 222.

19. See Marthe Bibesco, *Marcel Proust at the Ball* (New York: Citadel, 1956). Original French edition, *Au Bal avec Marcel Proust* (Paris: Gallimard, 1956 [1928]).

IV/3

Eugene Ionesco and "The Nostalgia for Paradise"

ASKED BY A JOURNALIST what he was doing to eliminate social inequalities and political injustice, Eugene Ionesco answered: "I don't pretend that my plays are going to save the world!" As he made explicit in that interview, and on many other occasions, Ionesco does not believe that the goal of an artistic creation is to foster political education. On the contrary, in his opinion, a politically oriented theater, even that of Brecht, becomes an instrument of propaganda and, in the last analysis, a new dogma no less tolerant and tyrannical than the old dogmatic systems.

However, Ionesco is the first to deplore the fact that the theater cannot "save the world"; meaning salvation, in the *religious*, and not the *political*, sense of the word. He would be happy to know that there is a "soteriological theater," able to communicate revelation, and thus modify the human condition. But he doubts that such a "soteriological theater" will ever be possible. Instead, he hopes that his plays will help his contemporaries to forget, at least for a few hours, the oppressive "historical moment," and thus to break through the automatisms, the clichés and the ideological opacities of everyday life. In other words, he is anxious to see the spectators recover the blissful spontaneity of their own imaginations. He repeatedly emphasized the decisive role of imagination, not only for what is usually called mental health, but, what is more important, for the new quality of life brought forth by an active and creative imagination. "Imagining is building, it's making, creating a world. . . . By first creating worlds one can 're-create' the real world in the image of the invented, imaginary worlds."[1]

Most of the products of imagination have a "religious" significance.

"Eugene Ionesco and 'The Nostalgia for Paradise'" was originally published as "Eugene Ionesco and 'La Nostaglie du Paradis'" in *Two Faces of Ionesco*, edited by R. C. Lamont and M. G. Friedman (Troy, NY: Whitson Publishing Company, 1978), 22–30, and is reprinted here by permission.

That is to say, they have related to primordial *excellence* a religious dimension.[2] A historian of religions cannot fail to notice the variety of religious symbols in Ionesco's works. Of course, a number of them are employed outside of their traditional settings; nevertheless, their original intentionality is not completely lost. Such is the case, for example, for symbols of ascension and flight, or those of "paradise" and the labyrinth. It is interesting to note that Ionesco places the labyrinth in opposition to "paradise." For him, the labyrinth is an exemplary image of Hell.

> The labyrinth is hell; it's time; it's space; it's infinity. Whereas paradise on the other hand is a spherical world, a total world with "everything in it," neither finitude nor infinity, a place in which the finite–infinite problem simply does not arise.[3]

The traditional religious symbolism of the labyrinth is unusually complex and discourages any hasty formulation. Nevertheless, the "infernal" elements recovered by Ionesco are indisputable. But in his personal understanding of the labyrinth one misses another important factor, namely its initiatory function. Entering and successfully traversing a labyrinth, without being lost in its mazes, is tantamount to a *descensus ad infernos* followed by a triumphant return to our world; thus constituting a successful initiation.[4] For Eugene Ionesco, the labyrinth represents exclusively an *Inferno* accumulating all the terrors of spatial and temporal infinity ("it's time; it's space; it's infinity"). Standing in contrast to Paradise, a "spherical world," a totality in which finitude and infinity are definitively transcended.

It is difficult to specify to what extent this *description* of the paradisical beatitude was influenced by Ionesco's readings of the Byzantine mystics.[5] Already as a young man, in Romania, he had perused certain mystical and theological authors,[6] and in France, after 1940, he considerably widened his horizon. He read not only Pseudo-Areopagytus, and some of the Greek Fathers, but also Cusanus, Buber, the Upanishads, many Buddhists texts and *The Tibetan Book of the Dead*. Occasionally one can discover in certain plays the effects of his readings. Thus, for instance, *Exit the King* reflects the powerful impressions left by *The Tibetan Book of the Dead* and the *Brhadaranyaka-Upanishad*. One cannot really speak of "influences," though, but only of the renewal of Ionesco's imaginary universes through his creative encounter with exotic and traditional religious worlds.

Whatever might *have been the impact* of Ionesco's theological readings on his description of "Paradise," there can be no doubt about the authenticity of his personal experience. His "Paradise" was the time spent in the country, at La Chapelle-Athenaise, when he was eight, nine and ten years old. In his Diaries, and in the *Conversations* with Claude Bonnefoy, he repeatedly evokes that lost beatitude. "At La Chapelle-Athenaise, time didn't exist. I just lived in the present. And living was a joy, a state of grace. [. . .] A kind of completeness. A symbolization, if you'll forgive the word, of paradise. La Chapelle-Athenaise is still for me the image of a paradise lost."[7] Leaving La Chapelle-Athenaise was, for him, equivalent to "being forced to leave my paradise."[8]

A happy childhood is frequently remembered as a "paradisic" existence, but what is noteworthy in Ionesco's case is the significant role played by these early experiences both in his life and in his *oeuvre*. More or less unconsciously, he was somehow able to recover, at least in part, and only for a few blessed moments, that primordial beatitude, the lost Paradise of La Chapelle-Athenaise. For him, those were "days of fullness, happiness, and sunlight."[9] Ultimately, Ionesco relates the ideas of perfection, serenity, clarity, and beatitude to a rather mysterious presence of light. The first French authors he admired—Valery Larbaud, Charles du Bos, Flaubert, Alain Fournier—all have in common a "style of light." He specifies: "In all of them I felt this same presence of light," that is to say the light of his "own childhood vision."[10] He confesses, however, that he does not know what corresponds to this light. "Really, I don't know what this light corresponds to. Obviously one mustn't immediately give it a mystical significance, but I should like to know its psychological significance, to know why I need it, to know why, every time I have a feeling of light, I become happy."[11]

Indeed, for him, "light is the transfigured world." Such an expression brings to mind the idiom of the Byzantine mystics, particularly the Hesychasts and Gregory Palamas in discussing the Light of the Transfiguration on Mount Tabor.[12] But for Eugene Ionesco this "miracle" is part of our world: "It is, for instance, the glorious transformation, in the springtime, of that muddy path from my childhood. Suddenly, the world takes on an inexplicable beauty."[13] Such a "transfiguration" may occur any time and in any circumstances. He relates an experience, when he received the visit of a friend, a pessimist, who was depressed by the meaninglessness of life, and the ugliness and dreariness of everything, including Ionesco's apartment. "At the time, I was living in a ground floor flat on the Rue Claude Terrasse. My daughter was still only a baby and we didn't have much room, we'd hung her nappies up to dry inside the house." And suddenly he noticed a glorious illumination of every object in the room. "For it had suddenly seemed to me that those nappies on the washing line had an unexpected beauty . . . a brilliant, virgin world. I had succeeded in seeing them through a painter's eye, seeing them in terms of light. From that moment, everything seemed beautiful, everything was transformed."[14]

Commenting on Claude Bonnefoy's observation, that in his *oeuvre* the theme of light is opposed to what may be called the theme of sinking in the mud and slime,[15] Ionesco admitted that these two contradictory themes reflect his antagonistic modes of being: "I feel either very heavy or very light, or else too heavy or too light." For him, "the theme of the wretchedness of man's condition is perhaps experienced [. . .] as weight and thickness."[16] In contrast, as we have seen, beatitude is connected to light and spontaneity.

His decisive experience, though, which he utilized in *The Killer*, took place in a Romanian provincial town, when he was 17 or 18 years old. The description deserves to be quoted integrally.

> It was in June, around mid-day. I was walking down one of the streets in this very quiet town. Suddenly it seemed to me that the world was both retreating and moving closer at the same time, or rather that the world had moved away from me, that I was in another world, more mine than the old one, and infinitely more light; the dogs in the courtyards were barking as I passed by in the street, but it was as though their barking had suddenly become melodious, or fainter, as if it were muffled; it seemed to me that the sky had become extremely dense, that the light was almost palpable, that the houses had a brightness, I had never seen before, an unaccustomed brightness, free from the weight of custom. It's very difficult to define it; perhaps the easiest thing to say is that I felt an enormous joy, I felt that I had understood something fundamental; that something very important had happened to me. At that moment, I said to myself: "I'm not afraid of death anymore." It felt like an absolute, a definitive truth. I told myself that later on, when I was sad or worried, I would need only to remember this moment to discover joy and serenity again. It sustained me for quite some time. Now I've forgotten that moment. Oh, of course, I can still remember it a little, but it's just . . . well, just a theoretical memory . . . I remember those moments because I've repeated them to myself, wanted to keep them alive in my memory. But I've never managed to "live" them again. Yes, it was a kind of miraculous moment that lasted for three or four minutes. It seemed to me there was no longer such a thing as weight. I could work with great steps, with huge leaps, without getting tired. And then, suddenly, the world became itself again, and it still is, or almost. The washing that was drying in the yards of the little provincial houses no longer looked like banners, like pennants, but simply like old washing. The world had fallen back into a hole.[17]

Without being a literal recovery of the "paradisic" state of his childhood at La Chapelle-Athenaise, this experience can be considered equally important for Ionesco's life and *oeuvre*. The encounter with the light is accompanied by a sense of joy and serenity, the certitude of eternity ("I'm not afraid of death anymore"), the revelation of the absolute truth and the impression of deliverance from the law of gravity. Experiences of light occur frequently in the history of different mysticisms as well as in religiously ignorant, or indifferent, individuals. It is particularly the latter case that is relevant for our topic. A number of books and monographs are devoted to such "spontaneous" (or "natural") experiences of light.[18] Although a great morphological variety, all these "spontaneous" light experiences contain some basic features in common: they come suddenly and unexpectedly; they are accompanied by the feeling of joy, happiness, peace and confidence, or by an intellectual illumination quite impossible to describe; they reveal a fundamental unity, purpose and meaning of the world and of human existence, an *Urgund* where contraries are reconciled. Some experiences may give the impression of taking place outside—or beyond—time; others seem to develop in time, the light continuously changing its colors (for instance, from bluish smoke to a violet haze and finally to a blinding golden incandescence).[19] Another common element is the sense of being born again, of *incipit vita nova*, of an "existential mutation" or of being "saved." And what is more, in many cases the subject's life was radically different and permanently transformed.

We will not discuss in any detail the differences, which are important, between these "spontaneous," "natural" light experiences, and those of the mystics belonging to various religious traditions. There is not only a question of *intensity* (for instance, the dazzling light that blinded Saint Paul on the road to Damascus, or the terrific vision of Arjuna in the *Bhagavad-gita*), but also one of dissimilarity between the light revealed as divine, personal presence, and the light which discloses an *impersonal holiness*. But we do not need to extend this comparative analysis. What should be noted is that ultimately each "mystic"[20] values his experience of the light according to his own theological (or philosophical) presuppositions. Nevertheless, whatever the nature and intensity of a light experience, such an experience always evolves into a religious experience: as it brings an individual out of his profane universe or historical situation, and projects him into an entirely different world—"transcendent" and "holy." Whatever his previous ideological conditioning, the light produces a break in the subject's existence, revealing to him—or making clearer than before—the world of spirit, of the sacred and of true freedom.[21]

These few remarks may help to estimate the role of light experiences and light symbolism in Ionesco's personal life and in his *oeuvre*. From the "paradise" of La Chapelle-Athenaise, to the sudden irradiance of a dusty street in a Romanian provincial town, to the illumination of that crowded room in *rue* Claude Terrasse, there is a secret but impressive continuity.

Eugene Ionesco could not doubt that *there is* Being, absolute truth, beatitude and freedom (in every sense of this term). He never emphasized the religious dimensions of his experiences and nostalgias, but in his conversations with Claude Bonnefoy he did not disregard a religious vocabulary ("paradise," "transfigured world," "original sin," "resurrection," etc.). In a certain way he feels, and he behaves, *naturaliter*, like a *homo religiosus*. The creative imagination, the "play" and what has been called his "humor and fantasy" are in the last analysis equivalent expressions of that prodigious *freedom*, which is not only political, social and spiritual, but also includes deliverance from the physical sense of weightiness. It is probably this profound understanding of the "religious" dimension of freedom—the freedom experienced in the fabulous and inexhaustible "play"[22] of the imagination—that explains Ionesco's serene detachment from any institutionalized form of religion.

NOTES

1. Claude Bonnefoy, *Conversations with Eugene Ionesco,* translated by Jan Dawson (New York: Holt, Rhinehart and Winston, 1971), 92. Original French edition, *Entretiens avec Eugene Ionesco* (Paris: Editions Pierre Belfond, 1966).

2. Eugene Ionesco speaks of "archetypes," using this term both in the neo-platonic (paradigms, exemplary models) and in the Jungian sense (structures of the collective unconscious).

3. Bonnefoy, *Conversations,* 39.

4. The initiatory function of the labyrinth has been acutely analyzed by W. F. Jackson Knight, *Cumean Gates. A Reference in the Sixth Aeneid to Initiation Pattern* (Oxford: Oxford University Press, 1936). Cf. also Paolo Santarcangeli, *Il libro dei labirinti. Storia di un mito e di un simbolo* (Florence: Vallecchi, 1967).

5. He states that among the books which influenced him are those of the Byzantines of the 12th, 13th and 14th centuries, and the Hesychasts; cf. Bonnefoy, *Conversations,* 28.

6. Like so many Romanian writers of his generation, Eugene Ionesco was, in the '30s, attracted by the Byzantine spirituality and the Eastern Orthodox traditions. For a number of intellectuals, such preoccupations were part of their endeavor to connect modern Romanian culture to its "autochthenous," i.e., "oriental" roots, in order to counterbalance the powerful influence of Western, particularly French, culture. However, by 1936–38, this concern for the autochthonous tradition became an ideological slogan of the right wing movements, and Ionesco lost his interest in the "reactualization" of Eastern Orthodox spirituality.

7. Bonnefoy, *Conversations,* 12.

8. Ibid., 16. When Ionesco contrasts the labyrinth to Paradise, "where the problem of finitude-infinity does not arise," (ibid., 39), he adds: "That was what

La Chapelle-Athenaise seemed to me: a place free from anguish."

9. Ibid., 10.

10. Ibid., 28.

11. Ibid., 28.

12. Cf. Mircea Eliade, *Mephistopheles and the Androgyne* (New York: Sheed and Ward, 1965), 61ff.

13. Bonnefoy, *Conversations*, 29.

14. Ibid., 29–30. In part, this experience is reflected in *The Killer*. "In the first act, Berenger enters a radiant city. In a world that has been disfigured, he discovers a world transformed; he regains paradise after leaving the rainy town, after leaving the world of limbo," (ibid., 30). Ionesco specifies that, for him, "radiant" means "shining with light."

15. On the social plane, this corresponds to alienation; ibid., 29.

16. Ibid., 36–37.

17. Ibid., 31–32.

18. The most notable is R. M. Bucke, *The Cosmic Consciousness* (Philadelphia: Innes and Sons, 1901). See also Warner Allen, *The Timeless Moment* (London: Faber, 1946); R. C. Johnson, *The Imprisoned Splendour* (New York: Harper, 1953); J. H. M. Whiteman, *The Mystical Life* (London: Faber, 1961), 25–45; Mircea Eliade, "Experiences of Mystic Light" in *Mephistopheles and the Androgyne*, 19–77; idem, "Spirit, Light, and Seed," *History of Religions* XI (1971), 1–30. Some relevant psychedelic-mystical experiences of preternatural light have been brought to the discussion by R. E. L. Masters and Jean Houston, *The Varieties of Psychedelic Experiences* (New York: Holt, Rhinehart and Winston, 1966), 307ff.

19. Cf. W. L. Wilmhurst, *Contemplation*, 142ff. as quoted in Johnson, op. cit., 306–307.

20. We use this term in its broadest sense, i.e., including the shamans, medicine-men, yogins and all species of contemplatives and ascetics.

21. Cf. Eliade, *Mephistopheles and the Androgyne*, 69ff.

22. It is not without significance that the Sanskrit word *lilā*—meaning "play," especially cosmic play—has been explained by the root *lelay*, "to flame," "to sparkle," "to shine." The term *lelay* may convey the notions of Fire, Light or Spirit. Indian thought seems then to have detected a certain relationship between, on the one hand, cosmic creation conceived as a divine game, and on the other hand, the play of flames. Likewise, in the Christian tradition, the "flame" is the exemplary epiphany of Spirit (as in *Acts* 2,3–4, where the Holy Ghost appears to the disciples in the form of tongues of fire); cf. Eliade, *Mephistopheles and the Androgyne*, 36ff.

IV / 4

Literary Imagination and Religious Structure

IN ONE OF HIS LESSER KNOWN BOOKS, *The Philospher and Theology*, Etienne Gilson wrote the following: "There are times when a person must have the courage to provide the critics with an easy method of getting rid of him." Well, I suppose I must have this courage because, instead of discussing literary imagination and religious structures *in general*, I will speak also of my own literary activity and its relation to my work as a historian of religions.

Now, in the Anglo-American academic milieu, not so long ago, it was rather unwise for a scholar to be also known as a writer of fiction. (Poetry was usually accepted; somehow, it was not taken seriously.) One of the luminaries of neo-positivism, Professor Ayer—the only living philosopher to be called a "second Hobbes"—thought that he could not better discredit Jean-Paul Sartre and the existentialist philosophers than by entitling his devastating critique of them in the journal *Mind*: "Philosophers-Novelists."

As you know, Bertrand Russell became famous for his inexhaustible and imaginative audacity, not only in philosophy and mathematics, but also in ethics, in politics and in his understanding of personal freedom (in his *Autobiography*, he did not hesitate to speak of his many extramarital love affairs). Nevertheless, Bertrand Russell did not publish, during his lifetime and under his name, the short stories which he so much enjoyed writing. He did not care about losing his respectability, but he did not want to endanger his reputation as a "serious" thinker. His literary pieces were brought out in a handsome volume only a few years after his death.

There are, of course, exceptions, and George Santayana is one of them. He *did* have the courage to sign and print his novel, *The Last*

"Literary Imagination and Religious Structure" was first published in *Criterion* 17.2 (1978), 30–34, and is here reprinted by permission.

Puritan. But one wonders if he did not do it on purpose, just to annoy his colleagues. Oliver, the hero of *The Last Puritan,* says he is going to become a professor because he does not think he is "fit for anything else." And another character remarks: "People must *teach themselves* or remain ignorant—and the latter was what the majority preferred." Santayana considered the profession of teaching almost exclusively as a means of subsistence—and especially as a means of being able to go to Europe every year. But, as I said, Santayana was an exception. During one of his classes, he suddenly looked through the window, then addressed the students: "I have a date with spring," he told them, and he left. And he never came back. . . .

As you know, things have changed in the last thirty years, at least in Europe. Jean-Paul Sartre brought out a volume of short stories, *Le Mur,* and his novel, *La Nausée,* a few years before *L'Etre et le Néant,* and almost at the same time, he became extraordinarily popular as a playwright. Likewise, Gabriel Marcel published philosophical books and many plays, and Merleau-Ponty was writing a novel in the very year of his death. Moreover, he told his friends that by working on this novel he was able to formulate his philosophical insights better and more adequately than in his theoretical books.

I must add, however, that, born in Romania near the turn of the century, I belong to a cultural tradition that does not accept the idea of the incompatibility between scientific investigation and artistic, especially literary, activity. As a matter of fact, some of the most original Romanian scholars have also been successful writers, and the greatest of Romanian poets—Mihail Eminescu—was also a philosopher and one of the most learned men of his time. Long before the new fashion of the French artist-philosopher, it was not uncommon for a Romanian scholar to be acclaimed as a poet, a novelist, or a playwright.

In my case, I soon discovered that such a double vocation was part and parcel of my destiny. While yet a very young man, I realized that no matter how captivated I might be by oriental studies and the history of religions, I would never be able to give up literature. For me, the writing of fiction—short stories, novellas, novels—was more than a "violon d'Ingres"; it was the only means I had of preserving my mental health, of avoiding neurosis. I shall never forget my first year at the University of Calcutta; from January until the beginning of the summer of 1929, I devoted myself exclusively to the study of Sanskrit. I worked some fourteen to fifteen hours a day and did not allow myself to read in any language except Sanskrit, not even, after midnight, a page from the *Divina Commedia* or the Bible. And suddenly, at the beginning of the summer, I sensed I had to escape from the prison in which I had locked myself. I needed *freedom*—that freedom which the writer knows only in the act of literary creation. For several days I tried, in vain, to resist the temptation to put aside the Sanskrit grammar, the dictionaries of Apte and Monier-Williams and Aniruddha's *Saṃkhya-sutravrtti,* and write the novel that was obsessing me. In the end, I *had* to write it; I wrote *Isabel and the Devil's Sea* in a matter of a few weeks, and only after that did I regain my desire to work. I returned then with enthusiasm to the study of Sanskrit grammar and Saṃkhya philosophy.

Twenty years later, on June 21, 1949, in Paris, when I was drafting a chapter of *Le Chamanisme,* I felt all of a sudden the same temptation to begin a novel. This time too I tried to resist. I said to myself, quite correctly, that it would be of no use to write a literary work in Romanian—a book which could not appear in Romania and for which I should have to find a translator and above all a publisher; since, at that time, I was completely unknown as a writer in France, it would have been difficult to persuade an editor to publish such a novel. In my *Journal* for that summer, I noted several desperate efforts that I made to ward off the temptation to begin *The Forbidden Forest.* For some time, I hoped I could continue working on *Le Chamanisme* during the daytime while devoting a part of the night to the novel. But soon I realized that I could not live at the same time in two worlds—that of scientific investigation and that of literary imagination—and, at the beginning of July, I interrupted *Le Chamanisme* in order to be able to concentrate on the novel. It was to take five years for me to finish it, because I did not find enough time, or the right "inspiration," except for two or three months a year.

I said to myself that my spiritual equilibrium—the condition which is indispensable for any creativity—was assured by this oscillation between research of a scientific nature and literary imagination. Like many others, I live alternately in a diurnal mode of the spirit and in a nocturnal one. I know, of course, that these two categories of spiritual activity are interdependent and express a profound unity, because they have to do with the same "subject"—*man*—or, more precisely, with the mode of existence in the world specific to man, and his decision to assume this mode of existence. I know likewise from my own experience that some of my literary creations contributed to a more profound understanding of certain religious structures, and that, sometimes, without my being conscious of the fact at the moment of writing fiction, the literary imagination utilized materials or meanings I had studied as a historian of religions.

So, it was with great joy that I read this observation by J. Bronowski: "The step by which a new axiom is adduced cannot itself be mechanized. It is a free play of the mind, an invention outside the logical processes.

This is the central act of imagination in science, and it is, in all respects, like any similar act in literature." This means, however, that literature is, or can be, in its own way, an instrument of knowledge. Just as a new axiom reveals a previously unknown structure of the real (that is, it *founds* a new world), so also any creation of the literary imagination reveals a new universe on meanings and values. Obviously, these new meanings and values endorse one or more of the infinite possibilities open to one for *being* in the world, that is for *existing*. And literature constitutes an instrument of knowledge because the literary imagination reveals unknown dimensions or aspects of the human condition.

In epic literature (novella, story, novel), literary imagination utilizes narrative scenarios. They may be as different as the scenarios attested in *The Quest of the Grail, War and Peace, Carmen, A la recherche du temps perdu,* or *Ulysses*. But in one way or another, all these creations of epic literature narrate something—more or less dramatically, more or less profoundly. Of course, the *forms* in which the narratives are presented—from *The Golden Ass* to *Père Goriot,* from Dostoevsky to *Absalom, Absalom!* and *Dr. Faustus*—can appear antiquated; in any event, few contemporary writers would dare to repeat epic formulas used by their great predecessors. But this does not mean, as has been believed, the "death of the novel"; it means simply that many of the classical forms of the "roman-roman"— the "novel as narrative"—are superannuated; that consequently we must invent new narrative forms.

This is not the place to enter into the recent fervent discussion about the decisive importance—in fact, the tyranny—accorded to language, an importance which, according to some, would justify not only "la nouvelle vague" of the novel, but also the other contemporary attempts to write unintelligible (or at any rate unreadable) prose. I wish only to recall that discoveries made recently in linguistics can help revive lyrical poetry, but they do not annul the importance and necessity of narrative literature. It would require too much time for me to analyze the function and significance of this literature. The specific mode of existence of man implies the necessity of his learning what happens, and above all what *can* happen, in the world around him and in his own interior world. That it constitutes a structure of the human condition is shown, among other things, by the *existential necessity* of listening to stories and fairy tales even in the most tragic of circumstances. In a book about Soviet concentration camps in Siberia, *Le Septième Ciel,* J. Biemel declares that all internees, almost a hundred in number, living in his dormitory, succeeded in surviving (while in other dormitories ten or twelve died each week) because they listened every night to an old woman telling fairy tales. So greatly did they feel the need for stories that every one of them renounced a part of his daily food ration to allow the old woman not to work during the day, so she could conserve her strength for her inexhaustible story-telling.

Quite as revealing in my view are the experiments carried out in several American universities in connection with the physiology and psychology of sleep.

> One of the four phases of sleep is called REM (Rapid Eye Movement); it is the only phase during which the sleeping person dreams. The following experiments were done: Volunteers were prevented from staying in the REM phase, but were permitted to sleep. In other words, they could sleep, but it wasn't possible for them to dream. Consequence: the following night, the persons deprived of REM tried to dream as much as possible, and if they were again prevented from doing so, they proved to be nervous, irritable, and melancholy during the day. Finally, when their sleep was no longer bothered," they gave themselves over to veritable "orgies of Rapid Eye Movement sleep," as if they were avid to recover everything they had lost during the preceding nights.[1]

The meaning of these experiments, it seems to me, is clear: they confirm the organic need of man to *dream*—in other words, the need for "mythology." At the oneiric level, "mythology" means above all *narration*, because it consists in the envisioning of a sequence of epic or dramatic episodes. Thus man, whether in a waking state or dreaming (the diurnal or the nocturnal modes of the mind), needs to witness adventures and happenings of all sorts, or to listen to them being narrated, or to read them. Obviously, the possibilities of narrative are inexhaustible because the adventures of the characters can be varied infinitely. Indeed, characters and events can be manifest on all levels of the imagination, thereby making possible reflections of the most "concrete" reality as well as the most abstract fantasy.

A closer analysis of this organic need for narrative would bring to light a dimension peculiar to the human condition. It could be said that man is *par excellence* an "historic being," not necessarily in the sense of the different historicistic philosophers from Hegel to Croce and Heidegger, but more particularly in the sense that man—any man—is continually fascinated by the chronicling of the world, that is, by what happens in his world or in his own soul. He longs to find out how life is conceived, how destiny is manifest—in a word, in what circumstances the impossible becomes possible, and what are the limits of the possible. On the other hand, he is happy whenever, in this endless "history" (events, adventures, meetings, and confrontations with real or imaginary personages, etc.) he recognizes familiar scenes, personages, and destinies known from his own oneiric and imaginary experiences or learned from others.

For me, a historian of religions and an orientalist, the writing of fiction became a fascinating experience in method. Indeed, in the same way as the writer of fiction, the historian of religions is confronted with different structures of sacred and mythical space, different qualities of time, and more specifically by a considerable number of strange, unfamiliar and enigmatic worlds of meaning. Each literary piece creates its own proper universe, and the creation of such imaginary universes through literary means can be compared with mythical processes. For any myth relates a story of creation, tells how something came into being—the world, life, or animals, man and social institutions. In this sense, one can speak of a certain continuity between myth and literary fiction, since the one as well as the other recounts the creation (or the "revelation") of a new universe. Of course, myth has also an exemplary value in traditional societies, and this is no longer true for literary works. One must keep in mind, however, that a literary creation can likewise reveal unexpected and forgotten meanings even to a contemporary, sophisticated reader.

In sum, as I have said, literary creation can be considered an *instrument of knowledge;* knowledge, of course, of other worlds, parallel to the everyday world. There is a structural analogy between the universe of meaning revealed by religious phenomena and the significant messages expressed in literary works. Any religious phenomenon is a hierophany, i.e., a manifestation of the sacred, a dialectical process that transforms a profane object or act into something that is sacred, i.e., significant, precious and paradigmatic. In other words, through a hierophany, the sacred is all at once revealed and disguised in the profane. (It is disguised for everyone else outside that particular religious community.) Likewise, in the case of literary works, meaningful and exemplary human values are disguised in concrete, historical and thus fragmentary characters and episodes. Investigating and understanding the universal and exemplary significations of literary creations is tantamount to recovering the meaning of religious phenomena.

This is why a writer or a literary critic is usually better prepared to understand the documents investigated by the historian of religions than, say, a sociologist or an anthropologist. Writers and literary critics *believe in the reality and the significance of artistic creations,* i.e., they are convinced by their own labors of the objectivity and the intellectual value of the *mundus imaginalis,* of the imaginary universe created or discovered by any significant author. As you know, a number of literary critics, in Europe as well as in the United States, interpret literary creations in a perspective borrowed from the historian of religions. Myth, ritual, initiation, cultural heroes, ritual death, regeneration, rebirth, etc., belong now to the basic terminology of literary exegesis. To quote one single example: there are a considerable number of books and articles analyzing the initiation scenarios camouflaged in poems, short stories, and novels. Such scenarios have been identified not only in Jules Verne's novels or in *Moby Dick*, but also in Thoreau's *Walden*, in the novels of Cooper and Henry James, in Twain's *Huckleberry Finn*, and in Faulkner's "The Bear." Quite recently, Professor Vierne, of the University of Aix-en-Provence, published a book entitled *Ritual, Initiation and the Novel*. And in his *Radical Innocence* (1966), Professor Ihab Hassan consecrates an entire chapter to the "dialectics of initiation," using as examples the writings of Sherwood Anderson, F. Scott Fitzgerald, Wolfe, and Faulkner.

More than ten years ago, while investigating precisely this interest of the literary critics in the initiation patterns camouflaged in novels, short stories and poems, I suggested that such research may also be significant for an understanding of modern Western man. And I would like to conclude with what I wrote then:

> The desire to decipher initiatory patterns in literature, plastic arts, and cinema denotes not only a reevaluation of initiation as a process of spiritual regeneration and transformation, but also a certain nostalgia for an equivalent experience. In the Western world, initiation in the traditional and strict sense of the term has disappeared long ago. But initiatory symbols and scenarios survive on the unconscious level, especially in dreams and imaginary universes. It is significant that these survivals are studied today with an interest difficult to imagine fifty or sixty years ago. Freud has shown that certain existential tendencies and decisions are not conscious. Consequently, the strong attraction toward literary and artistic works with an initiatory structure is highly revealing. Marxism and depth psychology have illustrated the efficacy of the so-called demystification when one wants to discover the *true*—or the *original*— significance of a behavior, an action, or a cultural creation. In our case, we have to attempt a demystification in reverse; that is to say, we have to "demystify" the apparently profane worlds and languages of literature, plastic arts and cinema in order to disclose their "sacred" elements, although it is, of course, an ignored, disguised, or degraded "sacred." In a desacralized world such as ours, the "sacred" is present and active chiefly in the imaginary universes. But imaginary experiences are part of the total human being, no less important than his diurnal experiences. This means that the nostalgia for initiatory trials and scenarios, nostalgia deciphered in so many literary and plastic works, reveals modern man's longing for a total and definitive renewal, for a *renovatio* capable of radically changing his existence.

NOTE

1. Mircea Eliade, *No Souvenirs* (New York: Harper and Row, 1977), 279–280.

Bibliography

THE FOLLOWING BIBLIOGRAPHY of critical and/or interpretative essays examining Mircea Eliade's fiction, art critical and/or creative texts is an introduction to that dimension of his *oeuvre*. This bibliography is neither comprehensive nor complete. For example, no book reviews are listed below. Only those essays published in English have been included for their availability and intelligibility to students beginning an inquiry into Eliade study. Additionally, I am confident that several new interpretative essays are "in press"; and in fact, Professor Eliade is himself completing a new French collection of his essays on the arts.

Students of any or all aspects of Eliade's *oeuvre* are deeply indebted to Douglas Allen and Dennis Doeing for their masterful *Mircea Eliade: An Annotated Bibliography* (New York: Garland Publishing, Inc., 1980). It is the first place to look for bibliographic references for either primary Eliade texts or interpretative materials.

Al-George, S. "Temps, histoire et destin" in *Mircea Eliade,* edited by Constantin Tacou. Paris: L'Herne, Cahiers de l'Herne #33, 1978. Pp. 341–346.

Apostolos-Cappadona, Diane. "To Create A New Universe: Mircea Eliade on Modern Art," *Cross Currents* XXXIII.4 (1982/3): 408–419.

Bălu, I. "Les débuts littéraires de Mircea Eliade" in *Mircea Eliade.* Pp. 381–389.

Bies, J. "Chamanisme et littérature" in *Mircea Eliade.* Pp. 330–340.

Cain, Seymour. "Poetry and Truth: The Double Vocation in Eliade's Journals and Other Autobiographical Writings" in *Imagination and Meaning,* edited by Norman J. Giardot and Mac Linscott Ricketts. New York: The Seabury Press, 1982. Pp. 87–103.

Calinescu, Matei. "Imagination and Meaning: Aesthetic Attitudes and Ideas in Mircea Eliade's Thought," *Journal of Religion* 57.1 (1977): 1–15.

———. "The Disguises of Miracle: Notes on Mircea Eliade's Fiction," *World Literature Today* 52.4 (1978): 558–564.

———. "The Function of the Unreal: Reflections on Mircea Eliade's Short Fiction" in *Imagination and Meaning.* Pp. 138–161.

Cioran, E. M. "Beginnings of a Friendship" in *Myths and Symbols. Studies in Honor of Mircea Eliade*, edited by Joseph N. Kitagawa and Charles H. Long. Chicago: The University of Chicago Press, 1982 (1969). Pp. 407–414.

Coates, W. A. "Littérature fantastique: métaphysique et occulte" in *Mircea Eliade*. Pp. 375–380.

Comstock, W. R. "Mythe et cinéma contemporain" in *Mircea Eliade*. Pp. 347–349.

Horia, Vintila. "The Forest as Mandala: Notes concerning a Novel by Mircea Eliade" in *Myths and Symbols*. Pp. 387–396.

Ierunca, Virgil. "The Literary Work of Mircea Eliade" in *Myths and Symbols*. Pp. 343–364.

Marino, Adrian. "Mircea Eliade's Hermeneutics" in *Imagination and Meaning*. Pp. 19–69

Masui, J. "Mythes et symboles" in *Mircea Eliade*. Pp. 355–363.

Moore, Albert C. "Religion and the Arts in the Work of Mircea Eliade," *Miorita, New Zealand Romanian Cultural Association Bulletin*, Volume 1.2 (1974): 1–8.

Nemoianu, Virgil. "Wrestling with Time: Some Tendencies in Nabokov's and Eliade's Later Works," *Southeastern Europe/L'Europe du Sud-est*, Volume 7.1 (1980): 74–90.

———. "Naming the Secret: Fantastic and Political Dimensions of Charles Williams' and Eliade's Fiction," *Bulletin of the American-Romanian Academy of Arts and Sciences* No. 4 (1983): 50–59.

Popescu, Mircea. "Eliade and Folklore" in *Myths and Symbols*. Pp. 81–90.

Ricketts, Mac Linscott. "Mircea Eliade and the Writing of *The Forbidden Forest*" in *Imagination and Meaning*. Pp. 104–112.

Simion, Eugen. "The Mythical Dignity of Narrative" in *Imagination and Meaning*. Pp. 131–137.

Spaltmann, Gunther. "Authenticity and Experience of Time: Remarks on Mircea Eliade's Literary Works" in *Myths and Symbols*. Pp. 365–386.

Stewart, Mary Zeiss. "The Royal Road Toward The Center: Fictional Hermeneutics and Hermeneutical Fiction in Eliade's *Two Tales of the Occult*," *Ohio Journal of Religious Studies*, Volume VI.1 (1978): 29–44.

Strauss, Walter A. "*The Old Man and the Bureaucrats: A Novella*, by Mircea Eliade," *The Western Humanities Review*, Volume XXXV.3 (1981): 276–280.

Uscatescu, George. "Time and Destiny in the Novels of Mircea Eliade" in *Myths and Symbols*. Pp. 397–406.

Vierne, S. "La littérature sous la lumière des mythes" in *Mircea Eliade*. Pp. 350–354.

Zancu, Liliana. "The Twilight Zone: Fantastic Elements in Mircea Eliade's *Doctor Honigberger's Secret* and *Serampore Nights*," *Yearbook of Romanian Studies*, Volume 6 (1981): 50–54.

Photographic Credits

THE EDITOR AND PUBLISHER wish to thank the custodians of the works of art for supplying photographs and granting permission to use them.

1. Courtesy of The J. Paul Getty Museum
2. Courtesy of The Cleveland Museum of Art, Cleveland, Ohio
   Purchase from the J. H. Wade Fund
3. Courtesy of the Michigan-Princeton-Alexandria Expedition to Mount Sinai
4. Courtesy of the Department of Anthropology, Smithsonian Institution
5. Courtesy of the Dumbarton Oaks Research Library and Collection, Washington, D.C.
6. Courtesy of The Cleveland Museum of Art, Cleveland, Ohio
   John L. Severance Fund
7. Courtesy of the National Museum of African Art, Eliot Elisofon Archives
   Photograph by Delmar Lipp
8. Courtesy of the Government of India Tourist Office
9. Courtesy of the Government of India Tourist Office
10. Courtesy of the Freer Gallery of Art, Smithsonian Institution, Washington, D.C.
11. Courtesy of The Cleveland Museum of Art, Cleveland, Ohio
    Purchase from the J. H. Wade Fund
12. Collection Museum of Modern Art, New York
    Mrs. Simon Guggenheim Fund
13. Courtesy of The National Gallery of Art, Washington, D.C.
    Gift of Katharine Graham
14. Courtesy of The National Gallery of Art, Washington, D.C.
    Gift of Eugene and Agnes Meyer, 1967
15. Courtesy of the Romanian National Tourist Office
16. Courtesy of The Cleveland Museum of Art, Cleveland, Ohio
    Thirty-fifth Anniversary Gift of Mr. and Mrs. Paul Mellon
18. Courtesy of UNESCO
19. Courtesy of the Embassy of Peru
20. Courtesy of UNESCO
21. Courtesy of UNESCO

Index

181